W9-CUD-150

The New Shell Guides

East Anglia

The New Shell Guides

East Anglia

Christopher Catling

Introduction by Ronald Blythe

Series Editor: John Julius Norwich
Photography by Geoff Doré

Michael Joseph · London

MICHAEL JOSEPH LTD

Published by the Penguin Group
27 Wrights Lane, London W8 5TZ, England
Viking Penguin Inc., 40 West 23rd Street, New York, New York
10010, USA
Penguin Books Australia Ltd, Ringwood, Victoria, Australia
Penguin Books Canada Ltd, 2801 John Street, Markham, Ontario,
Canada L3R 1B4
Penguin Books (NZ) Ltd, 182–190 Wairau Road, Auckland 10,
New Zealand

Penguin Books Ltd, Registered Offices: Harmondsworth,
Middlesex, England

First published in Great Britain in 1990

Text copyright © Shell UK Limited 1990

Photographs copyright © Michael Joseph Limited 1990

All rights reserved. Without limiting the rights under copyright
reserved above, no part of this publication may be reproduced,
stored in or introduced into a retrieval system, or transmitted, in
any form or by any means (electronic, mechanical, photocopying,
recording or otherwise), without the prior permission of both
the copyright owner and the above publisher of this book

Typeset in Linotron 10/11pt Plantin by Cambrian Typesetters,
Frimley, Surrey
Colour reproduction by Scantrans, Singapore
Printed and bound by Kyodo-Shing Loong Printing, Singapore

A CIP catalogue record for this book is available from The British
Library

ISBN 0 7181 3285 8

The name Shell and the Shell emblem are registered trademarks

Shell UK Ltd would point out that the contributors' views are not
necessarily those of this company

The information contained in this book is believed correct at the
time of printing. While every care has been taken to ensure that the
information is accurate, the publishers and Shell can accept no
responsibility for any errors or omissions or for changes in the
details given.

Title-page photograph: Wheatfield and St Michael's church at
Broome, near Ditchingham, Norfolk

Contents

We would like to thank the owners – the National Trust, English Heritage and private owners – for their permission to photograph and feature their properties in this book.

John Julius Norwich was born in 1929. After reading French and Russian at New College, Oxford, he joined the Foreign Office where he served until 1964. Since then he has published two books on the medieval Norman Kingdom in Sicily; two historical travel books, *Mount Athos* (with Reresby Sitwell) and *Sahara*; two volumes on the history of Venice; a book about Glyndebourne; an anthology of travel writing; *The Architecture of Southern England*; and *Byzantium: the Early Centuries*, the first volume of a three-volume history of that city. Since 1970 he has also compiled an annual anthology of poetry and prose, *A Christmas Cracker*. He was general editor of *Great Architecture of the World*, *The Italian World*, and *The Heritage of Britain*; he is now general editor of the *Oxford Illustrated Encyclopedia of Art*.

In addition he writes and presents historical documentaries for television and frequently broadcasts on BBC radio. He is Chairman of the Venice in Peril Fund, Co-Chairman of the World Monuments Fund and a member of the Executive Committee of the National Trust.

Christopher Catling was born in 1955 and lived in East Anglia for a number of years. After reading English at St Catherine's College, Cambridge, he worked at a publicity copywriter, spending several years in Hong Kong and China, before becoming a full-time author. He has written *The Economist Business Traveller's Guides* to China, South-East Asia and the Soviet Union, and a guidebook to Florence. He is currently researching the history of conservation.

Ronald Blythe is an East Anglian, born in Suffolk. He is an essayist and poet and has written a number of books about the region, including *Akenfield*. His latest book, *Each Returning Day*, is a study of diarists.

Cindy Buxton (F.R.G.S.) was born in 1950 in Essex. Her love of wildlife was nurtured by her father and many locals of East Anglia. She began making wildlife films for the Anglia Television series *Survival* in 1971. She has filmed in Africa, Iceland, the Falkland Islands, South Georgia, Ascension Island, the United Kingdom, New Zealand and Ireland. She has written two books, *Survival in the Wild* and *Survival: South Atlantic*.

Christopher Somerville lived in East Anglia for many years. He has written several books, presented series on radio and written on walking and travel for various newspapers. His current project is a journey round the islands of Britain.

Paul Jennings was the *Observer*'s first resident humorist with his column *Oddly Enough*. This was reprinted, with *Punch* and other pieces, in 15 of his 30 books, which include one novel for adults and three for children, and documentaries.

Ian Trethowan is a keen follower of horse-racing and has regularly visited Newmarket for over 40 years. He was a political journalist and broadcaster, becoming Director-General of the BBC. He is now Chairman of Thames Television and of the Horserace Betting Levy Board, and a Trustee of the British Museum and of Glyndebourne Opera.

St John Gore (C.B.E., F.S.A.) has for the greater part of his life worked for the National Trust, continuously as an adviser on pictures and for a decade as Historic Buildings Secretary. He is now retired. He is a Trustee of the Wallace Collection and of the National Gallery and since 1963 has been a member of the Executive Committee of the National Art-Collections Fund.

Geoff Doré was born in 1957. His interest in photography began while he was reading Zoology at London University. After graduating in 1980, he concentrated on naturalist photography and worked for the RSPB on research projects. He is now a full-time nature/travel photographer and has had his work published worldwide.

Introduction

RONALD BLYTHE

East Anglia is where England began, at least nominally. Settlers from Angle in Holstein arrived in south-eastern Britain in such numbers that it became known as Angle-land, or Engla-land. East Anglia preserves the original sharp-edged form of the name, derived, they say, from the actual shape of Angle in Holstein. These were the people whose golden looks so astonished Pope Gregory I when, walking through the slave-market in Rome, he saw a group of children and was told that they were Angles. In spite of his famous retort, *'Non Angli sed Angeli'*, he set about the immediate conversion of this fair race. But for centuries, and almost up to modern times, the characteristic features of the East Anglian face have been strong and irregular, like those in Flemish glass, and are those of a community which has had a long intellectual and commercial relationship with Europe's northern seaboard, and which historically has turned away from much of what has happened in the centre of this country. East Anglians were a tough lot who farmed in forest clearings and who yet existed in a marine climate and stared out to sea.

East Anglia is Suffolk and Norfolk and a sliver of Cambridgeshire, but never Essex. Essex, the land of the East Saxons, is another territory altogether. John Constable, watching one of his father's labourers rowing himself across the Stour from Suffolk to Essex, heard the man say, 'Farewell, old England!' Rivers large and minute intersect this wide arc of plain every few miles from the

Breydon Water and Berney Arms Mill, Norfolk Broads

Stour to the Wash, creating lovely shallow valleys to hold towns and villages. The myriad ports of the Middle Ages through which poured the wool fortunes, the herring profits and the philosophy which caused the Reformation, are now reduced to the single monster success of Felixstowe, plus a few old fishing harbours which are but pale shadows of what they were even only 50 years ago.

Coastal East Anglia, because of erosion as well as huge changes in its industries, can provide the traveller with one of the most moving and fascinating studies in decline and development in these islands. Everything from the Atlantis-like drowned medieval city of Dunwich to the disturbing implications of Sizewell B. But the finest sights to be seen all along the edge of East Anglia are the immense skies, the wild flowers and a parade of vast, lonely, beautiful churches, glorious artefacts whose towers were seamarks to guide and welcome the traders home to Godly and prosperous parishes. Some of these shore-line churches are cages for gulls, others fill up in the summer for festivals and jog along through the bitter winters with little, faithful congregations.

Confronted by the solidity of its agriculture, the wateriness of East Anglia can be under-estimated. Its early rulers, the Wuffinga dynasty, buried in ships at Sutton Hoo, might be called river princes, while certainly the ancient settlement patterns follow the intricate mesh made by streams and estuaries. The rivers have ravishing names, some Celtic, some homely, some English – Thurne, Alde, Blyth, Dove, Linnet, Lark, Yare, Deben, Waveney, Stour – and although in many places scarcely seen unless searched for, once traced they can still be recognised as the controlling features of a subtle landscape. They thread their way through corn and woods towards the heaths and wetlands which used to sprawl in immense, airy flats throughout coastal East Anglia, slow-moving yet positive and even rather grand.

A pleasant contrast to the all too-frequent prairie fields

The early inhabitants of the region kept clear of its forests, leaving these to the gods, and lived on the sandlings on East Anglia's wide and mysterious and only recently vanished moor, the Breckland, and on the flinty fields which still half-crush the crops on many river-bank farms. Glorious treasures often emerge from this poor soil – gold torques and the matchless Mildenhall and Sutton Hoo finds – as well as quantities of humbler artefacts to reveal that what was eventually to become the country of the North Folk and the South Folk had for thousands of years, since Britain was joined to Europe, been that of successive peoples. So, an old, old land whose Christian culture is in comparison but a thing of yesterday. An alternately open, grassy and densely wooded place, with the North Sea blowing into it and gnawing at its edge. Also, for all its apparent openness, a hidden and discrete corner of England which takes some degree of knowing.

There are over 1,300 parishes, nearly all of them displaying something superb or quietly good in the way of architecture. Their names are a roll-call of their founders, as well as an inventory of East Anglia's natural history, and they lie thick on the map. This was once the most densely populated part of Britain. Now, in spite of a flood of recent immigrants and official plans for many more, whole stretches of East Suffolk and North Norfolk in particular remain remote and even lonely, due partly to the closing-down of their shops, pubs, crafts, schools and even churches, but also partly to some kind of indigenous isolation which continues to keep themselves to themselves. The explorer will meet with greatly contrasting and sophisticated pleas for conservation – and a stubborn local belief in unchangingness.

The villages, though so close, stay distinctive and separate. While they are usually seen in terms of architecture, their real history is that of English agriculture through all its most important developments; one needs to walk on footpaths as well as in naves to get the full picture of East Anglia. The East Anglian farmer's tale is one of heights and depths, of wealth and genius and of slump and despair. A man who knew nothing of farming when he inherited large estates in west Norfolk, Thomas Coke, was one of the inspirers of the first Agricultural Revolution and soon after two Suffolk firms, Garrett's of Leiston and Ransome's of Ipswich, were inventing the machinery which would not only begin to obliterate the killing toil of sowing and harvesting, but would make possible the prairie grain-lands of North America. The Second Agricultural Revolution of the 1940s has proved all too successful, yield-wise, and East Anglia is beginning to count the cost and repair the damage caused by ruthless mono-culture, the stripping out of hedges and destruction of wildlife. The tragedy is that it has turned us away from a sight which filled our ancestors with gratitude and delight – an expanse of golden corn. To an East Anglian it is shocking to hear harvests abused, even monolithic ones. Mercifully, it is now increasingly shocking to kill everything else in order to grow crops. The old gamekeepers did this to preserve game.

The wonder of the district is its medieval church architecture. From Salle to Lavenham it is incomparable, and not all of it the result of the munificence of millionaire clothiers but often the gift of men and women of modest means who had their names picked out in flintstones and engraved on bells. Contrary to many other counties, numerous Norfolk and Suffolk churches were built and

paid for by freeman, not landowners, and could be said to be a part of the long history of independence and a radical response to life which has shown itself in rebellion, emigration and even in a kind of cussedness which is best summed up in Suffolk's unofficial motto, 'Do Different'. What is obvious is that East Anglia has always been a 'house of art', a place which feeds the imagination and makes great demands on the craftsman. The visitor can only be amazed by the quantity and the quality of the sacred buildings and their contents, 'cleansed' though so many of them were by the iconoclasts. Because a church was a community's only public building, and the ante-room to paradise, nothing was too good for it. Though it was built – very slowly, so that it would not buckle – with rubble, it was adorned with whatever would make it most beautiful. Masterpieces include the 14th-century retable, still with its original frame, at Thornham Parva, Suffolk, the bosses in Norwich Cathedral and the entire unification of flint, stone, paint and wood at Holy Trinity, Blythburgh, a work of art which has endured every kind of neglect, vandalism and natural disaster, only to emerge imperfectly 'complete'. East Anglia's saints were Felix, Fursey, Anna, Botolph, Ethelreda (Ely Cathedral was to grow from her little house in the Fens) and predominantly Edmund, England's Sebastian, at whose shrine at Bury St Edmunds the barons swore to force King John to sign a list of fundamental liberties for his people. These holy men and women are now shadowy figures in contrast with the bright stone, mortar and glass which survives at every hand. Equally strong and vivid to those who have read her *Revelations of Divine Love* is Julian of Norwich, an unknown lady who died some time after 1416.

There is one splendid city, Norwich, and numerous towns; the most important is Ipswich and the most delightful Bury St Edmunds, though a range which includes King's Lynn, Sudbury, Aldeburgh, Framlingham, Eye and Beccles, each so individual and unmatching, must leave out precedence. Some of these old market centres have been gutted to create glittering shopping malls, or have been locked in by post-war estates. Many surprise one by their essentially untouched scenes.

A small group of the nation's finest artists, all born during the 18th century, created a vision of East Anglia so potent and so lasting that not even the drastic changes of the late 20th century have managed to distort or banish it. Thomas Gainsborough and John Constable, neighbours in the Stour valley some 50 years and 20 miles apart, and 'Old' Crome (to distinguish him from his artist son) and John Sell Cotman in Norwich, continue to provide the popular image of the place. All of them worked amid magnificent buildings – wool churches, guildhalls, water-mills and classical Georgian mansions – and in agricultural surroundings which both Gainsborough and Constable, in their different ways, were to look back to as an ideal. The local climate, especially the light – so like that in Holland, it used to be said – preoccupied them. Although there has never been anything comparable to the Cornish 'school' in Suffolk and Norfolk, generations of artists have since worked close to these famous scenes, notably Wilson Steer at Walberswick.

It is only recently that George Crabbe, our chief poet, has taken over from

St Mary's church at Ufford still has the village stocks outside

Charles Dickens as a popular East Anglian literary figure. When people were steeped in Dickens they followed Mr Pickwick around Sudbury, Bury St Edmunds and Ipswich, where many of his adventures took place and where the actual inns and houses stand to this day. But the best Dickens country was the huge, wild heathland between Blundeston and Great Yarmouth, David Copperfield's early topography and peopled by Peggotty, Mrs Gummidge, Mr Barkis and other immortals. Dickens's wintry exaggeration of East Anglia has always pleased the natives, who like caustic sayings: 'Yarmouth is the strangest place in the wide world; one hundred and forty-six miles of hill-less marsh between it and London.'

During the 1940s Benjamin Britten combined two of Crabbe's verse tales to make an opera, *Peter Grimes,* and coincidentally made everybody recognise the excellence of the realist poet. With his unsparing descriptions of the inhabitants and his expert local botany, George Crabbe speaks now for the whole of East Anglia, not just Aldeburgh, an uncomforting giant in the land. For consolation we have Edward FitzGerald, an Irish gentleman promoting a Persian paradise in Suffolk, and the philosophical Sir Thomas Browne of Norwich, whose strange and lovely language influenced, among many others, Coleridge and Paul Nash. Chaucer too was an East Anglian and snatches of local Suffolk speech in use to this day can be heard in *The Canterbury Tales.* Norfolk and Suffolk are laden with poetry and stories, as all long dwelt-in territories are.

Norwich cathedral seen from Kett's Hill

The Stour Valley, near East Bergholt, was a favourite subject for Constable

Note on using the Gazetteers

Entries in the Gazetteers are arranged in alphabetical order. 'The', if part of the name, follows the main element: **Burnhams, The** (alphabeticised under B).

Entry headings consist of the name of the place or feature in **bold** type, followed by a map reference in parentheses: **Diss** (5/2C). The figure 5 is the map number; 2C is the grid reference, with 2 indicating the across and C the down reference.

If a name mentioned within the text of an entry is printed in capital letters – i.e. SUDBURY – this indicates that it has its own entry in its county Gazetteer.

Bold type is used for certain places, buildings or other features of interest or importance referred to within Gazetteer entries.

Every effort has been made to ensure that information about the opening to the public of buildings, estates, gardens, reserves, museums, galleries etc., and details of walks and footpaths, were as accurate as possible at the time of going to press. Such particulars are, of course, subject to alteration and it may be prudent to check them locally, or with the appropriate organisations or authorities.

Norfolk Gazetteer

Acle (3/3D)

A large marina on the River Bure, north-east of Acle, makes this small town, 8 miles west of Great Yarmouth, busy in summer with holiday-makers shopping for supplies. St Edmund's church contains fascinating graffiti, thought to date from the time of the Black Death, which raged in East Anglia around 1349; it refers to the 'brute beast plague that rages hour by hour'. The well-restored chancel screen is decorated with crossed arrows and crowns for the popular East Anglian king and martyr, St Edmund, and the lovely font of 1410 is carved with a *pietà*.

At Upton, 1½ miles north-west, St Margaret's church contains a painted flying dragon, once the weathervane, taken down when the tower was rebuilt in 1930.

Three miles east of Acle, the Stracey Arms windpump stands prominently beside the A47, near the pub of the same name. The brick-built water pump was built in 1883 and has been fully restored by the Norfolk Windmills Trust. It is open in summer.

Acres, The (1/5D)

Castle Acre, 3 miles north of Swaffham, is arguably the finest village in Norfolk. Approached from the south through the narrow flint gateway that leads on to the village green, it has something of the air of a French hilltop town. The gateway was built in the 13th century to defend, not the village, but the northern entrance to the castle; in fact, much of the present village lies within the castle bailey, which indicates just how large a castle this was in its heyday. Even now, the ruins are of an impressive height, and from the top of the motte there are wide-ranging views across the shallow marshy valley of the River Nar.

Although this little stream looks unspectacular today, in the past the Nar was navigable from the Wash at least as far as here. Castle Acre was, moreover, the site of an important ford across the river, which has existed since Roman times, if not before, for PEDDARS WAY passes through the centre of the village.

Recent excavations of the castle have thrown

Stracey Arms windpump, near Acle

up some intriguing facts about its development. The first castle, founded by William de Warenne, the Earl of Surrey, soon after the Norman Conquest, was essentially a dwelling house surrounded by a modest ditch and bank, more a symbol of power than a seriously defensive structure. It was not until the 1140s, during the Civil War between King Stephen and Matilda, that the walls were thickened, all the ground floor doors and windows blocked and the extensive surrounding curtain wall and earthworks built. The evidence suggests the castle never sustained an attack and was virtually abandoned by 1200, providing the villagers with a ready source of good-quality building material.

Small cottages now cluster all around the foot of the castle and up the steep narrow street that leads to Stocks Green, a broad manicured lawn, planted with limes and surrounded by scaled-down rural versions of grander Georgian town houses; the most commanding building is the 18th-century Ostrich Inn.

West of the village is the church of St James, set in a spacious churchyard and typically East Anglian, with a stalwart tower and gracious window tracery. The wooden wine glass-shaped pulpit is painted with the Four Doctors of the Church (Saints Augustine, Gregory, Ambrose and Jerome), and its screen includes the figure of St James, patron of the church, in pilgrim's hat and staff.

Further west, sheltering in a peaceful hollow by the River Nar, are the extensive ruins of Castle Acre Priory. This Cluniac institution was founded by the Earl of Surrey in about 1090, as a daughter house to the Priory of St Pancras at Lewes. The abbey church dates from this period. The grand west front is decorated with the full repertoire of English Romanesque motifs, including intersecting blank arcading and a corbel table of monstrous heads.

The elegant Prior's Lodging was inhabited from the dissolution of the Priory in the mid 16th century, until the 17th century, and contains contemporary fireplaces and fine moulded roof beams painted with Tudor roses. Of great interest are the associated agricultural buildings, and the stone-lined water channels that run

Ruins of Castle Acre priory

through the kitchen and reredorter, or latrine, before feeding the Priory fish ponds.

At **Newton**, a mile east of Castle Acre, the little church of All Saints hides unassumingly behind a belt of yew trees and is not at all like the soaring Perpendicular churches of most of Norfolk: just a simple building with whitewashed walls and a brick floor, but with a plain square central tower, a solid Saxon arch inside and a triangular-headed doorway.

The other two Acres, South and West, can be reached by a choice of narrow lanes, some so little used that grass grows up the middle and partridges scatter as you drive along. **South Acre** is a mile south on the opposite bank of the Nar to Castle Acre. St George's church stands opposite a Georgian house with double bow front and sheep graze among the tombstones carved with cherubs.

At **West Acre**, 2 miles further east, the ruins of an Augustinian priory founded in 1100 stand in the farmyard next to the church, beside the tall chimney of a lime-burning kiln. The 14th-century Priory gatehouse survives as the entrance to the farm. All Saints' church has some fine Flemish woodcarvings of the Annunciation, Nativity and Presentation in the Temple incorporated into the altar reredos. The window above, dated 1907, depicts members of the Hamond family, one in a pink hunting coat and others with splendid mutton-chop whiskers.

Alderford (2/4D) *see* Swannington

Anmer (1/4C) *see* Sandringham

Ashwellthorpe (2/4F)
This village, 2½ miles south-east of Wymondham, has mainly modern houses but the church of All Saints is worth a visit. Here, surprisingly, you step down into the chancel, not up, and discover the delicately carved figures of Sir Edmund Thorpe (d. 1417) in armour and his Lady in splendid horned headdress. At the rear of the church is a fascinating 17th-century Italian pokerwork chest, ornamented with flamboyant military figures, harbour scenes and townscapes.

On the road to **Tacolneston**, 2 miles south, is the delightful Dairy Farmhouse, a pleasing 17th-century building with a triple-storey porch and stepped gables. Opposite the church is another refined manor house, this time built in Queen Anne style. All Saints' church contains a painted screen panel of 1510 which, though sadly defaced, depicts the Temptation of St Anthony, based on the 1509 engraving by Lucas van Leyden, an indication that East Anglian artists were influenced by the work of their Dutch contemporaries.

Attleborough (2/3F)

Most of the houses in this small town date from the coming of the railway in the 1840s and several shops retain early bow fronts. One of the few early buildings is the timber-framed Griffin Hotel.

St Mary's church has one of the most impressive chancel screens in Norfolk, dating from the 15th century; massive and richly carved, it stretches the whole width of the church, partly obscuring the mighty columns of the Norman tower crossing behind.

Besthorpe Hall, a mile east, has fine walled gardens, which are open under the National Gardens Scheme. All Saints' church, next door, is a perfect, unspoilt example of 14th-century architecture.

Aylsham (2/4C)

John of Gaunt, Duke of Lancaster, determined that Aylsham, in north-east Norfolk, should be the principal town of all his landholdings in the county and so, from 1372 on, it began to develop as a market. The solid red-brick buildings that now surround the Market Place speak of the town's comfortable prosperity. Even the jet-black ravens on the front of the Black Boys Hotel, plucking grapes in a long plaster frieze, look contented.

Clarke's hardware store, north-east of the Market Place, has a fine bow front with cast-iron pillars; in Red Lion Street beyond there is scarcely a building later than the early 19th century and most have original and ornate shop fronts.

A handsome five-bay Georgian house terminates the northward view and, opposite, a flight of steps climbs to the churchyard of St Michael's church. Here, by the south chancel door, is the rose-covered grave of the great landscape designer, Humphry Repton (d. 1818).

The fine big church is filled with box pews, fitted during the 1824 restoration, though the unusual pulpit is dated 1637 and ornamented with *trompe-l'œil* receding arches.

North-west of the church, on the Blicking Road, is Aylsham Old Hall, a perfect late 17th-century house surrounded by Dutch-gabled

Chancel screen and wall paintings at Attleborough

farm buildings. In the opposite direction, Millgate Street leads down to the River Bure, with its imposing 18th-century mill, and Bridge House, once a pub used by ferrymen sailing to this former harbour in their shallow-bottomed craft.

A mile upstream, at **Ingworth**, the little church of St Lawrence stands on a knoll, with views down to the Mill House and its water meadows. The stump of the former round tower is now thatched, giving it an apsidal appearance and, inside, simple rustic pews, a brick floor and a higgledy-piggledy screen, composed of salvaged fragments, create a pleasing atmosphere.

Oxnead, 3 miles south-east of Aylsham, presents a pretty scene as you approach from the west, crossing the hump-backed bridge over the River Bure, with the old mill on the right. St Michael's church was partly rebuilt in red brick in the 18th century and the rustic tower, porches and gable ends add to the attraction of this simple church.

Another pretty clapboard water mill stands by the Bure as you enter **Burgh-next-Aylsham**, a

Chancel of St Mary's church, Burgh-next-Aylsham

mile further north. Hanging at the back of St Mary's church is a letter from Sir Gilbert Scott dated 1865, in which he compares the very fine Early English chancel to that at Lincoln cathedral and recommends restoration. This was put in hand in 1877, with such skill that the beautiful blank arcading, which Scott found in a fragmentary state, now completely rings the chancel.

Babingley (1/3C) *see* Castle Rising

Baconsthorpe (2/4B) *see* Barninghams, The

Bale (2/3B)
This small village lies just off the A148 between Fakenham and Holt. The church of All Saints is hidden by a noble group of holm oak trees that have grown as high as the tower. They were planted around 1860 to replace the Great Bale Oak, which was several centuries old when it died, and whose hollow trunk was for years used by a local cobbler as his shop.

The simple church contains at least five separate stained glass representations of the Annunciation, and there is another group of angels playing lutes and organs; some are standing on chequered floors, or painted floorboards, a stylistic detail of the 15th-century Norwich school of glaziers.

More excellent glass of the same period is to be found at St Andrew's church, **Field Dalling**, 2 miles north, an atmospheric church full of box pews and old gas lamps. This farming hamlet has several flint barns, some built quite recently but in a style that goes back centuries.

Banham (2/3G)
This delightful village, 5 miles north-west of Diss, surrounds a rectangular green. From the churchyard at its eastern end the view takes in a number of historic houses. On the right is the Priory, a fine Georgian house with Dutch gables and, beyond, Norfolk House has its own original 19th-century pedimented shop window. To the left, the Guildhall is a timber-framed building with a jettied upper floor. Further on, Church Farm House also has shaped gables.

The source of the brick to build these handsome houses is half a mile west of the village, at Hunts Corner, where the Bricklayers Arms is a reminder of the kilns that once stood here and supplied much of south Norfolk with brick and tile.

St Mary's church has an impressive rustic king-post roof, dated 1622, and a 14th-century effigy of a knight – wooden but painted to look like stone. A beautiful 16th-century Flemish stained glass Virgin and Child was inserted in the north aisle in 1962.

Barnham Broom (2/3E) *see* Kimberley

Barninghams, The (2/4B)

The tiny church of St Mary, **Little Barningham**, 5 miles south of Sherringham, contains a unique and surprising wood carving of a shrouded skeleton. He stands on the corner of a box pew, dated 1640, one side of which is carved with a conventional *momenti mori*. Another inscription, on the rear of the pew, records that it was paid for by one Stephen Crosbee, clearly a man with a macabre sense of humour, since the inscription continues: 'For couples joined in wedlock this seat did I intend'.

Further north is the entrance to Barningham Park, an interesting house that once belonged to the Paston family and was later remodelled by John Repton, while his better-known father, Humphry, landscaped the extensive gardens (open under the National Gardens Scheme). John very wisely retained the original 1612 façade, with its unusual two-storey-high dormer windows and some of the mighty espaliered trees in the garden still bear fruit, nearly two centuries after Humphry supervised their planting.

A mile further north, St Peter's church, **North Barningham**, has survived, although the village has not. It contains a notable set of brasses and monuments to the Palgrave family, whose once splendid house now lies in ruins to the east of the church.

More substantial ruins survive at **Baconsthorpe**, 1½ miles to the west. The so-called 'castle' was a large moated and semi-fortified manor house built by the Heydon family in the 15th century but sold for demolition in 1654, when the best stone was carted away and used to build FELBRIGG HALL. The remains, maintained by English Heritage, include the gatehouse and curtain wall as well as a steeping tank, dug when the site was used for wool processing, and are open all year round.

Barshams, The (2/2B)

These two small villages lie 2 miles north of Fakenham. Dominating the scene as you drive into **East Barsham** from the south is the

The Manor House, East Barsham

splendid brick manor house. Built around 1520–30 – some 40 years after OXBURGH HALL – it shows how far the skills of the brickmaker had developed in that time, for here the gatehouse, like the Manor behind, is highly ornamented with rubbed brick and terracotta finials and clusters of chimneys enriched with a multitude of raised designs.

West Barsham is a neat hamlet in the valley of the River Stiffkey, consisting of the Hall, farm and estate cottages, linked by a lane that is bordered by a neatly clipped holly hedge. The church of the Assumption has been almost wholly rebuilt but contains a delightful set of benches, designed by the children's book illustrator, Margaret W. Tarrant and featuring wild and domestic animals. In the nave there is a fine Italian marble relief carved with the Adoration of the Shepherds; the date of 1407 must have been added later, for it is in the Mannerist style of the 16th century, not that of the early Renaissance.

Barton Bendish (1/4E)

The name Barton derives from the Old English meaning 'barley farm' and often denotes a farm belonging to a monastery; there is ample evidence here, in the farm names, of former ecclesiastical ownership. As you approach this estate village, seven miles west of Swaffham, you pass St Andrew's Glebe Farm, St Mary's Glebe Farm and Abbey Farm.

The parish itself is now tiny but it once had three churches. St Mary's survives, a simple thatched church standing in a farmyard west of the village with a Norman beakhead doorway – rare in Norfolk – transferred here from the now demolished All Saints' church.

St Andrew's is the main church now and it, too, has an interesting doorway, pointed in the Early English style but with late Norman capitals and billet moulding. Simple box pews, dated 1623, fill the nave. The ornate wrought-iron candelabrum is the work of local people who also designed the richly coloured Ascension window, dated 1881.

Fincham is the next village to the west. St Mary's church must be visited for its square Norman font, carved with Adam and Eve, three gift-bearing Magi and the disembodied heads of an ox and ass looking over the manger, in the Nativity scene.

Some 3 miles south-west, St Andrew's church at **West Dereham** has an outstanding monument to Colonel Edmund Soame (d. 1706), the work of the local sculptor Robert Singleton.

Norman font in Fincham church

Barton Turf (3/2C) *see* Wroxham

Bawburgh (2/4E)

Four miles west of Norwich, Bawburgh is a delightful hamlet on the River Yare. As you walk to the peaceful little church of St Mary and St Walstan, down a path flanked by tall beech trees, it is hard to imagine that this was once a pilgrimage centre to rival Walsingham. Perhaps because St Walstan was only a humble farmhand, his shrine here had great popular appeal. This was built alongside the miraculous spring that gushed forth when Walstan was buried in 1016.

The present church may have been built at about the same time. It certainly has a Saxon round tower, now with a conical cap, and an arch on the north wall may have led to the first chapel of St Walstan.

The village of Bawburgh lies down in the valley, and is made attractive by the wide meadows either side of the River Yare and the triple-arched bridge in the centre. Straddling the river, to the west, is a 19th-century mill, now converted to houses but once owned by a miller named Jeremiah Colman, who moved to Norwich in 1823 to found his mustard empire.

Beachamwell (1/4E) *see* Swaffham

Beeston (2/2D) *see* Litcham

Belaugh (3/1D) *see* Wroxham

Billingford (5/4B) *see* Diss

Binham (2/2B) *see* Stiffkey

Birchams, The (1/4B)
In the chalk landscape of north-west Norfolk, the villages all hide in hollows. As you approach **Great Bircham** from the west almost nothing interrupts the view of rolling hills: no houses or pylons, just the white sails of Great Bircham windmill standing on one of the highest hills around. The fully restored corn mill is open daily in summer.

St Mary's is a simple church, full of 17th-century furnishings. A corner of the churchyard is maintained by the War Graves Commission: its Cross of Sacrifice, unveiled by George VI on 14 July 1946, is a memorial to 66 pilots from the UK, Canada, Australia and New Zealand who died on bombing raids from Great Bircham airfield.

St Mary's, at **Bircham Newton**, is a tiny Saxon church of the simplest type, with massive walls and a tall, narrow chancel arch. A grave slab by the altar is carved with a life-sized effigy of a priest in vestments; on the ogee arch above is the man in the moon and a whorl that represents the rays of the sun. This is just one of several interesting monuments in the church.

Blakeney (2/3A) *see* Cley-next-the-Sea

Blickling (2/4C)
Blickling, 1 mile north-west of Aylsham, is distinguished by Blickling Hall which in its long history has changed hands many times and now belongs to the National Trust. The house built by Sir Nicholas Dagworth in the 14th century was later bought by Sir John Fastolfe, whose name, slightly changed, was used by Shakespeare for his roistering comic hero. Fastolfe sold it to Geoffrey Boleyn, whose great-granddaughter Anne, Henry VIII's queen for three brief years, may have been born here. Finally, in 1616,

Blickling was bought by Sir Henry Hobart, and it was he who built the house that stands today, employing Robert Lyminge, who had previously designed Hatfield House (Herts), as his architect. Lyminge produced a simpler house here, but with the same splendid angle turrets and shaped gables, working within the confines of the moated site.

The result is a gentle house that seems to fit naturally into its setting, admirably enhanced by the richly planted gardens; the flowing beds of roses and colourful perennials were designed by Norah Lindsay in the 1930s and reflect the ideas of Gertrude Jekyll, as well as the experience that Mrs Lindsay gained working with Lawrence Johnston at Hidcote (Glos).

Equally memorable are the highly ornate plasterwork ceilings of the house, none more unusual than the series of allegorical figures in the Long Gallery. Here Sir Henry Hobart indulged his taste for moralistic emblems, copied from Henry Peacham's recently published book of woodcuts and verses, the *Minerva Britannia* (1612). Many of these emblems are as humorous as they are instructive; in particular the rhinoceros, whose armour plating is taken as a metaphor for human courage in the face of misfortune.

The brasses and monuments that fill St Andrew's church provide a portrait gallery of the people who were fortunate enough to spend some part of their life at Blickling Hall. Sir Nicholas Dagworth is commemorated by a splendid brass. There are several Boleyns and a brass to Ann Wood (d. 1612), who died giving birth to the twins she holds. The bearded 8th Marquis of Lothian (d. 1870), who inherited the Hall in 1850, is depicted in a sculpture by G. F. Watts; his widow, Lady Constance (d. 1901), is surrounded by youthful angels standing in the Hall gardens.

Blofield (3/2E)
Blofield, 8 miles east of Norwich, is bisected by the A47. The oldest part of the village lies to the south of the road, where 18th-century cottages cluster around the church of St Andrew and St Peter. This has an interesting font carved, not with the more typical Seven Sacraments or Evangelists, but with eight scenes from the Life of Christ.

All Saints' church, **Hemblington**, 2 miles to the north, has another unusual font – here carved with the Trinity and saints. Even finer is the series of wall paintings that illustrate not

Blickling Hall (National Trust)

only the usual figure of St Christopher but also far less common scenes from his life and martyrdom.

Blo Norton (5/3B) *see* Garboldisham

Booton (2/4C) *see* Reepham

Bracon Ash (2/4F) *see* Swardeston

Bradfield (3/1B) *see* Trunch

Brancaster (1/4A)

Brancaster lies less than a mile from the northern Norfolk coast. Very little now remains of *Branodunum*, Brancaster's Roman predecessor, except for some ditches to the east of the village. Until 1770, when the stonework was dismantled, the walls of this Saxon Shore fort stood to a considerable height, enclosing 6 acres. This was the northernmost fort in a defensive chain that

stretched round the English coast to Porchester, in Hampshire, built in the late 3rd century when Roman Britain was suffering repeated attacks from Frankish and Saxon pirates.

The site is now part of an extensive National Trust reserve. From **Brancaster Staithe** boats can be hired in the summer for trips to Scolt Head Island, a wild and lonely 3½ mile-long sand and shingle bank, part colonised by sea lavender and the breeding ground of numerous terns.

A mile to the west at **Titchwell** there is a car park and visitor centre which gives access to the sunken hides of the Titchwell Marsh bird reserve, run by the Royal Society for the Protection of Birds. The tiny church of St Mary, with its round tower and thin spike of a spire, has a pleasing Arts and Crafts stained glass window of 1889, illustrating the Sower in the Fields.

Breckles (2/2F) *see* Great Hockham

Bressingham (5/3A)
This hamlet on the A1066 lies 2½ miles west of Diss on the Suffolk border. To many people Bressingham is synonymous with the garden and nursery founded by Alan Bloom in 1926, and the hamlet is today surrounded by acres of fields covered in conifers, grown to satisfy the insatiable demands of suburban gardeners.

Bressingham Plant Centre is open throughout the year and Alan Bloom's Dell Garden is open on Sundays and occasional weekdays in summer. Since his 'retirement', Mr Bloom has built up a comprehensive collection of steam engines, ranging from fairground carousels to huge mainline railway engines and the collection is open to visitors on the same days as the garden.

The entrance to the Steam Museum is beside the church of St John the Baptist, rebuilt and furnished around 1527 by Sir Roger Pilkington.

In the flat agricultural fields north of Bressingham, the church of St Andrew at **Fersfield** is a delight. The slim, square Norman tower is surrounded by handsome yew trees and inside is a memorial to the 18th-century county historian Francis Blomefield. The Rectory, in which he wrote his history of Norfolk, stands opposite the church, surrounded by orchards and tall trees.

Brettenham (5/2A)
Three miles east of Thetford, Brettenham is a classic model village, consisting of substantial neo-Tudor brick farmworkers' cottages set in expansive gardens. The architect was probably Teulon, who rebuilt St Mary's church in 1852 and designed the neo-Gothic Shadwell Court in 1835–40. The Court is not visible from the church but the lodge houses near the church are a fine example of *cottages ornés*, with tree-trunk verandas, thatched roofs and Gothic windows.

The adjoining estate of **Kilverstone**, 2 miles to the west, is run as a Wildlife Park, specialising in animals and birds from Latin America, including Falabella miniature horses.

Rushford lies 1½ miles to the south-west, on the county boundary. St John the Evangelist is a large church, built to serve the college of priests founded here in 1342 by Edward Gonville, who also founded Gonville and Caius College, Cambridge. Much has changed since then: the chancel has gone, replaced by an apse scarcely ten feet deep. The remains of the college, south of the churchyard, have been incorporated into a Victorian Gothic house.

Bridgham (2/2G) *see* Harling, East

Brisley (2/2C)

A village about 8 miles north of East Dereham, whose extensive village green is one of the largest surviving in East Anglia and gives an idea of the appearance of the Norfolk landscape before much of the common land was enclosed. This process began as early as the 16th century and grew apace during the early 19th. On the edges of the common, the moated manor house and barns have scarcely been altered since the reign of Elizabeth I. St Bartholomew's church has fine furnishings, including a three-decker pulpit, and fine flowing window tracery.

Chapel keep at New Buckenham castle

St Margaret's church at neighbouring **Stanfield** is big, simple and barn-like. The sophisticated Early English lancet windows of the chancel, with their rich shafts and hood moulds, form an elegant contrast with the simplicity of the rest.

Buckenham (3/2E) *see* Strumpshaw

Buckenhams, The (2/3F)

These villages, a few miles south-east of Attleborough and separated by a mile from each other, make a fascinating pair. **Old Buckenham** surrounds a vast village green, at least a quarter of a mile across – big enough to accommodate ten football pitches with room to spare. Surrounding it are clusters of houses, threaded with attractively named lanes: Cake Street, Hog's Snout, Puddledock and Loos Wroo. Several ponds on the edges of the green probably represent old clay and gravel quarries.

New Buckenham is, by contrast, a very compact, planned village. After the Conquest the manor was given to William d'Albini, one of William the Conqueror's leading supporters, who built a castle (now gone) at Old Buckenham. His son, also called William, abandoned that earthwork and created New Buckenham in 1146. Here he built a new castle, the first known

example of a round keep in England, and laid out beside it a grid of streets, 200 yards square, and a broad market place surrounded by a bank and ditch.

All this survives, including the little chapel of St Mary, the town's first church (now incorporated into a barn to the east of the castle) and represents England's best example of a Norman new town. Many of the cottages are thatched and timber-framed, their oversailing upper storeys adding to the charm of the narrow streets. Standing on the green, the former market place, is the 1559 Court House, raised on Tuscan columns: the middle column served as a whipping post and still has its manicles of iron.

The new church of St Martin's, north of the market place, was built in 1254 and rebuilt by Sir John Kynvett in 1479, when the whole of the exterior was decorated with flint flushwork and the new roof was given its corbels representing the Apostles with their symbols. The font is an enjoyable piece, carved with wild men and lions, dated 'Feb 1 1619'.

Burgh Castle (3/3E)

There is little romance to the village of Burgh Castle, a couple of miles inland from Great Yarmouth, which is all caravan sites and bungalows, but the remains of the Roman fort, now maintained by English Heritage, are set apart, down an unmetalled track by the marshy shores of Breydon Water.

The fort was probably built in the 3rd century AD as part of a chain of fortifications running down the south-east coast, intended as a defence against Saxon raiders. Three sides of the rectangular fort walls survive to a height of 15 feet; the fourth side collapsed into the marshes and was robbed for building material.

Excavations revealed round huts of Celtic type within the interior, confirming that Burgh Castle was the site of a monastery founded by the Irish missionary St Fursa on land granted by King Sigeberht – around AD 635, according to Bede. The monastery was probably destroyed around AD 889 by Danish raiders.

Footpaths running from the fort round the eastern rim of Breydon Water provide a vantage point for studying the waders that feed in the extensive mud flats.

Burgh-next-Aylsham (3/1C) see Aylsham

Burgh St Peter (3/3F)

This village lies at the eastern extremity of a sparsely populated corner of Norfolk, contained within a great loop of the River Waveney, which seems reluctant to reach the sea; having flowed within sight of Lowestoft and the coast, it meanders for another 20 miles northwards to Yarmouth.

The riverside position of St Mary's church makes its curious 19th-century tower a navigational landmark. Built of brick, it consists of five cubes of diminishing size, stacked one on top of the other, with big angle buttresses. The rest of the church is pleasingly thatched and surrounded by Irish yews. The Boycotts were both patrons and rectors of the church in unbroken succession for 135 years and the pulpit, donated in 1819, is covered in brass plates to commemorate various members of the family.

All Saints' church, **Wheatacre**, is a good 1½ miles west of the village, and has another interesting tower, this time 16th century, of chequerboard flint and brick.

Burlinghams, The (3/2E)

North Burlingham stands just off the busy A47 Norwich to Yarmouth road, and St Andrew's church contains not only its own very fine chancel screen (dated 1530 and one of the latest examples in Norfolk) but also one from the church of St Peter which now stands in ruins close by.

Even richer is the church of St Edmund, **South Burlingham**, with its Norman doorways and splendid painted pulpit. A number of good bench ends, one carved with the Elephant and Castle, have survived and the chancel wall has a large wall painting depicting the martyrdom of St Thomas à Becket.

Burnhams, The (1/5A and 2/1A)

There are seven 'Burnhams by the Sea', but three of them, Westgate, Sutton and Ulph, have been combined into the newly created small town of Burnham Market, in northernmost Norfolk. Together, the seven form a delightful group of villages, connected by narrow lanes with high hedges, always just within sight of the sea. As you step out of one interesting church, the tower of the next beckons on the near horizon.

Burnham Deepdale is the westernmost of the seven, a neat village of pink and white chalk cottages. St Mary's church contains one of the finest fonts in East Anglia: square, Norman and carved with scenes illustrating the Labours of the Months.

The next village to the east is **Burnham Norton**, an unspoiled hamlet with scarcely a modern building in sight and views across the marshy foreshore where cattle graze, to the windmill above Burnham Overy Staithe. Norton's church, dedicated to St Margaret, is well to the south (almost in Burnham Market). Essentially Anglo-Saxon, it was considerably enlarged in the 15th century. King William's coat of arms, dated 1697, at the back of the church, is a rare example.

Immediately to the east is the 14th-century gatehouse of a Carmelite friary, exhibiting one of the earliest surviving examples of East Anglian flint flushwork.

Over the River Burn, **Burnham Overy** is full of surprises. At the entrance to the village there is a fine group of 18th-century mill buildings and, around the next bend, a curious house with two enormous female figures, like ship's figure-heads, supporting the front porch.

Another surprise is the awkward arrangement

Harvest scenes on the font, Burnham Deepdale

church. The battlements of the church tower are of great interest (binoculars essential) and are carved with biblical scenes.

The last of the Burnhams, **Burnham Thorpe**, is the most famous as the birthplace of England's great admiral, Lord Nelson (1758–1805). His father was rector of All Saints' church, a fine building in an unparalleled setting: to appreciate this fully it is best to approach along the unmetalled track from the east rather than by the southerly routes. The track starts higher than the church; then, as you descend towards the River Burn, the whole church is revealed below, set at the centre of a large rectangular church-yard with the moated manor house beyond.

The church was clearly intended to be seen from this direction, since the most elaborate flint flushwork decoration, normally reserved for the west tower, appears here on the east front. The interior was reroofed and extensively renovated in 1905, the centenary of the Battle of Trafalgar, and the south aisle contains an informative display on the life of Nelson.

Caister-on-Sea (3/4D)

In this suburb of Great Yarmouth, the extremes of antiquity and modernity stand side by side. The ruins of the 2nd century AD Roman town, maintained by English Heritage, are hemmed in by modern housing and caravan sites, just north of the A1064.

Caister Castle, a mile west of the town, occupies a more salubrious position. The castle, an early brick building, was built by Sir John Fastolfe (also of BLICKLING) in 1432–5, on his return from the Battle of Agincourt. In 1459 it passed to the Paston family after a lengthy dispute over the estate ownership, all of which is detailed in the famous Paston *Letters*. The gatehouse and moated walls have survived and

Burnham Market

of St Clement's church. The walls of the central tower are pierced only by domestic-sized door-ways with fanlights above, so that the nave and chancel are, in effect, two separate entities, invisible one from the other.

Burnham Market is the largest of the villages. There is a fine view of the wide village green, surrounded by grand houses and humbler rows of flint cottages, from the gate of St Mary's

the grounds are used to display a large collection of motor vehicles dating back to 1893. The castle is open to visitors in summer.

Caistor St Edmund (3/1E)

Impressive earthen ramparts and a deep ditch completely surround the site of the Roman town of *Venta Icenorum*, a mere 3 miles from the heart of Norwich and yet a lonely deserted place in which the imagination can easily conjure up the ghosts of former inhabitants. Having defeated Boudicca in AD 60–1, the Romans sought to civilise the conquered Iceni tribe by building this administrative centre in about AD 70. As so often with Roman new towns, the planners over-ambitiously laid out a street plan greater in area than was actually built up. The walls, added in the 3rd century, enclosed an area only a quarter the size of the original planned town.

Archaeologists working in the 1930s found Saxon cremations and evidence of settlement, but as Norwich began to develop as the new regional centre Caistor declined into a farming hamlet.

St Edmund's church lies within the earth ramparts in the south-eastern angle, and is built partly of Roman brick, partly of flint. One might speculate about the prior existence of an early Christian church, but the current structure is largely of the 13th century.

By contrast, **Trowse Newton**, 2 miles north, is a Norwich suburb with a busy main road, but well worth a visit for the surprising pulpit in St Andrew's church. Made in 1902, it is surrounded by the life-sized seated figure of King David, playing his harp, flanked by trumpet-blowing angels. Nikolaus Pevsner suggests that they once formed part of an 18th-century organ case; the figures are so bold and lively, they would not look out of place on a fairground organ.

Castle Acre (2/1D) *see* Acres, The

Castle Rising (1/3C)

Until the Middle Ages, the winding River Babingley was navigable from the Wash to Castle Rising, and the street called Havengate Lane may have been the site of a wharf. Up the river came the fine white Caen stone, used by the Norman d'Albini family to build their castle keep in 1138. This stands on a high mound south of the village, whose rectilinear street plan suggests that it was a planned town, laid out at the same time as the castle.

Caister Castle

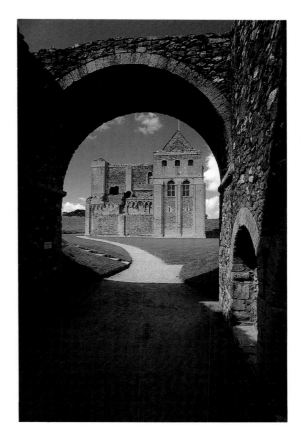

The d'Albini's castle, Castle Rising

The d'Albini's castle, now maintained by English Heritage, was regarded, even in its own time, as one of the finest in England, beautifully decorated with blank arcading and ox-eye windows: an elegant residence as well as a defensive stronghold.

The interior of the keep is approached up a ceremonial flight of stairs which could be barred at three points, making the castle impregnable. The rooms have vaulted ceilings and ornamented capitals – like a church – and numerous fireplaces.

Queen Isabella was imprisoned here in 1330, for her part in the murder of her husband, Edward II. Some say that the Queen's ghostly screams can be heard at times, but the historical evidence suggests that she lived comfortably enough and archaeologists have found the remains of an extensive apartment suite which may have been built specially for her.

The castle survives in its current remarkably complete state because it continued to be used as a hunting lodge well into the 16th century and a

Cley church and the River Glaven

proposal to pull down the tower in 1572 was fortunately rejected on the grounds that the value of the salvaged materials was too little to justify the labour.

To the south of the keep, the footings of a Saxo-Norman church, with central tower and apse, have recently been exposed. This church was submerged, not long after it was built, by the castle embankment, and replaced by the new church of St Lawrence in the village.

It may be that some of the masonry from the original church was reused at St Lawrence's, for the beautiful west front is ornamented with blank arcading, zig-zag and colonettes. Other genuine Norman work includes the imposing tower crossing and ornate triforium, and the massive font ornamented with feline heads.

On the green to the west of the church is an

church, alongside the A149, was built in 1894 as a gift of the future King Edward VII; it is of corrugated iron, but surprisingly atmospheric inside.

Cawston (2/4C) *see* Salle

Cley-next-the-Sea (2/3A)

Cley (pronounced 'Cly' and meaning 'clay') is at the centre of a great linked chain of nature reserves on the north Norfolk coast, where every spring and autumn bird watchers gather to observe rare migrant species. Cley was once a major port from which wool was exported to the Low Countries. Natural silting and deliberate land reclamation have now left the village accessible only to small craft, but traces of the old quay remain alongside the picturesque 18th-century windmill, now a private house.

St Margaret's church began as an ambitious building but was never completed and parts fell into ruin in the 16th century. The great and spacious nave contains many good bench ends and brasses, as well as numerous amusing figure corbels and the churchyard deserves exploring for the stories that are told on the tombstones.

From Cley churchyard there is a good view of St Mary's church at Wiveton, on the opposite bank of the River Glaven. No doubt conscious that the Cley parishioners enjoyed this view, the masons at Wiveton placed all the richest flush-work ornamentation on the side of the church that faces the rival village.

Not to be outdone by their neighbours, the people of **Blakeney**, a mile further west, built another magnificent church; the buttresses of its tall tower are carved with the *Instruments of the Passion*. For once, Victorian restorers did an excellent job and the sense of richness is enhanced by the 1887 chancel screen, organ and stained glass.

North of the church, narrow streets of cobbled cottages lead down to the Quay. From here it is possible to walk around the sea bank of Blakeney Eye and look across to the 3½ mile-long shingle ridge of Blakeney Point, Norfolk's first-ever nature reserve. (*See* 'Coastal Birds of East Anglia', p. 32.)

Ferries to Blakeney Point operate from the quay at **Morston**, the next village west, dropping passengers at the old lifeboat station, from where it is a short walk to the National Trust hide. Here, in summer, it is possible to watch nesting terns, plovers and oystercatchers, while winter visitors include a large colony of common seals.

unusually well-preserved 15th-century cross, standing 20 feet in height. To the east, the Trinity Hospital is occasionally open to the public: these 17th-century almshouses, endowed by Henry Howard, Earl of Northampton, retain their original Jacobean furnishings.

A mile north of Castle Rising, the near-ruinous church of St Felix, **Babingley**, is said to mark the spot where St Felix landed in AD 630, bringing Christianity to East Anglia. The newer

Coastal Birds of East Anglia CINDY BUXTON

East Anglia has long been famous for the richness of its birdlife and for its largely unspoilt habitats, despite the dramatic changes that have taken place in the English countryside in the last 40 years. The area is served by a wealth of conservation bodies and as a result few other areas in Britain have been so well documented, making my task very much easier. Having spent my childhood years in Essex and the last 12 years on the north Norfolk coast, I see East Anglia very much as my home. Of course I have my favourite places – like Blakeney Point, which always reminds me of many wonderful childhood holidays – but Cley Marsh is one of the first places I visit on returning from any long trip abroad. There is no doubt in my mind that the countless happy hours I spent being shown the wildlife along the north Norfolk coast by the local people laid the foundations for a future career as a wildlife film-maker.

There are countless reserves and protected areas, in some stretches almost continuous, along the Norfolk and Suffolk coastline. The coastal habitats where you will find large numbers of birds are the beaches, mudflats and salt-marshes. Mudflats and sandbanks spend half the time under the sea. Offshore, the faster currents allow only sands to be deposited, while inshore the sheltered conditions allow the build up of mudflats from extremely fine clay particles washed down the estuaries and off the salt-marshes. Waders can only feed when the mudflats are exposed by the tide, when they can find huge amounts of food. When the tide comes in they move on to the salt-marshes, which they use more as a safe haven than a feeding ground. Salt-marshes can, however, be dangerous places for birds to nest in because of the constant threat of an extremely high tide flooding even the upper marsh. Many small, sparrow-sized birds move across the marshes in winter, feeding on the seeds of the various plants. The shingle beaches and sand spits are of major importance as nesting sites for seabirds.

The Wash coast from the Norfolk border at Terrington Marsh to Snettisham is one of Britain's major wintering habitats for a variety of waders. Peak counts have estimated 74,000 knot, 52,000 dunlin, 18,000 oystercatcher, 8,300 bar-tailed godwit, 6,000–7,000 curlew and redshank, 3,000 plover, nearly 1,500 sanderling, 900 turnestone and 500 ringed plover, while some 14,000 shelduck winter here. Low tide reveals miles of mudflats which appear quite lifeless and are inaccessible and dangerous, even with local knowledge. As with other estuaries, the Wash is best visited some two or three hours before high tide, when large roosts of waders may be seen on fields adjacent to the coast as flood tides drive them off the mudflats. The Terrington Marsh region will sometimes reward the watcher with a passage of skua, kittiwake and wildfowl in autumn. In winter roving hen harrier, short-eared owl and merlin frequent the area. There are limited access roads to the coast at this point, so the majority of birdwatchers head instead for the coast around Snettisham.

This area is outstanding. The main attraction comes just before high tide when a huge movement of waders passes south down the coast. The disused gravel pits to the south of Snettisham beach, an R.S.P.B. reserve, form a major wader roost. During the higher spring tides every last patch of mud is covered by the sea and many waders seek a roosting place on the shingle ridges and on the islands in the gravel pits. Tern breeds here, as do oystercatcher and ringed plover. Snow bunting are often quite numerous and Lapland bunting and shorelark are regular. The pits, with their islands and shingle banks, can be seen from hides from where one can watch the birds gather and disperse without disturbance.

Further north, the sea between Heacham and Hunstanton is one of the best areas for watching winter sea duck and observing autumn seabird passage in rough seas. These are the only cliffs on the mainly low-lying Wash coast and from their tops many excellent sea watching days have been recorded over the years. Black redstart on migration can often be found among the beach huts, and offshore there are frequently quite large flocks of wintering sea ducks. Rafts of several hundred common scoter are frequent, with velvet scoter often up to 100 strong. Eider, too, can be seen in most months, but peak usually in February and March. A typical movement on an October day with a north-west wind would include large flocks of kittiwake swirling along the breakers every so often and small parties of gannet gliding against the wind. Arctic skua would be fairly frequent, with perhaps one or two late sandwich terns to rob them of their last meal.

Cley Channel, Blakeney

The north Norfolk coast for nearly 25 miles from Holme-next-the-Sea to Kelling is of great scenic beauty, comprising sandy beaches, mud-flats, shingle ridges, marram grass dunes, winding salt-water creeks, sheltering pine-forest dunes and fresh grazing marshes. Scolt Head Island was one of the earliest nature reserves to be established on the Norfolk coast. The main attractions on this island are the large colonies of nesting tern and plover in May and June. Breeding waders include redshank, oystercatcher and ringed plover. Turnstone, dunlin and bar-tailed godwit can be found along the salt-water creeks or on the shore. With some of the highest sand dunes on the coast there are unrivalled views over the mainland.

A visit to the similar Blakeney Point colony in summer is as traditional as the autumn migration pilgrimage. The sandwich tern has reached a maximum of 3,800 pairs in the last 10 years, while the common and little terns are declining. Because of its almost complete separation from the mainland, Blakeney Point continues to receive and hold masses of wind-drift small passerines whenever the autumn winds blow from the east or the north. About half-way along the Point, in the vicinity of 'Half-Way House' which is surrounded by bushes, walk slowly, with bino-culars ready, and you will find that redstart are common, wheatear keep more to open ground and sometimes black redstart appear; but hippolais, phylloscopus and sylvia warblers are less obliging and a patient wait may be required. Keep a look out for wryneck and red-backed shrike which

are both regular migrants. Later on in October the whole Point may be swarming with goldcrests and robins wind-drifted in from the Continent. From autumn and all through the winter grey plover, bar-tailed godwit, dunlin, turnstone, curlew and redshank are present.

For a complete change of scenery, yet still on the coast, visit the 3 mile stretch of pine trees at Holkham which is now firmly established on the ornithological map. There you may find extremely rare migrants like the rose-coloured starling, Bonelli's warbler, olive-backed pipit and rose-finch, to name but a few. The parrot crossbill bred for the first recorded time in Britain in 1984, at the Wells end of the pine trees; and it is this species, with the common crossbill, that attracts most bird watchers from February onwards. In April, the smaller winter migrants departing may congregate in their hundreds among the pine trees; these may include siskin, brambling and redpoll. In the Holkham area during the first two months of the year the flocks of wild geese reach their highest numbers of the winter, when several hundred pink-footed and white-fronted geese may be present as well as one or two thousand brent geese. Other winter attractions of the shore and marshlands are flocks of roaming snow bunting, one or two short-eared owls and the hen-harrier, while there is always a possibility of seeing a peregrine. Offshore in Holkham Bay during suitable weather conditions, there may be guillemot, razorbill, red-necked grebe, black-throated diver and goldeneye.

The variety and numbers of birds seen at Cley Marsh, as passage migrants, winter visitors or summer residents, have made it one of the most popular haunts for birdwatchers in this country. Over the past 150 years nearly 300 distinct species have been recorded, including a remarkable list of rarities and vagrants. Among breeding birds bearded tit, bittern, avocet and black-tailed godwit are a special feature. Ringed plover and oystercatcher breed on the marsh perimeter, while nesting wildfowl include garganey, gadwall and shelduck. Although the area has such an outstanding list of rare birds, including seabirds, geese, ducks, hawks and passerines, it reigns supreme for the abundance and variety of its waders, which can be seen from the hides on the reserve. In the spring avocet can be seen courting, making their nests and defending their territory against all comers. Spoonbill often arrive in late spring to while away the summer months on the reserve. Bittern can usually be heard booming and very occasionally this skulking resident may appear in front of one of the hides or be seen flying low from one clump of reeds to another. Ruff are usually present in spring on the Cley marshes in varying numbers, frequently 50 birds or more. Autumn storms, particularly from the north-west, drive many seabirds close inshore. All four skuas may be expected, with gannet, guillemot, razorbill, kittiwake, shearwater and petrel. There is never a dull moment at Cley, although remember to wrap up warm in the autumn and winter against the bitter east wind.

Suffolk has never been a county noted for seabirds, apart from waders, wildfowl, gulls and terns. Birdwatchers there have always been envious of their Norfolk neighbours, whose north-facing coast often sees spectacular movements of skua, shearwater, petrel and auk. It seems that as these exciting species pass south they are too far out to be seen from the Suffolk coast. To compensate for this, Suffolk has enjoyed the initial recolonisation of Britain by avocet, an impressive increase in the numbers of nesting little tern and each winter the substantial estuaries are home to tens of thousands of wildfowl and waders. Sadly, the latter sites are now under threat from development, both industrial and recreational.

The Suffolk estuaries are, however, internationally important for redshank, shelduck, ringed plover, grey plover, avocet and black-tailed godwit. Of special note is the Stour, which holds the second largest population of wintering black-tailed godwit in Britain – with over 1,000 birds present some winters – and the greatest concentration of waders and wildfowl in Suffolk. Huge numbers of dunlin are present, wheeling across the estuary in tight flocks if disturbed by a raptor. The Stour is also a very important habitat for 2,000-4,000 redshank, and grey plover, curlew, turnstone, ringed plover and oystercatcher all occur in fairly large numbers. Of the wildfowl the most numerous is the widgeon, followed by the shelduck, mallard, teal and the pintail. The only diving duck to occur regularly in any number is the goldeneye.

Havergate Island is a notable breeding sanctuary for avocets and four species of terns. Outside the breeding season there is an impressive list of breeders and wildfowl. About 100 pairs now breed on the island, their season extending from April to late August. Other breeding waders include redshank, oystercatcher and ringed plover. A colony of between 150 to 250 pairs of sandwich tern nests on the island in addition to thousands of black-headed gull, adding to the general clamour at the height of the breeding season in May. Spring wader passage may bring in scores of black-tailed godwit, some bar-tailed godwit, a few ruff, greenshank or even a kentish plover, while in autumn a wider variety may include turnstone, little stint and curlew sandpiper. In winter the island is well used by both duck and wader species.

The salt-marshes of Suffolk are of considerable importance for birds. Salt-marsh plants provide grazing for overwintering flocks of widgeon and dark-bellied brent geese, and the prolific supply of seed is exploited by large flocks of passerines, particularly linnet and twite. Areas of high marsh also provide secure roosting sites for waders, remote from human disturbance; the most important of these sites are found on areas of mature salt-marsh, for instance Waldringfield on the Deben, where good numbers of wintering black-tailed godwits can usually be found along the mudflats of the river, while dunlin may reach

Ringed plover (J. F. Young, Natural Selection)

Little tern with chick, in their typical shingle beach habitat (E. A. Janes, Natural Selection)

four figures. Fagbury on the Orwell estuary provides good viewing of winter duck species running into counts of hundreds. Salt-marshes also provide valuable sites for breeding waders, in Suffolk predominantly redshank, oystercatcher, avocet, black-headed gull, skylark, meadow pipit and, more recently, Canada geese.

The shingle areas associated with the Suffolk estuaries, such as Orford Ness and Landguard, hold large breeding colonies of little tern. Orford Ness also provides the habitat for breeding oystercatcher, ringed plover, avocet and a colony of approximately 8,000 pairs of lesser black-backed gull and 2,000 pairs of herring gull. Such large populations cause substantial nutrient enrichment of the shingle, promoting the establishment of permanent plant cover. Black redstarts nest on Landguard Reserve, along with a small well-guarded colony of little terns which are among Britain's rarest breeding seabirds. Sea watching here can be rewarding, with waders and wildfowl passing offshore. Thousands of brent geese move south in late autumn heading for the Essex marshes.

In spite of the lack of seabird numbers, more than 200 species are seen in the Minsmere Reserve, which is owned by the R.S.P.B. There are about 100 species breeding annually on the reserve – a greater variety than in any other comparable area in Britain. Avocets return in mid-March and more than 40 pairs usually frequent the scrape. Bitterns begin to make their famous booming call from the end of March at any time of day. Short flights low across the reeds are frequently made in the spring and summer. Other nesting birds are bearded tit and sandwich tern, which first arrive from Africa at the end of March or early April. Ever-secretive water rails find the dense cover to their liking and an estimated 40 pairs nest annually. A few pairs of

grey heron nest in the reed-beds – an extremely unusual site, for they more commonly nest in tree tops – and the rare marsh harriers establish their territories, causing a daily commotion to their lesser neighbours. In April and May there is a northward passage along the coast of goldfinches and linnets, probably returning from their winter foraging in southern Europe, and the reed-beds are alive with reed and sedge warblers. Common and little terns nest on the scrapes among noisy multitudes of larger sandwich tern and black-headed gull. The best time to watch out for the arrival of non-breeding passage waders is in May. These regular Minsmere specialities include the spoonbill – several adults usually spend some weeks on the reserve in summer. Vagrants which have been recorded in May include hoopoe, bee-eater and white-winged black tern. The greatest variety of wader species might be found between the end of July and mid-August; from then onwards, with the easterly or north-easterly winds, falls of passerines may occur in the coastal bushes. Another feature of the autumn is the high numbers of bearded tit – estimated 1,000 birds in the reed-bed, where large irruption flights take place from mid-September. In the winter months, water levels are raised to provide sanctuary for hundreds of teal, widgeon and shoveler.

It would be nigh impossible to mention every nook and cranny along such an extensive coast as East Anglia, and I do not claim to know all its birdwatching sites; such knowledge would take several lifetimes. Instead I have mentioned just a few locations and the birdlife you can expect to find there. To be honest, no matter where you go along the Norfolk and Suffolk coast, if you are prepared to devote a little time and patience, to move slowly and quietly and, finally, to be alert and look, then you will always find something of interest.

Cockley Cley (1/4E) *see* Swaffham

Cockthorpe (2/2A) *see* Stiffkey

Colby (3/1B) *see* Erpingham

Cranwich (1/4F) *see* Northwold

Creakes, The (2/1B)
The story of **North Creake**, 4 miles south-west of Wells-next-the-Sea, begins with the Abbey, a mile to the north of the village. These peaceful ruins have seen a tragic past, for the small

Seafront and pier, Cromer

Augustinian monastery, founded in the 12th century, was all but destroyed by fire in 1484 and shortly afterwards most of the community died of the plague. The transepts and chancel of the monastic church still stand to a considerable height and the cloister and chapter house survive in the adjoining farm. The ruins are maintained by English Heritage.

St Mary's church in North Creake was rebuilt in the late 15th century by Sir William Calthorpe. The pronounced uphill gradient of the church floor has the effect of focusing the eye on the raised chancel, and the huge nave has a fine hammerbeam roof carved with angels holding symbols of the Passion.

The River Burn (the creek that gave these two villages their name) flows through **South Creake** alongside the main street, in front of the houses whose gardens lie over little wooden bridges. St Mary's church has another fine roof.

Directly east of the church is the solid, simplified classical Congregational church of 1783 and, in the centre of the village, a ramshackle group of buildings that were built in the 1920s as a razor factory, founded by George Theophilus Money. Unfortunately he did not live up to his name and his 'Ace of Blades' factory went out of business not long after it was built.

Two miles east, at **Waterden**, the little church

of All Saints stands alone in fields. The brick mullioned and transomed windows inserted after the tower and north aisle collapsed give it a domestic appearance, but the double-splayed windows, long and short-work quoins and simple north and south doors all confirm that this is essentially an untouched Saxon church.

Cressinghams, The (2/1E)
Six miles south of Swaffham, **Great Cressingham** sits in the attractive valley of the River Wissey. St Michael's church stands on rising ground that shows off its ornate west tower to advantage. The chancel is Early English, but has a fine and ambitious Perpendicular east window.

Opposite the church, the remains of Great Cressingham Priory are incorporated into the existing farmhouse, a splendid building with polygonal turrets and an upper storey covered in Perpendicular blind arcading built of elaborately moulded brick.

Little Cressingham is 2 miles south-east on a tributary of the River Wissey, where the windmill and its adjoining Gothic gazebo have recently been restored by the Norfolk Windmills Trust. St Andrew's church is a dramatic sight, for much of the massive tower and west end is ruined and only the easternmost bays of the nave and chancel are roofed.

At **Hilborough**, 3 miles further west and just off the A1065, All Saints' church stands alone in a forest clearing. Lord Nelson's grandfather, father and brother were all rectors here. The finest part is the highly ornate west tower doorway, with its statue niches and huntsmen carved in the door spandrels. The angels in the nave roof have been decapitated, but those in the chancel survive intact, carrying symbols of the Passion.

From the churchyard the fine Georgian Hall, built in 1779, can be seen in its parkland setting. East of the church, a path leads down to the River Wissey, past a moated motte and a substantial but now empty 19th-century mill.

Cromer (3/1A)
Famous for its succulent crabs, Cromer was an important port long before it became a seaside resort. The fine medieval church of St Peter and St Paul in the centre of the town is a symbol of early prosperity; its great tower, 160 feet tall, served as a lighthouse for coastal shipping. Aspects of the town's maritime history are well explained in the little museum to the east of the church in Brook Street, which occupies a row of

former fishermen's cottages.

Cromer was already popular by the late 18th century (a character in Jane Austen's *Emma* calls it 'the best of all the sea-bathing places'), but major development began in the 1890s with the opening of railway lines to London and the Midlands. From this period date the pier and the imposing Hotel de Paris on the promenade, as well as all the attractive houses of the suburbs – their turrets, bay windows and balustraded balconies lend an Edwardian atmosphere to this unspoiled town.

As often happens with seaside resorts, a more up-market suburb developed away from the densely populated centre. **Overstrand**, 2 miles east, has several outstanding houses, which rank among the best of their time in all England.

Edwin Lutyens built the inventive Overstrand Hall for Lord Hillingdon in 1899; even more accomplished is The Pleasance, in Harbord Road, built for Lord Battersea in 1897, with gardens by Gertrude Jekyll.

The great architect was less successful in the nearby Methodist Chapel, at the east end of the village: an odd and ugly experiment. A little further east is an inspired neo-Tudor house called Sea Marge, built in 1908–12 by an architect who deserves fame; alas, no record of his name has survived.

Crostwight (3/2C) *see* North Walsham

Denton (3/1G) *see* Earsham

Denver (1/3E) *see* Downham Market

Deopham (2/3E) *see* Hingham

Dersingham (1/3B) *see* Snettisham

Diss (5/4A)

Diss takes its name from the Old English *dic*, meaning 'a ditch or pond', a most appropriate name since the town is built around a 6-acre mere, or lake. The southern end of Mere Street opens out into a public park, where a great variety of water birds come to feed and even to wander adventurously up the town's principal pedestrianised shopping street.

This leads uphill to the broad Market Place, with its raised pavement and Victorian Shambles, a pretty building with a cast-iron veranda that contains a small museum. To the east of the Shambles is the heavily timbered Dolphin Inn and, to the north, the much-restored St Mary's

church where the poet John Skelton was rector from 1498.

West of the church, Market Hill and St Nicholas Street form a triangle with Market Place and are lined with many fine half-timbered houses, some with carved corner posts, others with bold plaster pargeting. Alleys run back from the street fronts, some providing glimpses of the mere to the south.

Several of Norfolk's major roads converge on or near Diss, and at **Scole**, 2 miles east, there is not only a busy junction but also one of the most splendid coaching inns ever built, the White Hart. The big carved wooden inn sign dates, along with the building, from 1655 and hangs from the ornate brick facade – all Dutch gables, pilasters and giant chimneys betokening the fireside warmth that lies within. Such a sumptuous creation could easily be mistaken for the country home of a wealthy landowner.

At **Billingford**, a mile west, is a handsome five-storey windmill, kept in good order by the Norfolk Windmills Trust and open at weekends in summer.

Ditchingham (3/2F)

Four miles west of Bungay, Ditchingham is a dispersed village, centred around the park – landscaped by Capability Brown – and the fine early Georgian Hall which is open on occasions in summer.

St Mary's church is full of interest. The tall west tower is decorated with a flushwork frieze of thorn wreaths surrounding the Sacred Heart and the two 15th-century statues on either side of the south door are original, though restored. At the west end, the life-size bronze soldier in uniform is a remarkable and moving memorial to the victims of the First World War. The chancel screen is accomplished Victorian work, as is the rich floral painting of the chancel ceiling, while the north aisle window was designed in 1925 as a memorial to the local author, Henry Rider Haggard.

Hedenham, a mile to the north, has a delightful Hall, built in the 16th century of brick, with early 18th-century stepped gables and Venetian windows. It stands opposite the Mermaid Inn, which has an amusing inn sign.

Downham Market (1/3E)

This small town, right on the edge of the Fens, has few buildings of note, but the overall effect of yellow brick and rust-brown carstone, cut into brick-sized blocks, is pleasing. St Edmund's

Oaks at sunset, near Ditchingham

church is itself of carstone and stands high above the town, separated from it by an ugly concrete embankment. The churchyard commands views for miles across the Fens.

The market place is the focal point of the town. It is marked by an 1878 cast-iron clock tower, Big Ben in miniature, decorated with Gothic panels and painted pastel green and white. Near by stands Lloyds Bank, with a massive pedimented doorcase, and the 1887 Town Hall, all Dutch gables and Renaissance detailing that looks incongruous in yellow brick.

Further up the High Street is the folly-like Castle Hotel, heavily rusticated and battlemented, with a fine doorcase, all the more striking for being painted bright turquoise and green. At the top of the High Street, number 57, Canon House, now an antique shop, has an attractive Edwardian conservatory, complete with tufa grotto, squeezed between it and the next-door garage.

To the west of the town, the railway station and a small industrial estate stand on the site of a formerly important river port, through which ships, wherries and barges passed on their way to Cambridge, Bedford and the East Midlands. To understand the changes that have taken place since then, we must visit the great Denver Sluice complex, 3 miles south-west of the town — passing first, however, through the village of Denver.

Denver, almost a suburb of Downham Market, has a group of four houses, built in 1987, in local materials and with Dutch gables; a praiseworthy group but for the massive garage doors which spoil the integrity of the façades. Beyond it Denver Hall, with its lovely Tudor brickwork gatehouses and shaped chimneys, can be glimpsed over the high surrounding walls. Its neighbour, Ryston Hall, is a 17th-century house designed by Roger Pratt; the gardens and parkland were laid out by Sir John Soane and are open under the National Gardens Scheme.

The road to the river crosses Sluice Common, with its old brick farmhouses and magnificent windmill, open to the public, built in 1835 and retaining all its associated granary buildings.

Denver Sluice itself is an impressive piece of engineering, at the centre of a massive complex of rivers and drainage channels: the Rivers Wissey, Little Ouse and Ely Ouse, the Old and New Bedford Rivers, as well as numerous Lodes and Drains, all converge on the Great Ouse at this point.

The Dutch engineer, Vermuyden, built the first sluice at Denver in 1651, as part of a scheme to drain the fenlands owned by the Duke of Bedford. The oldest surviving sluice was built in 1834 and is still in use, though its original wooden gates have been replaced with steel doors. Alongside is the new Great Denver Sluice, opened in 1964. Together, they perform several vital functions; they control the flow of the rivers and, when necessary, can divert floodwaters into the Flood Relief Channel that runs parallel to the Great Ouse. They also serve as a lock gate between the tidal water of the Ouse and the freshwater rivers to the south, whose height remains constant. Finally, water diverted into the Cut-off Channel that forms a great loop through west Norfolk supplies drinking water for towns and cities as far south as Chelmsford and Colchester.

Many visitors come to Denver Sluice to walk southwards along the retaining banks of the Old and New Bedford Rivers. These two great drains were dug by Vermuyden, and run parallel for 22km, from Earith, in Cambridgeshire, to Denver. The space between, known as the Ouse Washes, are up to 1km wide and are deliberately flooded during winter, taking the river overflow, so that the fen fields either side remain dry.

As a consequence, a rich ecology has developed over the last 300 years; many rare and attractive water plants flourish in the ditches and river banks, as well as numerous species of fish, small and large, dragonflies, the rare large tortoiseshell butterfly, moths and small mammals. Above all, the Washes are an important breeding ground for all sorts of birds, from warblers to Bewick swans. The best place to see them is at **Welney**, 10 miles south-west of Downham Market, where the Wildfowl Trust runs a visitor centre with a car park and a series of hides.

Dunhams, The (2/1D)

Anyone who loves simple Saxon architecture will immediately warm to the church of St Andrew at **Great Dunham**, 6 miles north-east of Swaffham. The sturdy central tower is square, with double belfry windows separated by shafts and a cushion capital. The west end has a model example of long and short-work quoins and a blocked Saxon triangular-headed doorway.

The entrance is now through the south porch. The nave is ornamented with impressive blank arcading: this is now plastered, but in 1925 the construction was studied in detail and the arches were found to be made of reused Roman brick.

The tall tower arch, separating the nave from the rebuilt Victorian chancel, has imposts decorated in a variety of patterns, including rope moulding. Simple the church may be by comparison with later ecclesiastical architecture, but by Saxon standards it is an unusually ornate and accomplished building.

At **Little Dunham**, the church of St Margaret stands by the side of the Georgian rectory, surrounded by trees and parkland. A lovely 13th-century arcade runs the length of the nave, while the westernmost arch of that in the chancel rests on a big and puzzling male head; he has a monastic tonsure, but he also sports a pair of horns – the devil in disguise, perhaps?

Two miles south-west, the village of **Sporle** is made attractive by the streams that flow down either side of the long main street. St Mary's church contains simple, cartoon-like painted scenes from the life of St Catherine of Alexandria, dating from the early 15th century.

Earsham (3/2G)

Otters are now uncommon in the wild, and the Otter Trust at Earsham, on the county border 1 mile west of Bungay, Suffolk, provides a rare opportunity to study these delightful mammals at close quarters. The Trust is open daily in summer. The large collection includes both European and Asian otters, kept in natural enclosures along the banks of the River Waveney; a nature trail laid out along the river shows us the otter's natural habitat.

Denton lies in pleasant countryside 3 miles west of Earsham; the path to the church crosses one of the River Waveney's several tributaries. The large porch of St Mary's church has unusually well-preserved bosses of the *Nativity*, the *Resurrection*, the *Assumption* and the *Coronation of the Virgin* and the windows contain much English and foreign stained glass of the 15th to the 18th centuries.

East Barsham *see* Barshams, The

East Dereham (2/2D)

This town lies at the geographical centre of Norfolk, just off the A47. One of Harry Carter's most ambitious town signs (*see* SWAFFHAM) spans the High Street; it illustrates the legend that St Withburgha founded a nunnery here in AD 654 and was sustained during a famine by the milk of two deer. The name Dereham probably does mean 'a deer enclosure' and Withburgha, daughter of Anna, King of the

East Angles, has a well named after her to the west of the parish church; her bones used to lie here but they were stolen by the monks of Ely, whose own community was founded by another saintly daughter of King Anna, Etheldreda.

The parish church of St Nicholas was once at the centre of the town, which moved further west following a disastrous fire in 1581. Bishop Bonner's Cottages alongside the church were among the few groups of buildings to survive. Dated 1502, the thatched row is decorated with plaster pargeting and is now a museum.

Inside the church is one of Norfolk's finest Perpendicular Seven Sacrament fonts and a memorial window to the poet William Cowper who died in the town in 1800.

Yet another fire swept through the town in 1679, after which the huge Market Place, which once stretched from the church to the High Street, began to shrink as the new houses of Church Street and Quebec Street encroached upon the space.

The whole town now has a genteel, mainly

The Otter Trust at Earsham is open in summer

18th-century appearance, with only a few later intrusions into the general harmony; the big Corn Hall, with its mighty Corinthian columns, was built in 1857 and is now a cinema. The Congregational Chapel opposite was built in 1873 on the site of the house in which Cowper died.

South of the town is the little hamlet of Dumpling Green, where the writer George Borrow was born in 1803, and then Yaxham, a compact village surrounding St Peter's church, which has a Saxon tower.

At **Shipdham**, 3 miles further south-west, the lovely minaret-like structure on top of All Saints' church is a local landmark visible from afar; this inventive lantern, of two lead-covered onion domes, was an inspired addition of the 17th century and contemporary with the 1630 Commandment Boards and attractive Communion rails inside. The other treasure of the church is its lectern, one of the finest and earliest

Bishop Bonner's Cottages, East Dereham

surviving wooden examples in England, dating to around 1500 and carved with Tudor roses.

Two miles north-west of Dereham is **Gressenhall**, where the former workhouse has been converted into an excellent Rural Life Museum. The 'House of Industry' was built in 1776 and initially the regime was a progressive one; inmates farmed the surrounding fields, producing crops for sale and for their own consumption. Alas, the 1834 Poor Law introduced a harsher way of life, intending as it did to deter the poor from seeking parish assistance except as a last desperate resort. The 'Union', as it is known locally, continued in use until 1976, latterly as an old people's home. The museum draws on the collective memory of the local community for its displays, illustrating the changing face of Norfolk agriculture.

East Harling (2/2G) *see* Harlings, The

East Lexham (2/1D) *see* Lexhams, The

East Raynham (2/1C)
East Raynham lies on the A1065, 3 miles southeast of Fakenham. The way to the church leads past the lodge gates of Raynham Park. Beyond, on the hill, the Hall itself is visible. This important brick house of 1620–50, with bell gabled projecting wings, was built for Sir Roger Townshend. The design has been attributed to Inigo Jones but is more likely to be the work of Townshend himself and of William Edge, his master mason.

The widow of an earlier Sir Roger Townshend left money in her will of 1499 to provide the sumptuous Easter Sepulchre in St Mary's church. Sir Roger's helm is back on top of the sepulchre; it was stolen and sold at Sotheby's to an American buyer, who found it described in the Standard Textbook of European Armour and generously returned it to the church.

East Walton (1/4D) *see* Narborough

East Wretham (2/2F) *see* Thetford

Edingthorpe (3/2B) *see* North Walsham

Ellinghams, The (2/3F)
These two villages lie about 5 miles south-west of Wymondham. Time has taken its toll of the fine east window of St James's church, **Great Ellingham**, and the tracery mullions lean this

way and that, no longer parallel. In the south aisle, a prettily vaulted 14th-century niche is inhabited by a painted angel. The delicate 18th-century west gallery is in two stages, to accommodate choir and bellringers.

St Peter's church at **Little Ellingham** has a good stained glass window designed by C. E. Kempe. The 1855 lodge house, which stands in front of the Hall, is a curious structure: it is cross-shaped with a separate dwelling in each arm, and a great lighthouse-shaped clock tower rising from its centre.

Elsing (2/3D) *see* Swanton Morley

Emneth (1/1E) *see* Upwell

Erpingham (2/4B)

The village lies 4 miles west of North Walsham, just beyond the A140. The tall 15th-century tower of St Mary's church leaves you in no doubt as to where you are, for flushwork initials around the battlements spell out the name Erpingham. The east window contains excellent stained glass from a variety of sources.

Just east of the village, on the A140, Alby Gardens has an interesting collection of wild and wetland plants and is part of a working craft complex, created from restored agricultural buildings.

Two miles further east, at **Colby**, St Giles's church and the former rectory form a charming group, alone in the fields. The two-storeyed porch has an upper room with a fireplace and chimney disguised as a pinnacle. The door spandrels are carved with St Michael and a *St George fighting the dragon*.

Inside, the very fine font is carved with a

Raynham Hall, East Raynham

number of unusual scenes; as well as Evangelists' symbols, found all over East Anglia, the sculptor has added a *Virgin and Child*, kneeling benefactors, and a vignette of St Giles, the 9th-century hermit and patron of the church. The broad chancel is fitted with 15th-century Norwich school stained glass, and the 17th-century panelling is thought to have come from nearby GUNTON church.

Fakenham (2/2C)

This prosperous market town stands at the conjunction of the A148 and A1065. There is nothing here to detain the visitor very long. The Market Place has all the good buildings, nearly all late 18th and early 19th century, of brick, now mostly the premises of banks and building societies.

The church of St Peter and St Paul is just west of the Market Place, surrounded by a big churchyard which shows off the tall and ornate west tower. Restoration in 1864 robbed the interior of much of its character.

Felbrigg (3/1B)

The village is 1½ miles inland from Cromer.

Dovecot and walled garden, Felbrigg Hall

The Hall and St Margaret's church are equally worthy of attention. The Hall, owned by the National Trust, is the more imposing, but the little church, once at the centre of a village that was cleared in the 17th century, contains the best collection of brasses in Norfolk.

The famous Coningsby brass of 1608 was made in London by the finest craftsmen of the day and has remained in pristine condition. Equally magnificent is Sir Simon Felbrigg (d. 1416) and his wasp-waisted wife, Margaret. He was standard-bearer to Richard II and the family's fetterlock symbol appears all over the church tower and buttresses.

The estate was acquired from the Felbrigg family in the mid 15th century by John Wyndham whose descendant, Thomas Windham, began the present Jacobean mansion in 1615. The modest house was gradually extended and James Paine designed one of the finest rooms in the house – the Gothick Library – in 1754–5. The furnishings reflect the taste of the late 18th and early 19th centuries. The huge walled garden, covering 2½ acres, has recently been restored as a 'potager' or decorative kitchen garden, providing fruit, vegetables and cut flowers for the house.

Feltwell (1/4F) *see* Hockwold

Fersfield (5/3A) *see* Bressingham

Field Dalling (2/3B) *see* Bale

Fincham (1/3E) *see* Barton Bendish

Florden (3/1F) *see* Tasborough

Forncetts, The (2/4F)
St Peter's church at **Forncett St Peter**, 5 miles south-east of Wymondham, is both handsome and rewarding, a near-complete Saxon church with three different types of bell-opening in its tall cylindrical tower: circular, simple slits and more complex double triangular-headed openings with a central turned shaft. The tower arch inside is one of the most impressive of its kind, a full 15 feet tall but only just over 5 feet wide.

Perpendicular windows were added in the 15th century, but without spoiling the atmosphere of a simple rural church, and the bench ends, though mostly carved in the 19th century, are nevertheless convincingly medieval in style and subject matter. The 18th-century Rectory alongside makes a perfect companion, with its curvaceous bell-shaped gables.

Forncett St Mary, a mere half-mile away, is not special and has many modern houses but the road joining the two hamlets follows the wide marshy reed beds of the River Tas, hunting territory for barn owls.

Framinghams, The (3/1E)
St Andrew's church at **Framingham Earl**, 4 miles south-east of Norwich, is a fine example of a complete Saxon church; even the neo-Norman restoration does not detract from its delightful compactness and the tiny windows scarcely admit any light.

The Saxon church at **Framingham Pigot** was demolished in 1859. The replacement, St Andrew's, is a good example of rural Victorian church architecture, with an ornate tower gallery.

Fring (1/4B) *see* Shernborne

Fritton (3/3E) *see* St Olaves

Fritton (3/1F)
This dispersed village, 8 miles south of Norwich, consists of a sprinkling of cottages, scattered around a long, wild and marshy common, almost a mile in length.

The delightful church of St Catherine is well to the north and is reached up a grassy track. One wall of the church is painted with a *St George*, which may have been retouched, but is none the less enjoyable.

Morningthorpe, a mere half-mile west of Fritton, is a pretty wooded village and the church of St John the Baptist makes a fine group with the manor house next door. The neat churchyard is a mass of daffodils in spring and there is a 14th-century piscina in the chancel, prettily carved, though a figure in the spandrel mocks the onlooker by poking his tongue out at him.

Garboldisham (5/3A)
Garboldisham (pronounced 'Garblesham') lies on the busy A1066 between Thetford and Diss, just a mile over the Suffolk border. The church of St John the Baptist has a fine tower decorated with flushwork. The excellent glass was made in the 1880s, clearly under the influence of Morris and Burne-Jones and the richly coloured *Ascension* in the east window is filled with pre-Raphaelite angels holding the symbols of Christ's Passion.

A mile to the west of the village is a well-preserved stretch of Devil's Dyke, straddling the A1066, originally a Roman road.

South of Garboldisham, there is a post mill on the right-hand side of the B1111 before the left turning to **Blo Norton** on the county boundary. St Andrew's church contains a monument to Prince Duleep Singh (d. 1926) who settled in England after his father, the ruler of the Punjab, was exiled by the Imperial Government in India. The Prince, who is actually buried at ELVEDEN, Suffolk, was an accomplished historian and for some years rented Blo Norton Hall; this very fine timber-framed house, only just visible from the road, has scarcely changed since it was enlarged in the reign of Elizabeth I.

Gillingham (3/3F)
Peace has returned to this hamlet a mile from the Suffolk border at Beccles, with the completion of a new by-pass on the A143. Its three churches now lie along a leafy lane that was once the busy Yarmouth road. The first church you see, climbing the hill, is the unusually tasteful Roman Catholic church, built in 1898, of brick, in restrained classical style.

The second church, St Mary's, lies a little further north, and is an attempt to produce a copybook Norman church, built in 1858–9. The tiny nave displays every type of Romanesque ornamentation, including fat, spirally grooved pillars in the style of Durham cathedral. The interior is gloomy from the tiny splayed windows filled with Victorian glass but, even so, the church has an atmosphere all of its own.

The third church, All Saints, a hundred yards to the north, survives only as an ivy-covered tower, from where there are views eastwards to the Jacobean Gillingham Hall.

Gissing (5/4A)

The village is 5 miles north-east of Diss. The church of St Mary's has one of Norfolk's most pleasing round towers, pierced by Saxon windows, and two ornate Norman doors. The nave has a lovely, delicate double hammerbeam roof, so graceful that it seems weightless.

Two miles north-east, St Margaret's church at **Tivetshall St Margaret** is surrounded by an oasis of greenery in a flat landscape of hedgeless fields and pylons. Inside, instead of a rood, the chancel arch bears an enormous Elizabeth I coat of arms painted on ash boards, dated 1587, with the Ten Commandments below. Tudor arms are

very rare, and nowhere else does one so dominate the church.

Glandford (2/3A) see Holt

Gooderstone (1/4E) see Oxborough

Great Bircham (1/4B) see Birchams, The

Great Cressingham (2/1E) see Cressinghams, The

Great Dunham (2/1D) see Dunhams, The

Great Ellingham (2/3F) see Ellinghams, The

Great Hockham (2/2F)

The village, on the B1075 5 miles west of Attleborough, consists of a number of picturesque thatched cottages around a triangular green. The carved sign on the green depicts a horned figure, a reminder that Hockham once held an Easter Fair, at which horn objects were sold, and visitors were liable to be 'attacked' by a jester wearing a fearsome set of horns until they placated him with the gift of a farthing.

Holy Trinity church is in the grounds of Hockham Hall and contains some well-preserved

Double hammerbeam roof in Gissing church

15th-century wall paintings of the *Trinity* and the *Annunciation*.

Cranberry Rough, north-west of the village, is a Norfolk Naturalists Trust reserve and the breeding ground of rare White Admiral butterflies.

St Margaret's church, **Breckles**, a mile northeast of Hockham, by the side of the B1111, is late Saxon and full of fascinating detail. The tall tower arch of the round tower is decorated with a frieze of interlace and snakes biting their tails. The font is Norman but has a distinctively Celtic feel.

Great Massingham (1/4C) *see* Massinghams, The

Great Ryburgh (2/2C) *see* Ryburghs, The

Great Snoring (2/2B) *see* Snorings, The

Great Walsingham (2/2B) *see* Walsinghams, The

Great Witchingham (2/1D) *see* Witchinghams, The

Great Yarmouth (3/4E)

Yarmouth is far more than just a seaside resort; it is an historic town of considerable interest, with one of the most complete medieval town walls in England, numerous museums and much interesting architecture. Because it is still a working port, it is also a busy, noisy place; no one would call it charming, but the juxtaposition of ancient and modern often creates poignant contrasts and lends Yarmouth a unique atmosphere.

Nowhere is this more evident than along South Quay, where elegant merchants' houses, one built as early as 1596, face the port at which grain, timber and cement are unloaded into huge riverside warehouses.

Visitors to Yarmouth are often surprised to find that the town is built facing the River Waveney, not the sea. After a long and tortuous course through Norfolk, this river forms a three-mile long channel leading up to the point where it joins the North Sea. This channel provided a safe, calm harbour and the town grew up on the long narrow sand spit alongside.

Yarmouth has been compared to Manhattan because of its shape and rectangular street grid. Before the town was bombed in the Second World War, scores of narrow alleys, called Rows, led off the main north-south axis. Around this ancient core two distinct new areas developed: to the east, facing the sea, the late Victorian holiday resort; to the south, the modern port, revitalised after the decline of the fishing industry by the discovery of oil and gas in the North Sea.

The best place to begin an exploration of the town is St Nicholas's church, at the northern end of the Market Place. The church was largely destroyed in the war and cleverly rebuilt in its medieval form in 1957–60. The two massive aisles, each as wide as the nave, justify its claim to be the largest parish church in England.

Handsome Georgian houses form a miniature close south of the church. Squeezed in between two of them is the half-timbered house in which Anna Sewell, author of *Black Beauty*, was born.

Across the busy road from the church lies the big, broad Market Place, lined with shops of all periods from the 18th century to the 1960s, predominantly of red brick and pleasing in its homogeneity. At the north-eastern corner is the beautiful quadrangular Hospital for Decayed Fishermen, founded in 1702, with its statues of Charity and a chilly looking Neptune.

On the opposite corner, to the south-west, are a few of the Rows that survived the bombings of 1939–45. Both Market Row and Broad Row are lined with Victorian-fronted shops.

The left turn, southwards out of Broad Row, leads to Hall Quay and the administrative centre of Yarmouth. Here we find the Queen Anne-style Town Hall of 1882, the early 17th-century Duke's Head Hotel and several banks. To the west Haven Bridge, one of the busiest routes into and out of the town, was opened in 1930 on the site of its medieval predecessor. Moored nearby is the *Lydia Eva*, one of the last coastal drifters to operate out of Yarmouth and now a floating museum with exhibits on the history of the herring industry.

Hall Quay leads to South Quay and the most complete group of early houses in Yarmouth. Number 4 has a deceptive late Georgian exterior, but behind lies a house built by Benjamin Cooper, a merchant, in 1596. It is now a museum of domestic life and some fine Elizabethan rooms survive, with oak panelling, ornate chimney pieces and sumptuous moulded plasterwork ceilings.

Numbers 6 to 12 are fine 18th-century buildings with typical doorcases and balconies – one would not guess that number 12 was entirely rebuilt after the war. Row 92, alongside, leads to the remains of a 13th-century Franciscan friary,

Great Yarmouth docks

maintained by English Heritage. The next, and most splendid, of the South Quay houses is number 20, built in the 18th century by the wealthy merchant, John Andrews and now occupied by the Port Commissioners. Further south, in Row 117, is the Old Merchants House, a typical brick townhouse of the 17th century and another English Heritage property.

The Row leads to Tolhouse Street and the Tolhouse Museum, which for centuries served as the town's courthouse and gaol. The earliest part of the building, with its external staircase, dates to around 1235 and was used to fix the price of herrings and collect a portion of the seller's profits for the Borough Chamberlain. Now the Tolhouse is used as a museum, full of fascinating objects that illustrate Yarmouth's long history as a port, fishing centre and holiday resort.

The north end of Tolhouse Street leads into Yarmouth Way with its view, to the east, of the handsome church of St George, now a theatre and arts centre. The church was built in 1714–16 by John Price, who was inspired by Wren's church of St James Garlickhithe, as well as, perhaps, St Clement Danes. Stretching north

and south from the church are the ancient town walls, surviving almost complete as they were built in the 13th and 14th centuries.

A good mile south of the old town, ringed by light industrial factories, is the impressive monument to Admiral Lord Nelson, built by public subscription in 1819, ten years before the more famous column in Trafalgar Square – and at 144 feet only a foot shorter. Britannia stands in triumph at the top, above a viewing platform from which all Yarmouth is visible.

Returning north, the long, wide beach-side Parades are lined with amusement arcades, caravan sites, pleasure parks and fun fairs. The original late Victorian sea front clusters around Wellington Pier, itself a cross between a garden conservatory and an Art Deco cinema. Some grand Edwardian hotels survive nearby, though many were bombed and have been replaced by meaner structures. A little further north, on Marine Parade, the former home for ship-wrecked sailors has been converted into an excellent Maritime Museum.

Gressenhall (2/2D) *see* East Dereham

Guestwick (2/3C)
This village lies midway between Fakenham and

Aylsham, in northern Norfolk. The Saxon tower of St Peter's church is in an unusual position north of the chancel and may, perhaps, once have belonged to a second church sharing the same churchyard, as at LITTLE SNORING.

A little north of the church is the Old Meeting House, founded in 1652 and one of the earliest Non-conformist chapels in Norfolk. Originally timber-framed, it was given a brick façade in 1695 and 'improved' in 1840 when the stepped gables and porch were added.

Gunton (3/1B) *see* Thorpe Market

Haddiscoe (3/3F)

This village lies on the A143 7 miles south-west of Great Yarmouth. The church of St Mary's, and that of the next village, Thorpe, can boast two of Norfolk's finest Saxon round towers. Their picturesqueness was much appreciated by Norwich school artists and Sir John Arnesby, who lived in the White House on the edge of Haddiscoe village, often included the distinctive tower of St Mary's in his paintings. The tower rises through five stages: the lower four are Saxon with unusually ornate bell openings, the fifth is 15th century, of chequerwork, flint and stone.

The church also possesses two of the finest Norman doorways in Norfolk; the south door is especially striking with its seated figure in vestments – possibly representing *Christ in Majesty* – and splendid 14th-century ironwork.

St Matthias's church at **Thorpe**, a mile north, occupies a memorable position, standing alone on a hill with the flats of the Waveney marshes laid out below. The building is simple but for the tower, with its blind arcading below and ornate bell openings above.

Hales (3/2F) *see* Loddon

Happisburgh (3/2C)

(Pronounced 'Haysboro'.) The skyline around this cliff-top village in north-east Norfolk, is ringed by tall landmarks: several church towers, water towers, radio masts, the pylons of the gas terminal at Bacton, the candy-stripe lighthouse, built in 1791 and – best and most prominent – the soaring spire of St Mary's church.

Light reflected off the nearby sea floods the big nave of the church and winds batter it on a stormy day. The treacherous offshore sand banks have wrecked many a ship and the churchyard contains numerous graves – including

Nelson's monument, Great Yarmouth

those of all 119 of the crew of HMS Invincible, wrecked in 1801 on the way to join Nelson's fleet at Copenhagen.

The road to the beach is lined with thatched and flint cottages, dominated by the splendid butterfly-plan Manor House (now St Mary's Hotel and Country Club), built in 1900 by the Edwardian Arts and Crafts architect Detmar Blow.

Hardingham (2/3E) *see* Hingham

Harleston (6/1A)
Now by-passed, this pleasing market town off the A143, just a mile over the Suffolk border, can be enjoyed to the full by walking around its triangle of main streets, lined with elegant Georgian houses and original early shop fronts. Two of the best houses lie at the extremes of the town; at the south end, the Swan Hotel with its enjoyable wrought-iron inn sign and at the north the Candlers House, rated by Nikolaus Pevsner one of the best early Georgian houses anywhere in the country.

Harleston has its own Victorian church built in 1872, but for centuries the parishioners travelled the 1½ miles west to **Redenhall** for services. Here they were greeted by the elegant tower of St Mary's church, set high on a hill. This tower is built in the Suffolk tradition (it resembles that of EYE), with vertical stripes of flint and stone that serve to emphasise its great height. Inside, the brass lectern is very rare, with a double-headed eagle made around 1500, and the 15th-century vestment chest is Venetian, painted inside the lid with a fleet of galleys in full sail.

Harling, East (2/2G)
East Harling, 10 miles north-east of Thetford, has one of the most splendid churches of the Breckland region. The tower of St Peter and St Paul has battlements ornamented with figures of its patron saints and a pretty lead-covered corona and spire, added in the 14th century and copied by the builders of St Peter Mancroft, Norwich.

The 15th-century Norwich school stained glass depicting the life of the Virgin is outstanding and has survived only because it was removed and stored in the manor during the iconoclastic Commonwealth period.

All Saints' church, **Bridgham**, 2 miles west of East Harling, has Dutch gables to the nave and two fonts; one is 15th century and carved with

an Assumption scene – a rare subject on fonts – and the other is Norman, moved here from St Andrew's church, Roudham, now a picturesque, creeper-clad ruin.

Two miles north of East Harling, the little church of St Ethelbert at **Larling** lies at the end of a long field track. The Norman south door is richly carved with geometrical designs.

Harpley (1/4C)
The oldest houses in this pretty and compact

St Mary's church, Redenhall

village, a mile north of Little Massingham, cluster around the turning to Church Lane; William Kerning's Dutch-gabled almshouses, the 1845 National School and the Primitive Methodist Chapel founded in 1771 (rebuilt 1871) form a fine group of mellow brick buildings. Up Church Lane the church of St Lawrence stands high on a hill, entered through a wicket gate in the 15th-century south door, beautifully carved with the symbols of St Luke and St John.

The chancel of the church, rebuilt by the Rector, John de Gurney, in the 14th century, has a charming priest's door under a cusped ogee arch, matched by an elaborate piscina carved with a frieze of roses. Much Norwich school stained glass has survived, high up in the west window.

A mile north of the village is **Houghton Hall**, one of the 'finest examples of neo-Palladian architecture in England, built in the 1730s by Sir Robert Walpole, Britain's first Prime Minister. The Hall is approached through the village, relocated to the southern perimeter of the estate in the 1720s when the park was landscaped. The villagers benefited from the move, for Walpole built them sizeable cottages, facing each other across the broad lime avenue that forms the approach to the Hall, and all of limewashed brick.

Sir Robert Walpole's choice of the neo-Palladian style was not just a matter of personal taste, but an expression of his political position. Colen Campbell, who designed this house, rejected the extravagant Baroque style of architects such as Wren and Hawksmoor, in favour of a purer and more ordered form of classical architecture, in keeping with the rationalist spirit of the age.

Ironically, the classical simplicity of Campbell's original design, influenced by Inigo Jones's earlier Wilton House in Wiltshire, was modified into a more opulent design by James Gibbs, who added the stone domes, Venetian windows and rusticated window surrounds. Willam Kent's interior decorations, too, are lavish, especially the immense Stone Hall – one of the grandest rooms in England – and the State Rooms of the upper *piano nobile*. As a result it is now quite the most magnificent house in Norfolk, rivalled only by HOLKHAM HALL, and one of the grandest in England.

In 1860 the Hall was rejected as a possible home for the Prince of Wales in favour of Sandringham and so the house continues to be owned by descendants of Sir Robert in the female line. His huge stable block is used for breeding heavy horses and Shetland ponies and the beautiful parkland is grazed by a herd of white fallow deer. The house is open on Sundays, Thursdays and Bank Holidays in summer.

Heacham (1/3B)

Caley Mill, at the junction of the A149 and B1454, just east of Heacham, is the home of Norfolk Lavender. An early 19th-century water-mill and miller's cottage form the centrepiece of this fragrant garden, which contains a collection of all the known varieties of lavender. This is at its best in July and August, when the commercial beds are harvested, and the flowers dried or converted into scents and toilet waters. The grounds are open all year and guided tours are organised in summer.

St Mary's church contains a memorial, carved by a pupil of Rodin, to the Algonquin Indian princess Pocahontas, dressed in a stylish Jacobean trilby hat and great neck ruff. Pocahontas saved the life of Captain John Smith by laying her head over his when her father, Chief Powhaten, ordered him to be clubbed to death. She was only 12 years old at the time; seven years later, in 1614, she married in Virginia John Rolfe, originally of Heacham Hall. Back in England she was an immediate social sensation; alas, lacking immunity to the many diseases endemic in Jacobean England, she died only three years later, aged 22.

Two miles east, **Sedgeford** is a pretty village of carstone cottages with a stately and atmospheric church. The Saxon round tower is now dwarfed by the big Perpendicular edifice that has grown from it. The roof was renewed in the mid 19th century; before that, the church was open to the sky and parishioners carried umbrellas to services.

Hedenham (3/2F) *see* Ditchingham

Hemblington (3/2D) *see* Blofield

Hemsby (3/2D)

This uninteresting seaside resort lies 3 miles up the coast from Caister-on-Sea. In the porch of St Mary's church, however, there are some fine bosses illustrating the *Life of the Virgin*.

More interesting is **Winterton-on-Sea**, 2 miles further up the coast. Apart from the modern seaside bungalows, the Hotel Humanus, to the south of the village, has intriguing thatched 'rond hovels', inspired by South African mud

Sedgeford village sign

huts. The massive, seven-stage tower of Holy Trinity church stands 132 feet high, a landmark for sailors exceeded in height in Norfolk only by the towers at Cromer and Wymondham. The whole south face has been colonised by wallflowers, which put out a mass of tiny yellow fragrant blooms in spring.

West Somerton, a mile west of Winterton, is the burial place of Robert Hales, known as the 'Norfolk Giant', 7ft 8ins tall and 32 stone in weight. A suitably large coffin-shaped memorial covers his grave in St Mary's churchyard.

Hevingham (3/1C)

Three miles south of Aylsham, just off the A140, the church of St Botolph at Hevingham contains a number of stained glass panels illustrating Old and New Testament stories. Originally made in the early 16th century for Steinfeld monastery in Germany, they were looted at the end of the 18th century by French soldiers who found a ready market for them in England. They were given to the church by H. P. Marsham in 1881.

Much of the surrounding area is beautifully wooded, thanks to Robert Marsham, a keen naturalist and squire of the neighbouring village of Stratton Strawless, who planted many trees in the late 18th century; some of them still line the A140.

Heydon (2/4C)

This very attractive estate village, 4 miles west of Aylsham, lies at the end of a *cul-de-sac* that leads to Heydon Hall, an Elizabethan mansion built in 1581. The house passed to the Bulwer family in 1762 and nearly all the houses surrounding the village green date back to that time. A blacksmith's forge, still in use, faces rows of neat houses, some with pediments, some with stepped gables and all with pretty front gardens.

At **Thurning**, 3 miles to the north-west, the River Blackwater has been dammed to form a lake that fronts the hall. This is a Georgian building visible from the road, with a good group of red-brick stables and farm buildings.

Hickling (3/3C)

This village lies 2 miles inland from the northeast Norfolk coast. The lofty tower of St Mary's church is ornamented with a delicate geometric frieze and the north aisle contains an unusually early memorial slab, of around 1300, with a Lombardic inscription.

The village now spreads south for at least 2 miles to **Hickling Green**, with its tall windmill, and **Hickling Heath**, a busy port of call for Broadland holidaymakers. Hickling Broad was one of the first national nature reserves in this country to be so designated and the reed beds can be visited by appointment with the Warden. Swallowtail butterflies still breed here in profusion, but marsh harriers are nowadays seldom sighted and bitterns are even rarer: pollution from boats and agriculture has diminished what was once an outstanding habitat for every form of wildlife.

Hilborough (2/1E) *see* Cressinghams, The

Hindringham (2/2B)

This village is a mile to the west of the A148, between Fakenham and Holt. The 84-foot tower of St Martin's church is not the highest in Norfolk but, situated as it is on a hilltop, it seems much taller and is visible from afar, together with the windmill at Lower Green, north of the village.

St Martin's has a 'weeping' chancel, with a pronounced southward lean; there has never been a satisfactory explanation for this, though many like to think it symbolises the weeping head of Christ on the Cross.

At **Thursford**, a mile further south, St Andrew's church stands in the grounds of the Hall. Both buildings are Victorian and the graceless church is only worth visiting as an example of bold but bad architecture.

The Thursford Collection is half a mile north – an inspired museum of mechanical organs, Victorian fairground machines and traction engines, which is well worth visiting. All the machines work and the best time to go is on a summer evening when the organ music and multi-coloured lights create a magical atmosphere.

Hingham (2/3E)

This cosmopolitan small town in the depths of rural Norfolk, 4 miles west of Wymondham, comes as a wonderful surprise. The Market Place is surrounded by Jane Austen-style houses, all sash windows, ornate doorcases and fanlights.

Stretching almost the length of the north side of the Market Place is the impressive White Hart Inn, a meeting place of the local gentry which was rebuilt in the 1770s. It is strategically sited on the former coaching road which helped make Hingham such a prosperous place, once a venue for important corn and cattle markets.

Morley monument and chancel, Hingham church

This affluence did not, however, prevent a number of Hingham people in the early 17th century from choosing the uncertain future of a new life in America, where they founded the colony of Bare Cove – now renamed Hingham – in the state of Massachusetts. In 1637, these early settlers were joined by another local boy, Samuel Lincoln, great-great-great-great-grandfather of Abraham Lincoln. Not surprisingly, the ties between the two Hinghams remain strong to this day and St Andrew's church contains a memorial to the Lincoln family, unveiled by the American Ambassador in 1919.

The church also has an outstanding east window and a towering and impressive monument to Lord Morley (d. 1435), one of the most splendid 15th-century monuments in all England.

Three churches in the vicinity of Hingham are worth a visit: the tower of St Andrew, **Deopham**, is a fine example of East Anglian flushwork at its most ornate (*see* 'East Anglian Parish Churches', p. 88); St George, **Hardingham**, is pleasing just for its position on a hill, above gently rolling countryside, with a view south to the Elizabethan Old Hall. The New Hall is in the village, a mile away, an 18th-century house with dovecote and sunken rose garden which is open under the National Gardens Scheme. St Peter's,

Reymerston is approached down a leafy avenue and contains a complete set of 17th-century furnishings.

Hockwold (1/4G)
Hockwold, a mile from the Suffolk border north-west of Brandon, is now one large continuous village with Wilton. St Peter's church, surrounded by tall trees and alongside the Tudor red-brick Hall, is beautifully maintained by the Redundant Churches Fund. It has a fine roof carved with saints. The parishioners now use St James's church, Wilton, for their worship. The graceful spire is one of the few in Norfolk to be built of stone and the nave contains a fine set of benches: one is carved with a shepherd and his flock, another with Mercy ministering to prisoners.

The same motif occurs at St Mary's church, **Feltwell**, 2 miles north, along with another scene from the Seven Works of Mercy, the burial of the dead.

Holkham (2/1A)
Holkham lies on the coastal road of northernmost Norfolk, 1½ miles west of Wells-next-the-Sea. The village is almost synonymous with the name of Thomas Coke, generally known as 'Coke of Norfolk' (1752–1842), the pioneering farmer

Overleaf: St Martin's church, Glandford
Holkham Hall

whom many of his contemporaries thought mad because of his determination to produce sheep pasture from the sandy, saline soils of his estate, where scarcely a blade of grass once grew (*see* 'Coastal Birds of East Anglia', p. 32).

Coke was successful; fortunately, however, he did not put the whole of his estate down to crops. He left the shore, which is one of the finest beaches in East Anglia, sheltered by stands of pine, big enough to absorb all its visitors and still not feel crowded and with a gently shelving pure sand beach where the shallow sea quickly warms under the summer sun.

Holkham Hall, which is open in summer, is approached up an avenue of noble holm oaks and lines of neo-Tudor cottages. Few would describe the neo-Palladian house as beautiful. It was begun in 1734 by Thomas Coke, great-uncle of the agriculturalist, who built it in rather sombre yellow-brown brick. Like Walpole at Houghton Hall (*see* HARPLEY), he employed William Kent to design the house and the furnishings for the palatial suite of inter-connected State Rooms. These are hung with pictures by – among others – Gainsborough and Van Dyck, and used to display a fine collection of antique sculptures acquired in Italy. Coke's scholarly bent is well reflected in the fine Library, decorated in gold and white.

Today the Hall is the centre for a number of attractions: an agricultural and domestic bygones museum, craft centre, pottery and garden centre.

St Withburga's church, dramatically sited in the grounds of the Hall close to the lake, was completely rebuilt in 1870, preserving monuments from the earlier church carved in 1639 by Nicholas Stone.

Holme-next-the-Sea (1/4A)

Two miles up the coast from Hunstanton, Holme is a pleasant village of narrow lanes and rose-covered cottages where the Roman PEDDARS WAY finally meets the sea. The great stretches of marshy shoreline are little visited by sunbathers, but hundreds of bird watchers gather to watch the spring and autumn migrations and observe rare species. Observatories at Holme and neighbouring Thornham form part of a linked chain of reserves running along the NORFOLK COASTAL PATH from here, eastwards for 45 miles to Cromer.

Thornham is another attractive village with varied architecture. Red House, at the southern end, is a charming 18th-century building with fine wrought-iron railings and gates. Unmissable is the 1858 school at the west end of the village, a typically Victorian Gothic extravaganza with a bell turret.

Holt (2/3B)

A great fire destroyed much of Holt in 1708, so that this pleasant market town, on the A148 7 miles from Cromer, is now principally Georgian in appearance. At the north end, a 10 foot-high milestone, erected after the fire, records the distances to all the neighbouring villages and big houses. St Andrew's church, east of the Market Place, was gutted and then over-restored in 1864 but contains some good stained glass.

On the eastern edge of the town is Gresham's School, founded in 1555 and relocated here from the centre of the town in 1900, when it became a public school. The school's buildings run the panoply of the architectural styles of the 20th century.

More curious is Home Place, a mile to the east, a convalescent home built by the Arts and Crafts architect E.S. Prior in 1903–5. This eccentric building, all of pebbles, takes its cue from local vernacular styles and reflects Prior's belief in using only local building materials.

A mile west of Holt, **Letheringsett** is built on either bank of the River Glaven and linked by an ornate cast-iron bridge of 1818. Facing each other east of the church, are the historic water mill – still producing stoneground flour and poultry feed – and the Hall, now a home for the elderly, fronted by a massive Doric portico.

The gardens of the Hall and of several other properties in the village are open under the National Gardens Scheme; all are linked by the river which has been channelled into attractive pools, cascades and waterfalls.

At **Glandford**, 2 miles to the north, St Martin's church was rebuilt in 1900 for Sir Alfred Jodrell of nearby Bayfield Hall and the richly carved hammerbeam roof, the rood, screens and choir stalls show that no expense was spared. Beautiful views stretch in both directions from the churchyard, up and down the River Glaven.

The model village, also built by the Jodrells, consists of pairs of charming flint cottages with shaped gables. One contains a little museum of shells and fossils from all over the world, collected by the fisherman-artist John Craske (1881–1943).

Cottage at Horsey Mere

Horning (3/2D) *see* Wroxham

Horsey (3/3C)
This tiny village, with a delightful little thatched church, sits on the marshes a mile from the coast and 7½ miles north of Great Yarmouth. Since the 17th century, measures have been taken to drain the surrounding marshes and turn them into agricultural land. The New Cut, west of Horsey, is one of a series of linked channels designed for both navigation and drainage. As the water table dropped and the peat contracted, some of these dykes were left higher than the land they were built to drain and windpumps had to be constructed to raise the waters. One fine example, at Horsey Mere, has been restored by the National Trust and is open during the summer; from its viewing gallery several others, now derelict, can be seen dotting the marshes.

Horsford (2/4D) *see* Horsham St Faith

Horsham St Faith (3/1D)
This suburb of Norwich, north of the city's airport, retains something of the atmosphere of a village. Ruins of the original Benedictine Priory of St Faith, founded in 1105, survive at Abbey Farm next to the church.

Recent restoration work in the farmhouse has uncovered an outstanding series of 13th-century wall paintings in what was once the refectory. They illustrate the life of Robert Fitzwilliam who, according to legend, was imprisoned while returning from a pilgrimage to Rome. After praying to St Faith he was miraculously released and founded this priory in gratitude. It is hoped that, after full conservation, the house will occasionally be open to the public.

The church of St Mary and St Andrew stands opposite a row of 16th-century houses; a boss in the porch is carved, most unusually, with the saltire crucifixion of St Andrew.

Two nearby churches in the spreading Norwich suburbs are worth visiting. St Peter's church at **Spixworth**, 2 miles east of Horsham, contains one of Norfolk's best monuments, to William Peck (d. 1635) and his wife, carved realistically in their funeral shrouds by a pupil of Nicholas Stone. At **Horsford**, 1½ miles west of Horsham, All Saints' church has a beautiful Victorian stained glass window, designed by the Royal Bavarian Institute for Stained Glass. It portrays three sisters, all of whom died of tuberculosis, in an alpine setting.

Houghton Hall (1/4C) *see* Harpley

Houghton St Giles (2/2B) *see* Walsinghams, The

Hunstanton (1/3A)
Hunstanton lies on Norfolk's north-west coast to the east of the Wash. The town's transformation into a popular seaside resort began in the 1860s, at the initiative of Hamon le Strange of Hunstanton Hall, and was boosted by the arrival of the railway in 1862. The station has now gone, so have the Sandringham Hotel which stood alongside and the 1870 pier; even so, New Hunstanton still has the genteel air of a late Victorian seaside town, with large turreted villas grouped around a green.

The charming beach has firm sands, numerous rock pools and dramatic striped cliffs behind; coastal erosion has exposed a colourful sequence of rocks, consisting of rust-brown carstone overlaid by red and white chalk. The best exposures are at the northern end of the Promenade, where the 1830 lighthouse stands beside the ruins of St Edmund's chapel.

Seaside development later spread to Old Hunstanton, a mile to the north, where the cliff top is lined with 1930s beach houses, flat roofed with balconies to take in the view and surrounded by trim privet hedges. Here and there older houses and farm buildings of pink and white chalk survive.

St Mary's church enjoys a memorable setting opposite a duck pond, surrounded by high beech and chestnut trees. It was handsomely restored in 1857. The steep-pitched lead roof is supported inside by a massive and complex series of timbers. Several members of the le Strange family are commemorated by stained glass and monuments, none of which is more splendid than the brass of Sir Roger le Strange (d. 1506), a youthful figure with flowing locks, surrounded by members of his family, with his arms raised in greeting.

Beside the high walls and yew hedges south of the churchyard is the ancestral Hall of the le Strange family, with a moat and a Renaissance garden; all that the visitor can see, alas, is part of the Jacobean gatehouse range.

South of the park and only accessible on foot, is the Ringstead Downs chalkland nature reserve, one of the prettiest sights in all of Norfolk. The reserve, noted for its lime-loving plants and butterflies, nestles into the deep slopes of a dry valley; at the bottom, a group of unspoiled 18th-century farm buildings and a pond fed by a mineral spring form the most charming picture.

Ringstead itself is a picture-book village, in which the cottages are built in a delightful polychrome mixture of carstone and flint, brick and chalk, both pink and white.

Ingham (3/2C) *see* Stalham

Ingworth (2/4) *see* Aylsham

Itteringham (2/4B)

The early 18th century must have been a period of prosperity for this handsome village on the River Bure 7 miles west of North Walsham, for several of its fine brick houses were built at around this time. Hill Farmhouse is dated 1704 in black letters on its shaped gable end and nearby Manor Farmhouse may be a little earlier – a splendid building with the owner's coat of arms in the pediment. St Mary's church, on the north bank of the river, has good wall panelling and box pews of similar date.

Half a mile further north, a tributary of the Bure feeds the moat that surrounds Mannington Hall, built around 1460. The house, which is open by appointment, survives much as it was built, despite external alterations carried out in

Mannington Hall

the late 19th century by Horatio Walpole, Earl of Orford, who filled the grounds of his estate with Gothic sculptural fragments.

The present owners have created a fine series of gardens around the house, which are open for most of the year. A Rose Festival is held every June, when the comprehensive rose collection is in full bloom.

Kenninghall (2/3G) *see* Wilby

Ketteringham (2/4E) *see* Wymondham

Kilverstone (5/2A) *see* Brettenham

Kimberley (2/3E)

Kimberley, 2½ miles north-west of Wymondham, consists primarily of a triangular green surrounded by thatched houses and the Regency lodge houses to Kimberley Hall. The church of St Peter, which stands on the green, has some excellent stained glass which came from the cloisters of the 16th-century German monastery at Steinfeld and the chancel is almost completely floored with memorial slabs.

Two miles north, **Barnham Broom** has a pretty group of mill buildings, straddling the River Yare. Upstream, the red-brick Old Hall, built in the time of Henry VIII, is just visible. Opposite the Hall, the church of St Peter and St Paul has a stately tower, its pinnacles carved with figures of the Evangelists, and a well-preserved screen painted with East Anglian saints: St Edmund, St Walstan and St Withburgha.

King's Lynn (1/3C)

Lynn, as it is known locally, is often cited as an example of the complex issues that face conservationists. The sterling work of the King's Lynn Preservation Trust has resulted in the survival of many fine buildings, particularly in the streets that lead down to the Great Ouse. Tragically, however, the core of the town has been ripped apart to create supermarkets, car parks and service roads.

Back in the late 1950s, when these policies were being debated, the docks that had been so busy hitherto were in decline and the population waning. Successful attempts were made to attract new industry and the population expanded as a result of an overspill scheme negotiated with the London County Council. The number of ships using the docks began to grow again. Sadly, the new housing estates and factories that ring the

town have no architectural merit. Even today, large areas along the river are zoned for redevelopment which will alter the whole appearance of the waterfront.

Nevertheless, there is still a great deal to be said in praise of King's Lynn; the riverside streets are full of character and the waterfront, with its few remaining warehouses, captures the imagination and speaks of stormy crossings across the North Sea to Denmark, Sweden and the Baltic – the old ports of the Hanseatic League with which the inhabitants of King's Lynn once did a brisk trade.

The town was originally called Bishop's Lynn

because it was founded by Herbert de Losinga, the first bishop of Norwich, in about 1100. Before that, there were a number of scattered late Saxon settlements among the marshes, sustained by salt panning. The bishop founded the priory of St Margaret's, of which the church remains; the area beside the church, the Saturday Market, became an important trading point. The town developed so rapidly that by 1150 the second church, St Nicholas, had been built further north, with its own Tuesday Market.

The river was wider in the 12th century than it is today; the curvaceous line of Queen Street probably marks the original waterfront. Silting,

Guildhall, King's Lynn

rubbish disposal and deliberate reclamation pushed the river bank westwards and by the 14th century there were already a number of warehouses and merchants' houses along the quay.

In 1536, with the Dissolution of the Monasteries, Lynn was appropriated by Henry VIII and changed its name; but it remained a busy harbour: out of East Anglia and the East Midlands came wool, salt and grain to be transshipped at Lynn in exchange for fish, timber and furs from Germany and the Baltic, wine from France, dried fruits from Spain and coal from Newcastle.

When the railway came to Lynn in the 19th century, two new deep harbours were opened in the north of the town alongside the station: the Alexandra Dock (1869) and the Bentinck Dock (1883). After the Second World War Lynn began to diversify its industry; Campbells, the soup manufacturers, were the first of the new arrivals. The firm's original factory, on the south-eastern approach to the city, is now surrounded by a sea of hypermarkets and industrial units. Beyond this, the road enters King's Lynn through the narrow South Gate, last rebuilt in 1520 and once part of the city's medieval defences.

Saturday Market, besides St Margaret's church, is now a car park and a good place to begin an exploration of the oldest part of the town. The most striking feature of the exterior of St Margaret's is the massive Norman masonry of the south-west tower: all that remains of the original church since the rest was almost completely rebuilt in the 18th century after the spire collapsed in a gale, destroying much of the nave.

Inside, in the south aisle, are two outstanding brasses, the largest in England and particularly interesting for the little vignettes of agricultural and banqueting scenes that surround the figures of the deceased.

The interior of the church is dominated by the imposing Snetzler organ, made for the church in 1754 at the request of the organist, Dr Charles Burney, father of the novelist Fanny.

The handsome red-brick Regency house by the church was the birthplace of Fanny Burney. St Margaret's Place leads south to Nelson Street, where Hampton Court, a jettied building painted red, sits squarely on the corner with a courtyard behind. The western side of the quadrangle was originally a warehouse facing the harbour and though the front range dates from 1500, the south range incorporates part of a 13th-century merchant's house.

Nelson Street curves markedly at its eastern end, following the line of the original harbour. The view on turning right into Bridge Street is unpromising; this part of Lynn was bombed in the last war and is now covered by the vast Hillington Square housing estate. A little way up, though, on the left, is the timber-framed Greenland Fishery Inn, built in 1605. The name is a reminder that, in the 17th and 18th centuries, the nearby banks of the River Nar were used for rendering down the blubber of Greenland whales to produce lamp oil.

Retracing our steps down Bridge Street and Church Street, we return to the south side of St Margaret's churchyard, Priory Lane. Here, on the right, is a row of 14th-century buildings, remains of the original Priory, now converted to houses.

St Margaret's Lane leads down to the South Quay and the Great Ouse. Over the centuries the river has silted up, so that most boats now moor at the deeper docks further north. Here the river is wide and at low tide exposes silt banks which are a favourable feeding ground of wading birds. West Lynn church is clearly visible on the opposite marshy bank. On the right of the quay is the handsome red-brick Hanseatic Warehouse, dating from 1428 and, with its steep-pitched roof and shuttered hatches for admitting sacks, barrels and bales, much like those on the waterfronts of Copenhagen and Amsterdam.

The first turning right, College Lane, leads past Thoresby College, founded in 1500 by Thomas Thoresby to house the chaplains and trainee priests of the Trinity Guild. The surviving buildings are mostly 17th century, with handsome shaped gables on the eastern (Queen Street) front.

We are now back in Saturday Market and facing the Guildhall complex. This famous group, with its handsome flint chessboard façade, is a surprisingly successful blend of buildings of four different periods. The Guildhall proper, built in 1421, has a massive Perpendicular window; to the left is the Elizabethan extension with its eroded arms of Elizabeth and James I in a pediment above the fine Jacobean doorcase. This was used as the Town Hall until 1895 when the neo-Gothic extension to the left was added. To the right of the group is the former gaol, built in 1784, with a pair of manacles above the door. Today the gaol is used as the Tourist Information Centre and leads into the Guildhall, which houses the city's magnificent collection of royal and civic regalia.

Heading north up Queen Street, we are now following a route which the late Sir John Betjeman called his favourite walk, the best in Europe. The neo-Tudor Burkitt Homes almshouses on the right were built in 1909 of brick and terracotta around an attractive courtyard; Clifton House, on the left, has an extraordinary 17th-century doorcase of massive barley-sugar twist columns.

Charles II presides over the Customs House

King's Staithe Lane leads down to the waterfront again and Purfleet Dock. Alongside Purfleet is the perfectly proportioned Custom House of 1683, designed by Henry Bell, a successful merchant and twice mayor of Lynn, as well as an accomplished architect (*see* p. 142). The building served as an exchange, presided over by the rather stern figure of Charles II who stands in a niche on the north façade.

He looks down King Street, with its varied architecture and long lanes leading back down to the river. Ferry Lane, as its name suggests, leads to a small pier, from which a ferry operates on weekdays, crossing the Great Ouse to West Lynn. The journey is worthwhile for the views, back across the river, to King's Lynn itself.

Number 27 King Street is now an excellent museum of social history and, next to it, the former Guildhall of St George, the property of the National Trust, is now part of the Fermoy Arts Centre, the focus of the lively King's Lynn Festival which takes place every July.

The spacious Tuesday Market is a huge open square lined with cheerful buildings: the delightful Duke's Head Hotel, built in 1683, is painted pink and white and surmounted by a huge broken pediment and the Corn Exchange opposite, built in 1854, is ornamented with a pretty statue of Ceres.

St Nicholas Street leads north-east out of the square to St Anne's Street. St Nicholas's Chapel stands to one side of this street and the churchyard is entered through a fine set of wrought-iron gates, dated 1749. In the churchyard, to the south, the little cottage dated 1635, with an elaborate Dutch gable, was once the home of the parish exorcist.

Around the eastern periphery of the town are several curiosities for those who are determined to tour comprehensively. At the junction of St James Street and London Road, the 15th-century tower of Greyfriars, all that remains of the Franciscan friary, is the focal point of an attractive public garden. Close to it, in the angle of Greyfriars Road and London Road, is the extraordinary Victorian neo-Tudor Public Library and, in Greyfriars Road itself, the walled Jewish cemetery.

On the opposite side of London Road, the public park known as 'The Walks' leads to Red Mount Chapel. This was built in 1485 by the prior of St Margaret's to house a relic of the Virgin and to attract pilgrims travelling to Walsingham. The unusual enterprise resulted in an even more extraordinary edifice built in the shape of an octagon and encasing a series of staircases leading to an inner chapel, which in 1505 acquired a beautiful, delicate fan-vaulted ceiling.

Knapton (3/2B) *see* Paston

Langley (3/2E) *see* Loddon

Larling (2/2G) *see* Harling, East

Lenwade (2/3D) *see* Lyng

Letheringsett (2/3B) *see* Holt

Lexhams, The (2/1D)
Five miles north of Swaffham, East and West Lexham are attractive estate villages of solid and picturesque flint and brick cottages and farm buildings in gently hilly countryside. St Nicholas's church at **West Lexham** is attractively situated on top of a hill and has the simplest of Saxon round towers, just a cylinder of rendered flint.

From the road to **East Lexham** there are views over the Nar valley. St Andrew's church forms a pretty group with the early 18th-century Church Farm, all surrounded by woods. The Saxon tower here is more elaborate, built in two stages with twin bell openings and a classic example of long and short-work in the southwest corner of the nave. The neat village down by the river consists of a group of praiseworthy modern estate cottages, built in flint and brick with ox-eye windows and classical detailing, surrounding a small green with a pavilion.

Litcham (2/1D)
Litcham, 5½ miles north-west of East Dereham, is almost a small town, with many handsome red-brick Georgian houses along its main street. The tower of All Saints' church is of the same brick: built in 1669, it was paid for by Matthew Hulcott, a wealthy local tanner who lived in the Dutch gabled former priory at the south-east end of the village. Litcham is surrounded by marshy, undrained common land, now a 60-acre Nature Reserve with a marked trail.

A mile south at **Beeston**, the church of St Mary stands alone in a bleak, hedgeless landscape. The high wide church is notable for the golden patina of its untreated woodwork and for its splendid hammerbeam roof, with figure carvings and ornate parclose screens.

Little Barningham (2/4E) *see* Barninghams, The

Little Cressingham (2/1E) *see* Cressinghams, The

Little Dunham (2/1D) *see* Dunhams, The

Little Ellingham (2/3F) *see* Ellinghams, The

Little Massingham (1/4C) *see* Massinghams, The

Little Ryburgh (2/2C) *see* Ryburghs, The

Little Snoring (2/2B) *see* Snorings, The

Little Walsingham (2/2B) *see* Walsinghams, The

Little Witchingham (2/4D) *see* Witchinghams, The

Loddon (3/2F)

This small market town off the A146, 5 miles north-west of Beccles, is now by-passed and peaceful, with many good Georgian red-brick houses and a Gothic fantasy of a school built in 1857. These buildings line the big square Market Place, with Holy Trinity church to the east. The church is full of memorials to generous patrons, among them one of Norfolk's finest monuments, the figure of Lady Williamson (d. 1684), carved in white marble by Joshua Marshall and an entirely realistic portrait of an elderly lady. Lady Williamson was the biggest single contributor to the rebuilding of St Paul's Cathedral after London's Great Fire of 1666.

The River Chet flows north of the town, lined by marinas and an old water mill, now an art gallery. On the opposite bank, Chedgrave is now a suburb of Loddon with much recent housing, but it also boasts a good Norman church, All Saints, with much 17th-century glass said to have come from Rouen Cathedral.

At Hardley, 1½ miles north-east, St Margaret's church stands in isolation overlooking the marshes, while at **Langley**, 2 miles west, St Michael's church is reached by a path across the fields, next to the Grange. Here is more of the stained glass thought to have been looted from Rouen Cathedral. It was brought here in 1787 by Lady Beauchamp Proctor, whose home, Langley Park, lies across the path from the church and is now a school. It was built in the 1740s by Matthew Brettingham, who worked on HOLKHAM HALL, and is a scaled-down version of that house, in red brick.

A mile to the south-east of Loddon, back on the busy A146, is the village of **Hales**. The church of St Margaret is a beautiful and unspoilt example of simple Norman architecture, consisting of a round tower, thatched nave and an apse, ornamented with graceful blank arcading. Scarcely anything later than the 12th century intrudes; even the few windows that were inserted later do not detract from the timeless atmosphere.

Raveningham, a mile east of Hales, consists only of the Hall and St Andrew's church. The Georgian house is surrounded by extensive walled gardens and a large nursery specialising in rare and exotic plants. It is open in summer. The Hall is the home of the Bacon family, and the church is full of delightful memorial tablets that remind us, proudly and often, that the head of the family is England's premier baronet.

Seething lies 2½ miles out of Loddon to the south-west. The pretty church dedicated to St Margaret and St Remigius has a thatched nave and round tower, topped by a thin lead spirelet. The nave is covered in wall paintings, not all of them well-preserved and some overlying others in a confusion of faded colours. Clearly discernible are the big St Christopher, three noblemen and a skeleton from the Three Quick and the Three Dead, and some gleeful devils. The Seven Sacraments font, dated 1485, is one of the finest and best-preserved in the county.

Long Stratton (2/4F) *see* Strattons, The

Lophams, The (5/3A)

These are twin villages just north of the A1066, 8 miles east of Thetford. **North Lopham** is a long village with much modern infill housing between the older timber-framed and thatched cottages. The initials of all the benefactors who contributed to the rebuilding of St Nicholas's church, in the late 14th century, are inscribed for posterity in big Gothic script on the tower.

South Lopham's church, of St Andrew, is even more impressive with a powerful Norman central tower, robust as a castle keep and ornamented with four tiers of blank arcading. The nave is also Norman and has a 15th-century hammerbeam roof.

Just over a mile south, the ancient Lopham Ford forms the Norfolk/Suffolk county

boundary. Speeding past in a car along the B1113, it is easy to miss the two insignificant muddy ditches either side of the road. That on the west is the source of the Little Ouse; that on the east the source of the Waveney. They flow in opposite directions, the Ouse to the Wash and the Waveney to the sea at Lowestoft, which makes this little spot the shallowest watershed in the land. Before the road was built, the two rivers would often meet in the middle, thus making Norfolk effectively an island.

Lopham Fen, to the east, is a wetland site of international importance; the 300 acres of spring-fed marshes are home to many small invertebrates, and the pools formed from ancient peat cuttings are the habitat of the unique Fen Raft Spider.

Lower Sheringham (2/4A) *see* Sheringhams, The

Ludham (3/2D) *see* Potter Heigham

Lyng (2/3D)

This attractive village, almost on the River Wensum, lies 4 miles north-east of East Dereham. The church of St Margaret has an original 15th-century door carved with elaborate tracery and a fine altar frontal of the same date.

Just west of the village is a scene that Constable would have enjoyed: an 18th-century bridge across the river, partnered by a weir and red-brick former paper mill, all made the more charming by the dappled sunlight that filters through the tall surrounding trees.

Downstream by 2 miles is another scenic mill group. Sayer's Mill at **Lenwade** is a white clapboard building, surrounded by flooded gravel pits that are maintained as a nature reserve.

On the opposite side of the river to Lyng, just over a mile to the north, is **Sparham**. St Mary's church contains 14th-century panels painted with scenes from the Dance of Death – a theme common in continental churches but very rare in England.

Martham (3/3D)

The core of this big village, 2 miles inland from Hemsby, surrounds a green, with the massive tower of St Mary's church at its northern end. Much of the excellent church is Victorian, with an east window of ravishing colour and an

St Andrew's church, South Lopham

astounding cusped chancel arch under hammer-beam roofs.

At Martham Ferry, north-west of the village, the River Thurne links several of the Broads and is, in consequence, not only a busy marina but also the starting point of several attractive walks along the river bank and Heigham Sound. (*See* 'The Norfolk Broads', p. 124.)

Rollesby, 2 miles south of Martham, is a peaceful hamlet with a fine Georgian farmhouse and a row of thatched cottages, one dated 1583.

Massinghams, The (1/4C)

These villages lie 9 miles east of King's Lynn. **Great Massingham**'s butterfly-shaped village green is dotted with duck ponds and surrounded by 18th- and 19th-century cottages, all of brick and flint laid in a chequerboard pattern. St Mary's church stands at the heart of the village, entered through the elegant Early English south porch.

At **Little Massingham**, the hamlet to the north, St Andrew's church has a good hammer-beam roof – not 15th century as it seems, but an excellent example of recent craftsmanship.

Mattishall (2/3D)

Narrow lanes, former sheep droves, converge on this village 2½ miles south-east of East Dereham, which was an important centre of the wool trade until the 18th century. All Saints' church stands in the centre of the village surrounded by Georgian houses, several with early shopfronts. It was wool wealth that paid for the fine hammerbeam roof inside the church.

Mattishall Burgh, just to the north, is growing fast around a core of ancient farmhouses; the 16th-century Grove Farm has ornate octagonal chimneys. St Mary's church at **North Tuddenham** stands alone in fields 2 miles to the north-west, a Perpendicular building that was restored in highly idiosyncratic taste by the Revd Robert Barry between 1851 and 1904.

Melton Constable (2/3B)

For 700 years Melton Constable Hall, 3 miles south-west of Holt, was the home of the Astley family. The existing Hall was built between 1664 and 1687 and is one of the earliest examples of Dutch-influenced architecture in Norfolk. The magnificent plaster ceilings were made by the same craftsman who worked at FELBRIGG Hall.

The Astleys owned the estate in continuous succession from 1236 until 1956, when it was sold. It was then deliberately neglected but, after a protracted rescue campaign, the future for this important house, now under new ownership, looks considerably brighter: it will form the centrepiece of an arts and conference centre, planned to open in the 1990s.

The church of St Peter is an intriguing building, with a Norman central tower and curious south transept, whose purpose is revealed inside: the whole of it served as a family pew for the Astleys, the floor raised high above the nave to enable the squire to survey the congregation.

The village of Melton Constable was a new town, founded in 1881 at the junction of four railway lines linking north, east, south and west Norfolk to the Midlands. Today, all the lines and the station have gone, but everything else has survived unchanged, with houses of different sizes for the railway workers and the foremen, a school, pub and Railway Institute.

North-west of the village, visible from the B1110, is an impressive battlemented tower topped with a glass-walled observatory, built by the Astleys at the time of the Armada in 1588 and later repaired and used again as a look-out tower during the Napoleonic and the two World Wars.

Merton (2/2F) *see* Thompson

Methwold (1/4F) *see* Northwold

Mileham (2/2D)
At the centre of this long village 5 miles north-west of East Dereham is a circular Norman motte on one side of the road and, opposite, the rectangular moated outer bailey surrounding Burghwood Manor. A 10th-century Viking sword, now in Norwich Museum, was found here, and the Manor was the home of Sir Edward Coke, Chief Justice under Elizabeth I. Since then the village has been part of the Holkham estate and preserved behind the Manor is a 20-acre field system in which Thomas Coke, who built the present HOLKHAM Hall, conducted experiments in crop rotation in the 1770s.

Tittleshall, 1 mile north, was also part of the Holkham estate and there is a splendid series of Coke family memorials in St Mary's church, including two fine busts by Roubiliac and a monument by Nollekens.

Morningthorpe (3/1F) *see* Fritton

Morston (2/3A) *see* Cley-next-the-Sea

Mulbarton (2/4E) *see* Swardestone

Narborough (1/4D)
Five miles north-west of Swaffham, this village is split by the busy A47. On the opposite side of the road from All Saints' church, the grounds of Narborough Hall are planted with magnificent specimen trees and contain one of Norfolk's few Iron Age encampments, now hidden among the trees of Camphill Plantation. On the right, as the road crosses the River Nar, the village mill now operates as a trout farm and is fronted by a pretty brick bridge and mill race.

A mile further east, St Mary's church, Narford stands in the grounds of the Hall and contains an accomplished bust by Roubiliac of Sir Andrew Fountaine (d. 1753), who succeeded Newton as Warden of the Royal Mint and was a noted collector of antiquities. The magnificent Hall still belongs to his descendants and has a gracious 18th-century three-bay front, built in rust-brown carstone. Inside there are important frescoes by the early 18th-century Venetian artist Antonio Pellegrini.

East Walton, 2 miles north of Narborough, is interesting for the common west of the village, known locally as the Ramparts. The great mounds and hollows are a classic example of Ice Age pingos, formed when a lens of ice expanded to push the soil aside and then collapsed on thawing. The boggy hollows support an interesting variety of rare plants.

Necton (2/1E) *see* Swaffham

New Buckenham (2/3F) *see* Buckenhams, The

Newton (2/1D) *see* Acres, The

Newton Flotman (3/1F) *see* Tasburgh

Norfolk Coast Path
This long-distance footpath, opened in 1986, runs from Holme-next-the-Sea, where it meets PEDDARS WAY, to Cromer, 45 miles to the east. The whole of the coast through which the path runs is designated an Area of Outstanding Natural Beauty – a unique region of sand dunes and salt marshes, with numerous nature reserves and Sites of Special Scientific Interest. One moment passing through busy ports, the next through lonely marsh systems, the path provides an opportunity to study the rich and diverse flora and fauna of the region.

The Countryside Commission has published a full and detailed guide to the route.

North Barningham (2/4B) *see* Barninghams, The

North Burlingham (3/2E) *see* Burlinghams, The

North Creake (2/1B) *see* Creakes, The

North Elmham (2/2C)

Elmham's long village street is lined with high brick and flint walls that hide the bigger houses from view. These include Elmham House, with its extensive park, wild garden and vineyards which are open under the National Gardens Scheme.

Opposite the park entrance are the extensive remains of a Saxon cathedral – one of only two that survive above ground in England. The other is at SOUTH ELMHAM in Suffolk and around AD 680 they served, respectively, the dioceses of North Folk (i.e. Norfolk) and South Folk (Suffolk). In 1072 the North Folk see moved to Thetford and in 1094 the two dioceses were combined into one with a cathedral at Norwich.

Marsh systems on the Norfolk Coast Path

North Elmham's cathedral has survived because Henry le Despenser, Bishop of Norwich, had the ruins converted into a hunting lodge in 1370. In 1903 archaeologists found substantial quantities of wine jugs and drinking horns, suggesting that the bishop enjoyed a life of considerable indulgence.

A mile south-east of Elmham is the hamlet of **Worthing**, with its pretty mill and pond, set in the ecologically rich Wensum valley. St Margaret's church is a tiny and appealing Saxon building with a round tower and decorated Norman doorway, standing alone by the river.

North Lopham (5/3A) *see* Lophams, The

North Pickenham (2/1E) *see* Swaffham

North Runcton (1/3D)

Three miles south-east of King's Lynn, this village surrounds a broad green and has a very appealing early 18th-century church. All Saints is small, classical and genteel; it has been attributed to the architect Henry Bell, who also designed the Custom House at KING'S LYNN.

St Margaret's church, Worthing

The delightful interior is almost square, with four columns supporting a Wedgwood-blue dome decorated with angels.

Less good can be said of the ranch-style houses that surround the common, west of the village, but in between them are some attractive cottages decorated with galletting: small stones pushed into the mortar joints between the square-cut carstone blocks.

North Tuddenham (2/3D) *see* Mattishall

North Walsham (3/1B)

North Walsham, 3½ miles from the north-east Norfolk coast, was already a prosperous market town when the arrival of the railway in the 1870s made it even more so. The legacy of that is the number of engineering firms still operating on its outskirts. The handsome Market Cross, in the middle of the town, has three tiers of bell-like roofs, each diminishing in size and was rebuilt after a fire destroyed much of the town in 1602.

Not all the buildings were destroyed, for many a timber-framed house survives down the numerous narrow alleys that run off the Market Place, albeit disguised beneath later rendering. Evidence of pre-railway age prosperity is found in the fine Georgian bow-fronted houses higher up the hill, to the west of the town.

St Nicholas's church lies to the north of the Market Place. The stump of its collapsed tower still reaches an impressive height – it once stood 147 feet high but partially collapsed in 1724 and again in 1835.

Two miles north-east of North Walsham is the village of **Edingthorpe**. All Saints' church stands alone amid fields on a rise that commands views of the nearby villages. The unspoiled church, with its drum-shaped tower and thatched nave, contains much to enjoy: wall paintings of St Christopher and the Seven Corporeal Works of Mercy, a delicate chancel screen with elaborate wheel tracery above the central arch and heavy oak doors, one with its original 14th-century ironwork.

A mile south, at **Witton**, St Margaret's church is equally isolated and high enough up to command views of the sea and the distant lighthouse at HAPPISBURGH. The nave has stood since Saxon times and has two original round windows.

All Saints' church at **Crostwight**, a mile south, is another lovely church, standing in fields and still lit by oil lamps. The north doorcase is carved with the figures of Adam and Eve together with others boiling in a cauldron in punishment for their sins. The theme continues inside, with a 14th-century wall painting of the Seven Deadly Sins, as well as scenes from Christ's Passion.

Northwold (1/4F)

A mile north-west of Weeting, a minor road off the B1106 leads towards Northwold following the low, broad rampart of Fossditch for nearly 3 miles. Excavation has yielded little information to archaeologists, other than that the ditch and bank were dug some time after AD 390, perhaps by native Britons, perhaps by Anglo-Saxon immigrants, to define a territory. Others believe it may mark the boundary of a late Roman agricultural estate.

St Andrew's church at Northwold has much decorative flushwork on the tower buttresses and, inside, one of the few surviving Easter Sepulchres in England and one of the finest, dated to the end of the 14th century. These are believed to have been associated with the Holy Saturday ritual, celebrating the Resurrection. Many were destroyed by 17th-century iconoclasts.

The tower of St George's church in the neighbouring village of **Methwold** is visible from afar; the splendid spire rises 60 feet from the pretty octagonal corona, which itself stands on top of a 60-foot three-stage Perpendicular tower. The fine nave roof is ornamented with angels and there is a beautiful rood screen, carved in 1900 by an unknown artist.

Opposite is the delightfully eccentric Vicarage. It was originally timber-framed, but a brick façade with stepped gable was added in the 16th century. Running up the middle of the gable is a projecting chimney ornamented with trefoil-headed blank arcading, very like the decoration of the gateway at OXBURGH Hall, but with some additional wayward and inconclusive serpentine squiggles.

Two miles south-east of Northwold, on the A134, is the village of **Cranwich**. St Mary's, set back from the main road, is a pretty thatched church surrounded by tall trees. The tapering round tower has circular openings, carved with an intricate interlace pattern that forms a continuous double figure of eight. Inside is a simple tower arch, very tall and narrow. The Victorian harmonium is worth noting for the patented 'mouse-proof' pedals.

Easter Sepulchre in St Andrew's church, Northwold

Norwich (3/1E)

Norwich is a city with its own distinctive character. The visitor receives a strong sense of its special atmosphere by spending a while in the Market Place, the focus of the town's commercial life. Here, in what is still called an open market, though the stalls are covered by brightly striped awnings (locally called 'tilts'), the lanes that thread beneath the canvas are so narrow that one is constantly forced to stop, watch, let others pass by and listen to the conversation of the locals and the frequent visitors from Holland and Scandinavia. Historically the links between Norwich and northern Europe have been strong; before the railway, it was as fast to travel by sea to Amsterdam as to London and Dutch influence is visible everywhere in the city's architecture.

Foreigners, indeed, created Norwich, for the

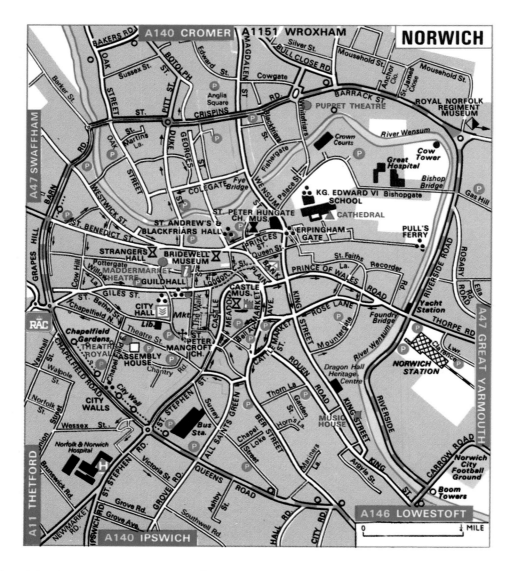

earliest inhabitants were Anglo-Danish settlers. The city's name first appears on the coinage of King Athelstan, minted around AD 930. Norman invaders built the first castle in 1067, a timber fort on top of a great earthen motte, replaced by a stone-faced square keep around 1100. At the same time they founded the church of St Peter Mancroft and laid out the Market Place on a greenfield site, still described several centuries later as the French Borough.

The cathedral was begun in 1096, by which time Norwich was already one of England's five most populous towns, along with London, York, Lincoln and Winchester. The walls were completed in the 14th century and survive in parts to an impressive height. The 4-mile circuit enclosed an area bigger than London, although the space within the walls was not all built up at once. Not until 1810, when the sprawling city began to absorb the surrounding villages, did Norwich exceed its medieval boundaries.

Early prosperity was based on wool, exported to the Low Countries along the Rivers Wensum and Yare. The discovery of early medieval dye pits in Westwick Street suggests that the town was involved in wool processing as well as trading the raw commodity. This made the city rich, but it could also be rough; there were anti-Jewish riots in 1144 and in 1272 much of the Priory was burned down by rioting citizens in protest against the monks' attempts to tax their annual Tombland market.

In 1348 Norwich was one of the richest towns in England, with a population of 6,000, but in 1349, the worst year of the Black Death, more than a third were carried away by plague. Recovery must have been swift, for many of the town's numerous churches were enlarged and embellished, at great expense, over the next two centuries.

During the 16th and 17th centuries, Norwich swung between the extremes of religious tolerance and repression. After the Reformation the city became a centre of Protestantism, attracting refugees from France and the Low Countries whose skills boosted the already buoyant cloth-weaving industry. The migration was not always one way, for during the mid 17th century as many as 3,000 local Non-conformists sought refuge in Holland from the High Church policies of Archbishop Laud.

Relative decline came with the industrial revolution, for Norwich lacked either the fast-flowing rivers or the readily accessible coal to compete with the newly mechanised mills of the Midlands and the North. Norwich was kept alive by the sheer diversity of her industries; the railway, which came in 1845 creating a swift link to London, encouraged new firms to expand.

By the mid 19th century, the demand for housing was such that vast areas ringing the city began to be built up. One of the earliest estates was South Heigham, south-west of the city, developed by the philanthropic Colonel C. W. Unthank, who insisted on a high standard of housing. Equally far-sighted was the group of campaigners who, in 1884, secured the preservation of Mousehold Heath, to the north-east of the city, as a public open space. The Heath continues to be a much-cherished piece of land from which to enjoy splendid views of the cathedral, and the city's 32 surviving Anglican churches.

In recent years, the city has been a magnet to firms seeking to relocate from less-favoured parts, particularly as the shuttle services from the city airport make the Continent as close as London.

New offices are beginning to rise on the former railway marshalling yards south-east of the city and, further east, planners have learned from past mistakes and are building housing estates with a village character, set around winding streets.

One consequence of the recent growth is the unresolved traffic problem. Visitors are well advised to leave the car behind and arrive by train. Stepping out from the splendid French Empire railway station, you face the River Wensum with its yacht basin and floating restaurants, a departure point for tours of the Broads. By crossing Foundry Bridge and turning right to the riverside path, modern Norwich is soon left behind. After about 100 yards the path reaches Pull's Ferry Water Gate, built in the 15th century to guard the river approach to the cathedral. A canal once led from here to cathedral itself, cut in the 11th century to carry the Caen stone, Swedish iron and Baltic timber used in the construction. The last of the licensed ferrymen, aptly named John Pull, died in the early 19th century and his name has been associated with the gate ever since.

The filled-in canal now forms a path that leads into the peaceful cathedral close. The broad green at the centre of the close is surrounded by handsome red-brick and flint houses with colourful gardens. To the east the most pleasing house of all, bearing the date 1682, was converted from the former priory brewhouse.

From the close there is a magnificent view of the cathedral. It is not easy to distinguish between the genuine Norman masonry and the Neo-Norman, for both the south transept and the bold crossing tower were comprehensively restored between 1830 and 1856, copying the massive bulls-eye windows and blank arcading that make the tower such an unusual and confident structure. The spire was added around 1480 by Bishop Goldwell making the cathedral, at 315 feet, in England second only in height to Salisbury.

The interior presents fewer archaeological teasers: the nave is all one homogeneous flow of solid Norman architecture, from floor to triforium. Above, and harmonising remarkably well, is the delicate clerestory and vault, added at the same time as the spire and studded with figure bosses carved with biblical scenes.

Despite the appearance of uniformity, however, there are some telling details that help to explain the cathedral's history. Two bays at the eastern end of the nave differ from the rest. Their fat, round piers, incised with spiral grooves, are typical of the earliest style of Norman English church architecture at the turn of the 11th and 12th centuries, the date of the cathedral's foundation. In 1094 the Bishop of East Anglia, Herbert de Losinga, transferred the see from Thetford to Norwich and work on the new cathedral began two years later. The western continuation of the nave was completed, in a

different style, under de Losinga's successor, Eborardus, sometime before 1145.

These same piers are coloured the rose pink characteristic of limestone that has been subjected to intense heat. Any one of several fires could have been responsible; the most significant took place in the Tombland riots of 1272, when the priory was all but destroyed and the cathedral itself set on fire. Following this the cloister was entirely rebuilt between 1297 and 1310. It has a remarkable series of bosses, close enough to the ground to be studied in detail without binoculars. The best group is by the Prior's Door, just off the south aisle. The doorway itself is magnificent and by great good fortune has survived unmolested by iconoclasts.

While exploring the cloister, many visitors make a detour to the grave of Nurse Edith Cavell, executed by the Germans in 1915 for helping Allied prisoners to escape from occupied Belgium. Her grave, always covered with flowers, lies outside the east end of the south transept.

The next stage in the cathedral's history began with another disastrous fire. The timber spire was struck by lightning in 1463 and the conflagration spread to destroy the nave roof. It was replaced by today's soaring lierne vault, built in stone as a precaution against further fire and completed in 1472, under Bishop Lyhart. His successor, Bishop Goldwell, added the finishing touches: the splendid chancel vault and the stone spire.

By the mid 17th century the cathedral was in a sorry state. Most of the priory buildings were looted for stone at the Dissolution and the chapels of the east end, stripped of their lead roofs, fell into disrepair. They were expertly restored in the 1930s and contain a rare and important series of painted panels.

Starting at the south-east, St Luke's Chapel, maintained by the city's Guild of Plumbers, Painters, Glaziers and Bellfounders, contains six scenes from the Passion and Resurrection of Christ, hailed as the finest work of the Norwich School of painters. It was commissioned in 1381 by Bishop Henry le Despencer to commemorate the defeat of the local version of the Peasants' Revolt. St Saviour's Chapel stands on the site of the former Lady Chapel and was rebuilt in 1930–2 as the chapel of the Royal Norfolk Regiment. Five painted panels were brought here from St Michael at Plea after restoration in

The soaring nave of Norwich cathedral

the 1950s. Their rich colour and animated figures are as good as any of the finest Italian paintings of the same period, the late 14th century. Continuing round the ambulatory, after the Jesus Chapel is the Treasury, used in the middle ages to display holy relics and nowadays for an exhibition of church plate from all the parishes of Norwich. The vault is covered in early 14th-century frescoes, recently restored to pristine freshness.

Directly opposite the west front of the cathedral is the splendid Erpingham Gate, built in 1420 by Sir Thomas Erpingham. Before passing through to admire the sculpture on the other side, note the beautiful buildings of the Carnery College to the right, the school founded in 1316 by Bishop Salmon. The chapel of St John is now used by the King Edward VI School. The Erpingham Gate presents its fairest face to the town, rather than to the cathedral. Its tall, deeply recessed arch is ornamented with finely carved female saints and in the topmost niche is the kneeling figure of Sir Thomas himself.

He looks down on Tombland, whose name refers to the table tops of the merchants who used to trade in this former market place. Now it is a broad thoroughfare, lined with Georgian and older houses. Number 14 is a fine timber-framed merchant's house, built in 1549.

At the north end of Tombland, Palace Street leads to Palace Plain, where the 15th-century gateway to the Bishop's Palace stands near a smart group of Georgian houses. One of these was the home of the artist John Sell Cotman (1782–1842). Further down Bishopsgate are the charming little Dutch-gabled Adam and Eve public house, the Great Hospital (founded in 1249 as an old people's home) and, finally, the oldest bridge in Norwich, the 14th-century Bishop Bridge.

The way north leads to Whitefriars Bridge and the noble, creeper-clad Yarn Mill, built 1836–9. This originally housed steam-driven looms, but the cost of shipping coal down the coast from Newcastle proved uncompetitive and the mill was converted to a print works in 1902.

North-west of Palace Plain, Quayside is lined with attractive Regency houses and leads to the 1829 Fye Bridge, built in medieval style, with cutwaters. The bridge marks the beginning of Magdalene Street, whose houses were well restored in the 1950s by the Civic Trust and deliberately painted in bold colours. Several of them have medieval courtyards.

Just west of Magdalene Street, off Colegate,

are two of the city's oldest Non-conformist churches. Both the Old Meeting House of 1693 and the Octagon Chapel, built in 1756 by the Presbyterians, are handsome classical buildings.

If you return via Fye Bridge and Wensum Street, the first turning on your right is Elm Hill, a narrow, winding, cobbled street and the city's conservation showpiece. The houses, partly dating from the 15th century, are painted in blue, green, white, yellow and pink limewash and form a remarkably harmonious group. Elm Hill is the focal point for a cluster of museums. In Princes Street, St Peter Hungate contains a display of church art and in St Andrew's Street the church and adjoining 14th-century friary buildings serve as a museum of civic portraits dating back to the 16th century. Opposite, the 14th-century Suckling House, named after the merchant family that built it, has been converted to an arts cinema, the only one in England with a scissor truss roof. Just beyond, on the left, the narrow Bridewell alley contains Colman's Mustard Shop and museum and the Bridewell Museum of local crafts and industries.

Old Meeting House, Norwich

One more museum lies further west, in Charing Cross. Strangers' Hall was begun in the early 14th century and each successive owner contributed something to it. The beautiful open hall was built in the 15th century, given its crown post roof in the 16th and its splendid staircase in 1627. The last owner presented the house to the city in 1922, together with a collection of furniture that illustrates changing tastes in design, from the simplicity of the Tudor period to the elaborate decors of the mid 19th century.

From Charing Cross, Guildhall Hill climbs to the Market Place. On the right is the flint-chequered Guildhall, begun in 1467 and now the Tourist Information Centre. The mayor and aldermen moved out in 1938 when the new City Hall was completed. This building, along the west side of the Market Place, still provokes criticism. Some like its clean functional lines, others regard it as a gross intrusion that has ruined the Market Place. It is undeniably bold, with a 200-foot high clock tower dominating the city, but it also has some fine details, such as the Assyrian lions that flank the portico and the bronze doors inset with scenes from the city's history.

St Peter Mancroft, high up on the south side of the Market Place, holds its own against this competition with its ornate stone tower and rhythmic run of clerestory windows. The east window contains a complete set of 15th-century glass, 42 panels illustrating the lives of various saints.

The area west and south of the Market Place has been substantially redeveloped, but a comprehensive tour of the city should take in the impressive Norwich Union Insurance Office in Surrey Street, designed by the local architect George Skipper in 1906. More of Skipper's versatile work can be seen in Red Lion Street, rebuilt in 1900 when the road was widened for trams and in the Royal Arcade, which links Gentleman's Walk on the east side of the Market Place with the street called, descriptively, Back of the Inns. Skipper designed the arcade in 1899 and though the entrances are all flamboyant Art Nouveau tilework and stained glass, the bow-fronted shops of the interior are as restrained and as elegant as in London's famous Burlington Arcade.

Heading north, all routes lead to the pedestrianised London Street, offering intriguing views in both directions. Framed in the western exit is the Guildhall and the City Hall tower; to the

Detail from the east window, St Peter Mancroft, Norwich

east, the elegant National Westminster Bank was built in 1924 but in a style reminiscent of one of Sir Christopher Wren's City of London churches.

From here it remains only to visit the castle. The battlements of the massive keep provide an excellent vantage point from which to look down on the medieval streets to the west, while the eastward view is of the old cattle market site, due to be developed as a Heritage Centre and car park. To the north, two fine classical

buildings have been converted into studios by Anglia Television: the 1882 Agricultural Hall to the right and the 1866 Crown Bank on the left.

The pristine state of the stone surface of the keep is due to refacing carried out in 1834, while the castle was still in use as a prison. In 1894 it was converted to a museum and art gallery. The art gallery has many paintings by artists of the

Guildhall and the Market Place, Norwich

Norwich School, particularly John Crome (1768–1821) and John Sell Cotman (1782–1842), who painted the city and surrounding countryside in faithful detail and vibrant colour.

Further exciting works of art await discovery at the Sainsbury Centre in the grounds of the University of East Anglia, 3 miles west of the city centre. The route to the university passes the imposing Roman Catholic Cathedral of St John, designed by George Gilbert and John Oldrid Scott, sons of the architect of St Pancras railway station in London and completed in 1910. It would have been even more of a landmark if it had been furnished with the intended spire – as it is, many first-time visitors to Norwich mistake it for the cathedral proper.

The University of East Anglia was founded in the early 1960s in the grounds of Earlham Hall. The 1642 flint and red-brick Hall is now surrounded by terraced student residences, designed in 1967, overlooking the River Yare. The river feeds an artificial lake, created from the gravel pit dug to supply materials for the new university.

The Sainsbury Centre, designed by Norman Foster, was opened in 1978. In this undeniably well-lit and flexible space, the art collection donated by Sir Robert and Lady Sainsbury is brilliantly displayed. Stimulating juxtapositions of works of art from many ages and countries – from tribal art to Henry Moore – make this a uniquely enjoyable gallery to visit.

Old Buckenham (2/3F) *see* Buckenhams, The

Outwell (1/2E) *see* Upwell

Overstrand (3/1A) *see* Cromer

Oxborough (1/4E)
The village lies 5 miles south-west of Swaffham. Oxburgh Hall is a perfect medieval manor house of rose-coloured brick, set serenely amid undrained marshland and surrounded by a moat. The house was built in 1482 by the Bedingfeld family, who still live here, though the house was given to the National Trust in 1952.

The Hall was built at a time when ceremonial gatehouses were fashionable, and the magnificent example here, 80 feet high, has survived untouched as an imposing example of early English brickwork. The two octagonal turrets flanking the entrance are ornamented with panels crowned by triplets of cusped arches: close inspection reveals the shapes of the individually moulded bricks used to create this pattern. Inside we find more inventive brickwork, in the handrail of the turret staircase and the vaulting. The roof of the tower offers a good view of the restored garden parterre; on a clear day Ely Cathedral can be seen on the western horizon.

Much of the Hall itself was demolished in 1775 when the accommodation was modernised, which unfortunately means that the splendid Great Hall roof, said to have been as magnificent as that of Westminster Hall, has gone. The rooms that replaced the hall were redecorated in 1830–60 and reflect early Victorian taste, many of the interior fittings having been designed by Pugin.

One room, however, is vivid with the colours of the embroidered wall hangings worked by Mary Queen of Scots and her guard, Elizabeth Countess of Shrewsbury ('Bess of Hardwick'), during the early years of Mary's long captivity in England from 1570 onwards. Mary herself did not visit Oxburgh; the embroidery was a Bedingfeld family heirloom.

The church of St John the Evangelist, just outside the grounds of the Hall, is partly in ruins following the collapse of the spire in 1948. Now only the chancel is roofed, but fortunately the Bedingfeld Chantry survived unscathed. This contains two lavish and unique, monuments of pink, almost waxy, terracotta, elaborately decorated with Renaissance ornament. These monuments, thought to date from around 1523–5, were made by Flemish craftsmen, influenced by Italian motifs.

At **Gooderstone**, the next village east from Oxborough, the bulb-filled Manor gardens are open in spring under the National Gardens Scheme.

Oxnead (3/1C) *see* Aylsham

Paston (3/2B)
This hamlet, 3 miles north-west of North

Oxburgh Hall (National Trust)

Walsham, is memorable for the massive and noble reed-thatched barn west of the church, dated 1581 and recently well restored. The barn is all that remains of the Pastons' original home, one of several that this large and influential family once owned.

The famous Paston *Letters*, penned by various members of the family in the mid 15th century, are largely concerned with the management of these estates. Alas, the substantial wealth that the Pastons made from the wool trade was squandered by the second Earl of Yarmouth in the late 17th century, and of all their properties, only CAISTER Castle has survived. The monument to Dame Katherine Paston (d. 1628) in the little thatched church of St Margaret, indicates the wealth and influence of the family in its heyday. It is said that John Donne penned her epitaph and the life-like figure of the plump Dame was carved by Nicholas Stone, master mason to James I.

Outside the church modernity intrudes upon the scene, for the view over the fields is of the huge and intrusive North Sea Gas terminal at

Bacton, built from 1968 onwards to receive natural gas from the North Sea.

Turning away from this, narrow lanes lead inland for a mile to **Knapton**, where the church of St Peter and St Paul has a splendid double hammerbeam roof, all the more beautiful for its unusual width and rich colouring: it is made of red-brown Irish oak and many of the angels retain their original paint. An inscription dates the roof to 1504.

Peddars Way

This long-distance footpath runs for 45 miles from Knettishall, just on the Suffolk side of the county boundary, to Holme-next-the-Sea, where it links up with the NORFOLK COAST PATH. The path follows a Roman military road, built soon after the Boudiccan revolt of AD 61, probably to enable troops to patrol the territory of the rebellious Iceni tribe and later providing access to the vast imperial estates of north Norfolk.

It is not known why the road was built to disappear into the sea. One plausible explanation suggests there might have been a ferry port at Holme-next-the-Sea, connecting Norfolk, via

Peddars Way, near Swaffham

the Wash, to Lincolnshire. The Roman road survived because it continued to provide a useful communication route for sheep drovers, pilgrims and pedlars. The name Peddars Way first appears on a 1587 map and may simply mean footpath – from the Latin *pedester*, to go on foot.

Although the Way is dead straight for much of its length, it is by no means monotonous. It passes through the varied terrain of Norfolk, from the southern Breckland to the rolling chalk hills of the north, by way of CASTLE ACRE and many a tranquil hamlet or farmstead. A complete and detailed guide to the route has been published by the Countryside Commission.

Pickenhams, The (2/1E) *see* Swaffham

Potter Heigham (3/3D)

This village lies in the heart of the Norfolk Broads. Broads Haven Marina, alongside the medieval bridge which crosses the River Thurne, has become one of the biggest centres of the Broads boating industry. A little downstream from the bridge is a charming polygonal house under a pith-helmet of a roof: at first sight it looks like a windmill, but in fact it is the top section of the helter-skelter from Yarmouth pier, converted to a holiday cottage.

The village proper, with its pretty thatched church of St Nicholas, housing a unique 18th-century brick font, lies well away from the tourist bustle.

Ludham, 2 miles west, also receives a stream of boating visitors, but the attractive village of thatched cottages, built in long rows, retains its old-world charm. The church of St Catherine contains two great rarities: a very well-preserved painted chancel screen of 1493 and a rood painting of around 1535–8, now beautifully restored.

The marshes around Ludham have several lonely ruins, accessible only on foot or by water. St Benet's Abbey lies by the River Bure, 2 miles south of the village. Founded in 1020 on land granted by King Canute, the abbey fell into ruin at the Dissolution of the Monasteries and the tower of an 18th-century brick windmill now rises from the middle of the gatehouse.

North-west of Ludham is the charming open-framed Boardsman's Mill at How Hill, open daily. At nearby How Hill Farm the water gardens, open under the National Gardens Scheme, are enlivened by the beautiful Swallow-tail butterflies that breed in the surrounding fens.

Pulhams, The (2/4G)

The large church of St Mary Magdalen at **Pulham Market** speaks of the prosperity of this former market town, now an attractive village of colour-washed cottages surrounding a green. Enjoyable flushwork decorates the tower and south porch, though restoration has robbed the interior of much architectural interest.

Better is the neighbouring church of St Mary the Virgin at **Pulham St Mary**, 1½ miles southeast, where the legend of the local king and saint, St Edmund, is carved on the parapets and the sumptuous south porch is profusely carved with little trumpet-blowing angels. Crowning the porch are figure pinnacles and cresting. This is 15th-century work; inside, the fine chancel is all Early English, 13th century, with a lovely piscina on slender shafts, painted with floral motifs in the 1886 restoration.

Quidenham (2/3G) *see* Wilby

Ranworth (3/2D)

The large marina on nearby Ranworth Broad ensures that this hamlet receives large numbers of visitors in summer. First stop on their itinerary is the church of St Helen, which contains England's finest painted chancel screen, dating from around 1419. Special features of this exquisite work are the two wings to the north and south which form side chapels, each with a group of four saints over the altar. The two opposing wings are painted with splendid depictions of the eternal struggle between good and evil.

Just east of the village is the Broadland Conservation Centre, with a permanent exhibition centre that floats on the marshes and a trail constructed of duckboarding that illustrates both the challenges facing conservationists and the rich wildlife of the Broads. A little to the north of the village, Old House sits by the side of the Ranworth Inner Broad. Its beautiful water gardens are open in spring, under the National Gardens Scheme.

There is another extensive woodland and water garden, open in summer, at **South Walsham**, a mile south of Ranworth, maintained by the Fairhaven Garden Trust and planted around the shores of a peaceful, privately owned broad. Lord Fairhaven, former owner of South Walsham Hall (now a leisure centre), donated the fine 17th-century Italian altar frontal in St Mary's church; his memorial (he died in 1973) is a fine piece of modern carving.

Ranworth's superb painted chancel screen depicts various saints

Raveningham (3/2F) *see* Loddon

Redenhall (6/1A) *see* Harleston

Reedham (3/3E)

The village clings to the bank of the River Yare, around a railway bridge that pivots to allow tall-masted ships through. The nearby chain ferry is the only crossing for vehicles between Norwich, nearly 15 miles to the west and Great Yarmouth, nearly 10 to the east.

The big church of St John the Baptist was gutted by fire in 1981, but the interior is nevertheless full of atmosphere – a great barn-like space. Plaster stripped from the walls after the fire has revealed that the Saxon nave wall was constructed from alternate courses of herringbone and horizontal tiles. A ready source of building material existed just 3 miles down-stream, in the Roman fort of BURGH CASTLE (*Gariannonum*).

Opposite the church are two unusual enter-prises: Hales Snails, not open to the public, breeds edible snails that are even exported to France and Pettitts, open in summer, combines the business of taxidermy with the breeding of Falabella miniature horses.

Reepham (2/3C)

A number of East Anglian villages have two parish churches in the same churchyard, but this attractive small town, 7 miles north-east of East Dereham, has the unique distinction of three – although one of them, All Saints, has been in ruins since a fire in 1513. The churchyard lies at the point where three parishes meet and it may have been more economic in labour and materials to build all three churches on the one site. Certainly the two surviving churches are much alike, in architectural style. St Mary's (the easternmost) is now the church of the combined parishes; St Michael's, used as a day centre and Sunday School, has a splendid pulpit and fine Jacobean woodwork.

The Market Place is surrounded by good Georgian buildings, including the fine old Brewery House Hotel of around 1700, with its inscribed sundial: 'I do not count the hours unless they are sunny/happy.' Opposite, several pretty buildings of brick and timber frame have projecting polygonal bays, now used as shop fronts.

A mile east of Reepham, **Booton** boasts one

of the most extraordinary churches in East Anglia, known with good reason as 'the Cathedral of the Fields'. St Michael's was the creation of the Revd Whitwell Elwin, incumbent from 1849 to 1900, editor of the *Quarterly Review* and friend of many contemporary writers, including Scott and Thackeray. Elwin began rebuilding the village church in the 1870s and lavished a fortune on it, choosing architectural features that he liked from the books in his own well-stocked library; his design thus includes details from as far afield as Venice and the early Coptic churches of Egypt. The result of this eclectic approach is surprisingly successful. The unifying element of the church is the splendid stained glass depicting a procession of angelic girls; the great roof, too, is full of angels with flaming wings. Altogether, this magnificent monument to Victorian enthusiasm is not to be missed.

Reymerston (2/3E) *see* Hingham

Ringland (2/4D) *see* Weston Longville

Rollesby (3/3D) *see* Martham

Rougham (1/5C)
This village 5 miles north of Swaffham has been transformed during the 20th century. The distinctive half-timbered and jettied estate cottages are Edwardian, and at that time Rougham Hall was extended. The Hall was originally built in 1693 for the North family, who planted the impressive avenue of lime trees which still leads past the church and up to the Hall.

Early this century St Mary's church was also excellently restored. The pleasing nave roof is deceptive, for its apparently medieval sweeping blades and fretwork in fact date from 1913.

To the north-east, the two **Weasenhams, All Saints** and **St Peter**, are attractive villages; both churches were however comprehensively restored in the 19th century.

Runcton Holme (1/3E)
Four miles north of Downham Market, St James's church stands apart from this all-modern village. A yew-lined walk leads to the brick porch which shelters a fine Norman doorway ornamented with saltire crosses. The nave contains one of Norfolk's most sumptuous Jacobean pulpits; the back support for the tester

is carved with leaping dolphins and the friezes have thistles, hearts and roses.

Two miles to the south, at **Stow Bardolph**, the church of the Holy Trinity seems rather dull until you enter the Hare mausoleum, built in brick in 1624, which is full of monuments. Easily missed in the far corner is the mahogany cupboard that contains the highly eccentric waxwork monument of Sarah Hare. The stalls in the chancel have some fine carving and at the back of the church is a three-dimensional Charles II coat of arms.

More excellent woodwork is found in St Mary's church, **Wimbotsham**, half a mile further south. The bench ends depict a series of animals, real and imaginary and were carved by James Rattee, one of the best master craftsmen of the 19th century.

Rushford (5/2A) *see* Brettenham

Ryburghs, The (2/2C)
Great Ryburgh underwent a considerable expansion in the mid 19th century with the coming of the railway. The line has now been taken up, but the big brewery in the centre of the village and the station master's house remain.

The prettier end of the village is to the east, where St Andrew's church, with its Saxon carstone and flint round tower, stands by the River Wensum. The rest of the church was modernised at several points in the 19th and 20th centuries.

East of the church, the road crosses the river and climbs Clay Hill to the site of the ruined church of All Saints, **Little Ryburgh**. The churchyard is still used and is presided over by a large white marble angel, visible for miles around, which stands over the Smith family vault.

Saham Toney (2/1E)
This village, 8 miles south-east of Swaffham, is built around a large circular mere, a typical Breckland landscape feature dug, like the Broads, to extract peat and then used as a valuable source of water in a region whose sandy soils do not easily retain moisture.

The west doorway to St George's church is squeezed up against the brick wall of the adjacent Georgian rectory – owned by New College Oxford, patron of the living.

Two miles south-west, **Threxton** lies in pretty countryside of river meadows dotted with old farm buildings. There could be no more appropriate setting for All Saints' church – a small Saxon building with a round tower and massive outward-leaning walls.

St Olaves (3/3E)

This scattered hamlet forms a gateway to the south-eastern extremity of Norfolk, parts of which were in Suffolk until the recent county boundary revisions. The region is almost an island, surrounded for the most part by the River Waveney. The A143 crosses two bridges to reach the village; the first over the railway and the New Cut, a drainage and navigational channel dug in the 18th century, and the second over the river itself.

The entrance to St Olaves's Priory is immediately after this second bridge. Founded as an Augustinian priory around 1216, the remains include a church and part of the cloister, with an undercroft of brick – an early example of the use of this material. The Priory is now maintained by English Heritage. Just north, by the riverside, Priory Mill is a tiny boarded trestle mill, well restored by the Norfolk Windmills Trust.

St Edmund's church at **Fritton**, 1 mile east, is a charming building with a Saxon tower and a thatched apsidal chancel. Surprisingly, the chancel, entered through a low arch, has a barrel-vaulted ceiling.

Fritton Lake Country Park lies in the valley below the church. Its main feature is the long narrow lake, dug like the Broads for peat extraction and later used as a site for duck decoys. The lake and surrounding woods are still visited by many birds.

Salhouse (3/2D)

Salhouse lies 5 miles north-east of Norwich. The little thatched church of All Saints has a Sacring bell above the chancel screen, close to the Elizabethan hourglass pulpit. The bell is a rare, if not unique, survival from the Catholic practices of Mary I's reign, and was rung during the consecration of the host.

Just north of the village is the Hoveton Great Broad Nature Trail, accessible only by boat, laid out on duckboarding through the wet alder woodlands and fens that ring this large broad. It is designed to explain the origins of the Broads and their rich ecology. Swallowtail butterflies are plentiful here.

At **Woodbastwick**, 2 miles east, the church, the cottages and the well on the green are all thatched, making this a most attractive village.

Misericord carvings, Salle church

The church of St Fabian and St Sebastian was well restored in 1878 by Sir George Gilbert Scott, who retained as much as possible of the older work, including the chancel screen.

Salle (2/4C)

(Pronounced Saul.) Little remains of this village 4 miles south-west of Aylsham except the massive and noble church of St Peter and St Paul, which towers over peaceful open country-side. Great local families built this outstanding church to last and so it has, untouched by later restorers. Their coats of arms are carved in a frieze all the way round the 111 foot-high tower, above a doorcase carved with censer-swinging angels. The Royal Arms of Henry V are there too, helping to date the building to around 1405–20.

Inside it is the monumental scale of the church, its spaciousness and grace that impresses, rather than any particular details. It scarcely seems possible that such a huge edifice should be supported by such slender nave columns; part of the secret lies in the structure of the roof, whose weight and outward thrust is partly born by the tall aisles. This soaring space

The church of St Peter and St Paul at Salle rises out of the landscape

is the ideal home for one of Norfolk's finest and tallest font canopies; here the original yardarm and pulley, used to lift the cover from the font, have survived, spanning out from the high bellringers' gallery.

The church is equally rewarding for its large collection of memorial brasses, commemorating those who contributed to the building of the church. None, however, commemorates Anne Boleyn, the ill-fated second wife of Henry VIII, who some people still believe to be buried here rather than the Tower of London.

Two miles east, St Agnes's church at **Cawston** rivals Salle in grandeur. Its tower, at 119½ feet, is actually taller, and the magnificent and awe-inspiring hammerbeam roof is one of Norfolk's finest.

A mile east of Cawston, by the side of the B1149 and marked by a National Trust plaque, is the Duel Stone, that commemorates a duel fought between Henry Hobart of Blickling Hall and Oliver La Neve of Great Witchingham Hall in 1698.

East Anglian Parish Churches ST JOHN GORE

Flint and Oak

East Anglia is a level land, interwoven with small meandering rivers. It is a country – because it is flat – of all embracing skies and – because of the proximity of the sea, for it is bordered by the sea to the north, east and south – its skies are limpid and nacreous. The same sky is the property of Holland and, with East Anglia's kinship to that country, Dutch elements are to be found in its buildings and the influence of the Dutch 17th-century artists is evident in the work of its three great landscape painters, Crome, Constable and Gainsborough. It is a country of flint, brick and thatch, but little stone; of chalk and clay; a country of modest yeomen's houses and colour-washed villages. Above all it is a country of parish churches.

It has been said, and there seems no reason to disbelieve it, that there are more medieval churches in East Anglia than in any other corresponding area of the British Isles. Today the number in Suffolk is around 450 and there are even more in Norfolk (though Domesday, admittedly indifferent to unpropertied ecclesiastical buildings, records only 243 in Norfolk as against Suffolk's 364). The implication is that East Anglia was more densely populated in the 14th and 15th centuries than the rest of the country.

This was a period of growing prosperity. Much of the East Anglian land was suitable for grazing sheep and much of the new wealth was created from their fleeces. The cloth trade, recalled in the names of villages such as Kersey, Lindsey or Worstead, was one of the factors which led to the construction boom in the late 14th and 15th centuries. Another was the coastal trade and the fisheries; and riches, as elsewhere, arrived as spoils of war.

Throughout this period churches were being built, rebuilt or enlarged. Funds came from much the same sources as they do today, private or corporate. But an additional element, singular to the time, was the way in which the new rich used their wealth to commemorate themselves: in a tower, a chantry chapel, a set of pews or a splendid new roof. A cynic might take the view that these benefactors were intending to buy a passage to Eternity; and no doubt that was part of the bargain. Lord Clark in his introduction to the excellent series of guides published by the Suffolk Historic Churches Trust, observed that 'without the doctrine of Purgatory the number of fine buildings would have been substantially reduced, and without the fear of hell they might not have existed at all.'

Today, not surprisingly, there are more churches than villages. In certain cases, following the Black Death for example, the village may have been re-sited. The church sometimes gives the impression of having receded from its community. Often it was built on the periphery of the village; on occasions, apart from it altogether, as it might be adjacent to the house belonging to the local landed family. On a domestic scale, the little church of Badley in Suffolk (now redundant, but cared for, even to the extent of preserving its pulpit cushion) is remote and isolated, in unkempt fields, looking like a scene drawn by an 18th-century topographical watercolourist, perhaps Michaelangelo Rooker who stayed in Suffolk on one of his antiquarian peregrinations. On a majestic scale, a subject for Turner, the great church at Salle (Norfolk) looks benignly down upon a few terraced cottages aligning the road below.

The size of Salle – where to all intents and purposes the village has vanished – poses the question: was the congregation once so large that a church of these dimensions was essential? It is true that under Edward VI and Elizabeth I attendance at services was compulsory; it is also a fact that the church was the centre for secular as well as for spiritual purposes. It fulfilled the function of a village hall; and space was needed at the east end of the nave, for instance for the performance of morality plays. A study of the population at various periods would be necessary to determine to what extent the church was built as a symbol of glorification, and to what extent it was dictated by the needs of the parish. It is unlikely that the answers would be consistent.

Local building is dependent upon the geological structure of the land and in East Anglia it is chalk and clay which predominate. To the west of a line of demarcation drawn roughly from Windsor to Norwich the substructure is chalk; to the east, clay. A stone-built church in this part of the country is a rarity. But freestone, transported from Northamptonshire (the nearest source) or Caen (the most accessible) was used for quoins

Deopham church at harvest time

and architraves, tombs and monuments, but most prominently for the columns of nave arcades. (Local stones, found mainly in the east and to a greater extent in Essex, are nothing to write home about: the yellow septaria and the rather unprepossessing conglomerate known as pudding-stone. Used together, sometimes with the addition of brick, they resemble nothing so much as Donegal tweed.) In East Anglia, however, the chief building material is flint, found in abundance in both the chalk formation and the tertiary stratum of the eastern coastline.

Flint is used decoratively as well as structurally. Combined with available stones and bound with mortar it is the main building material in almost every parish church, the rough stones generally in the past concealed by rendering, today unfortunately on occasions exposed and glutted with cement. But used decoratively flint has an unique characteristic: when fractured or 'knapped' it reveals a shiny, crystalline surface, like a deep pond touched by sunlight. The knappers' skill transformed, first by fracturing, then by chipping, a rough irregularly shaped stone into a tidy, rectangular, dark-coloured facet. Laid together, shining side outermost, the pieces fitted so closely that only a shadow of binding material was needed. The next step, in the early 14th century, was to combine the knapped flint with ashlar

stone or brick in a chequered pattern, a form of decoration which reached its apogee in the flushwork creations of the 15th century, among which the little church at Gipping (Suffolk), once a private chapel, is an example of a complete building so treated, having the appearance of an inlaid casket.

In many churches flushwork embellishes parapets, clerestories or plinths. But pre-eminently it is found as the decorative enrichment of 15th-century porches, regarded by Pevsner in his volume on Suffolk as among the greatest glories of the county. These porches do indeed give the impression, particularly today when their original purpose is lost, of a jewel attached to the fabric. In the early Middle Ages, when porches did not exist, many of the ceremonies central to church ritual took place at the church door. It was only later, when pews were conceded to the congregation, that porches, often of wood in imitation of stonework (a few remain) came into common use. Huizinga notes in *The Waning of the Middle Ages* that 'at the end of the Middle Ages an intense melancholy weighs on people's souls.' But at least in their worship they were better accommodated than their forbears.

If the porch is the cynosure of the church, the

The single hammerbeam roof at Wymondham is one of the finest of its kind

tower is its symbol. Unlike in Italy, where the militant towers of warring families rivalled each other for supremacy, or France where the sheer height of cathedrals such as Amiens or Albi dwarf their surroundings, the belfries of England are its discreet landmarks. A distinctive feature of East Anglia is the number of Saxon round towers (once fulfilling a defensive role) – some hundred of which are still in existence in east Norfolk and less than half that number in north-east Suffolk. These were the result of Scandinavian influence – or of parsimony: having no angles there was no need for stone quoins. They were, however, the forerunners of the majestic flint towers of the 15th century: the filigree elegance of Hessett, the uncompromising strength of Lavenham (both in Suffolk); or the tower of Deopham in Norfolk recalling Proust's description of Combray – like hands joined in prayer. Baedeker, that most resolute of *Ciceroni*, in holding the idiosyncratic view that Cromer, 'the English Etretat', is perhaps the most charming spot in East Anglia, praises in particular its church tower.

If flint is the most recognisably ubiquitous feature of these churches, their other most notable characteristic is oak, of widespread growth in the region but never used to better effect than in its parish churches. The East Anglian school of carpenters (the carpenter's importance was acknowledged by his being known simply as 'the wright') was unsurpassed throughout the kingdom. Numerous examples attest to the ingenuity, craftmanship, architectural skill and sense of proportion of these builders of the Middle Ages. Their crowning glory was the roofs: with tie-beams and kingposts; low pitched with arched braced tie-beams; and then the single and double hammer beams, soaring to the sky, supported above a choir of angels with outspread wings and demure comportment. Of these great roofs Blythburgh, Mildenhall, Needham Market and Barking in Suffolk, Wymondham, Ringland and Cawston in Norfolk, are among the masterpieces of their genre.

Within the churches woodwork proliferated; and in the successive periods of iconoclasm, from Reformation to Commonwealth, to be followed by the 'improvers' of the 19th century, the joiners' work, being easily destructible, suffered dearly – and none to more doleful effect than the delicate chancel screens. The roods were in any case condemned to destruction by the order of Elizabeth I in 1561. None I think survives. But the chancel screens escaped this proscription, though the easiest way to demolish the rood itself may well have been to chop down the screen. Often remaining fragments of the screens are to be discovered, used for purposes for which they were not intended, an attached decoration to a chancel stall perhaps, or to form a squire's enclosed pew. Nor did parclose screens escape a similar form of vandalism.

The introduction of screens, the purpose of which was a seemly division between the secular nave and the sanctified chancel, is likely to have coincided with the widening of chancel arches from late Norman times onwards. The rood group, the image of the crucified Christ with the Madonna and St John, had always been a subject of veneration, second only in importance to the altar itself. The absence in the majority of cases of this ritualistic division between the temporal and the hallowed, the church militant and the church triumphant, must in our churches today, apart

The font cover at Ufford church

from the stained glass, be one of the most poignant contrasts with the church of the Middle Ages. The screens in East Anglia have to be imagined as brightly coloured and gilt and, following the local pattern, comprising a dado painted with the figures of saints above which rose the traceried panels surmounted by the loft and the rood. (Fine examples of wooden screens are at East Harling, Ranworth and Attleborough in Norfolk, which has been mercifully spared in this respect more than other counties; and in Suffolk, Southwold, Bramfield and Yaxley.)

The effect of these screens, to the layman already a vivid and tantalising barrier, with the roods magically lit from clerestory or candle-beam, was further enhanced by the treatment of the west side of the chancel arch: the tympanum decorated with a canopy of honour (as at Woolpit in Suffolk) or painted with a Last Judgement. Today these Dooms are hardly discernible; all, if they exist at all, are abraded or fragmentary – 'a dim doom' as Pevsner describes the one at Bacton, Suffolk. An equally dim example belongs to Norfolk's wonderful church of Walpole St

Bench carving at Wiggenhall St Mary the Virgin

Peter. Perhaps others remain to be discovered, as has happened in a few instances in recent years, for example at Brent Eleigh (Suffolk), beneath Victorian plaster. A final touch of splendour was the ornamentation of the celure, the easternmost bay of the nave roof, its timbers painted and gilt, the culmination of the composition.

Before coming down to earth as it were, to the benches, stalls and pulpits, there is one other category of woodwork to be mentioned, namely the font covers. They share with the screens the ethereal lightness of carving; and, like the screens, they were highly vulnerable. A 13th-century decree enjoined their use for maintaining the purity of the water. 17th-century iconoclasm saw to it that this suspect function was subverted. Their numbers tragically diminished, of the few that remain the most romantic is at Ufford (Suffolk), a frail forest of stems and pinnacles, which at the touch of a finger can be raised so that the lower portion slides telescopically over the superstructure. Trunch in Norfolk still possesses one of the rare font canopies.

From the fragility of the screens and font covers, we turn to the muscular and robust: the pews and the stalls. Uncommon before the end of the 14th century – until then the congregation was expected to stand or kneel – they were essentially a 15th-century implementation. It is unlikely that they were ever painted and their darkened polished patina has today become an established element in the fabric of the building. (The ginger colour of Victorian replacements is an indictment of Victorian supererogation.) Oak in its untreated state develops with age a lighter tonality. Rarely is oak of this description found today. When it is, as at Shingham in Norfolk, its silvery greyness, complementing pale washed walls – interior walls were always plastered – bestows upon the church a balanced harmony and, now that the paintings which may once have covered the walls have been obliterated, a glow that is tender and moonlike.

The characteristic shared by East Anglian bench ends is their shaped, rather than square-topped (as in the west of England) style. In most cases ogee pedimented standards are surmounted by elaborate finials, the so-called 'poppy-heads' (the derivation of the word is likely to be from *puppis*, a poop). They were fashioned in a multiplicity of designs: animals, figures, chimera, monsters, plants and domestic scenes. Subsequently a further opportunity for decoration presented itself: the carving of the armrest – which immediately precluded the possibility of the eastern facing buttress being used for its intended purpose. The provision of this extension was logical, for it concealed the infelicitous appearance of the seat of the pew extending beyond the standard. One wonders whether the addition of a west buttress – as, for example, at Atherington in Suffolk – which served no such logical purpose, had any other *raison d'être* than to provide yet another platform for the carver.

The carving on these East Anglian bench ends – see, for excellent examples, the two Wiggenhalls in Norfolk – is unsurpassed by that of any other locality in the country. Its proliferation, variety and virtuosity, its stretches of imagination, its humour and lack of solemnity – these are a constant source of diversion. Designs are never duplicated; if they are it is almost certain that they are Victorian interpolations. It has been implied above that the inspiration for the scenes portrayed is drawn from everyday life or from bestiaries. Very seldom is it taken from religious texts, though the Seven Sacraments and Works of Mercy appear on bench ends at Wilby in Suffolk.

Our early cathedrals were essentially French in their conception, but when, after Beauvais and the Sainte Chapelle in the mid and second half of the 13th century, the building impetus lagged in France, a new life began in England with the Decorated style. The parish churches of the 14th century were an unique artistic growth and a national achievement. But we do not see either them or their magnificent Perpendicular successors as the entities that they originally were. Medieval architecture was comprehensive. The glass, the sculpture, the wall paintings with their didactic themes, were not seen in isolation but in a blaze of unified colour; and the church, which dominated the life of the community, must have spread a message that both daunted and raised the spirit of the medieval worshipper. The great tradition of church building to all intents and purposes ended in East Anglia with the Reformation; 17th- and 18th-century additions were few in number but almost always congruous: for example, the chancel added in 1745 to the unpretentious nave of Shotley in Suffolk, or the post-1633 furnishing of the Norfolk Wilby.

In many of these churches we may still enter a higher order of reality where, by the architecture alone, a mood of reverence and awe will be induced; in others we may be affected by the melancholy of their faded harmony. But none is inviolate and it is seldom that we will not be aware of abuses: of Tudor savagery, Puritan fanaticism, or the well-intentioned but generally maladroit zeal of the Victorians; and nor, I regret to say, of the misapplied rectitude of our own day, the source of which is a lack of understanding of the conception of the wholeness of a church.

Only discord can result from painting a monument in vivid colours or a wall in washing-powder white when the rest of the interior is no longer polychromatic. To reveal irregularly shaped stone architraves, never intended to be seen (or even to display, as sometimes occurs, newly embroidered hassocks not on the floor where they belong, but above, as if they were works of art), can only, however ephemeral, be to the detriment of an otherwise coherent nave. And out of doors things are not always much better. The design and siting of a new rectory will almost inevitably do an injustice to the unspoilt setting of a church. One recognises the need but deplores the execution. The unnecessary sales of so many serviceable or adaptable old parsonages is now also a matter for concern.

Today the churches of the eastern counties are more conspicuous than ever before. The country, bowing to the demands of agriculture, has been opened up. Elm disease has taken its toll of the indigenous trees of the region; and the wind, which Celia Fiennes noted in 1698 as having 'a pretty power . . . not well to be endured' and

Lady Chapel, Long Melford church

which caused Defoe concern in the case of Ely (he feared that it tottered with every gust), has in the ferocious storm of 1987 added to the devastation.

So some of the mystery of these churches, their surprise appearance, has gone. But there are few that cannot still inspire us: where we will find artefacts or atmosphere, nobility or serenity, unexpected grandeur or unassuming domesticity, antiquarian enlightenment or architectural sophistication. This is the transcendant legacy to which we are the heirs.

Acknowledgement
Any general introduction to the subject of East Anglian parish churches cannot fail to draw upon received knowledge and thus be liable to the charge of plagiarism, however unconscious. A primary debt must be to the vast display of knowledge in Sir Nikolaus Pevsner's *The Buildings of England*. For both Norfolk and Suffolk churches, Munro Cautley's volumes are indispensable. And the lucid and entertaining descriptions in the *Shell Guides* of the 1950s and 60s – Norfolk by Lady Harrod, Essex and Suffolk by Norman Scarfe – have served East Anglia with particular distinction.

Salthouse (2/3A) *see* Weybourne

Sandringham (1/3C)

The 7,000-acre Sandringham Estate and its surrounding Country Park, 5 miles north-east of King's Lynn, consists largely of sandy soils; this same sand was pushed southwards during the Ice Age to create the dunes and heath of the Breckland. Both regions once supported extensive warrens, in which rabbits were farmed for their fur and meat; they are now planted with conifers to stabilise the soil.

This habitat is ideal for the raising of game birds – wherein lay the attraction of the estate for the Prince of Wales, the future Edward VII, whose New Year shooting parties established a tradition that is still followed by the Royal family. The estate was bought for him for his coming of age in 1861. The original Georgian house was pulled down and replaced by a new building in Jacobean style, to which a lavish turreted ballroom and rooms for bowls and billiards were later attached.

The medieval church of St Mary Magdalene, already comprehensively restored in 1857, was further extended in 1890. It is replete with treasures: notably the splendid wood-panelled baptistry and Florentine marble font, the gift of Edward VII in 1911, and the solid silver altar and reredos given by an American, Rodman Wanamaker, in 1920.

The house and grounds and the exhibition of Royal cars are only open when the Royal family is not in residence at Sandringham.

Several generations of the family have each added something to the gardens. George VI had the lovely north garden laid out with box hedges and pleached lime alleys, interplanted with lavender and roses. In the spring and summer a succession of rhododendrons and azaleas put out their colourful blooms and the lakes, excavated in the 19th century, are fringed with irises, primulas, arum lilies and giant gunneras.

The charms of the garden form the theme of the great wrought-iron Norwich Gates at the entrance to the grounds; presented by the people of Norfolk to Edward, Prince of Wales as a wedding present, they form a sumptuous composition of interwoven flowers and leaves.

Outside the grounds, numerous nature trails thread through Sandringham Country Park, best visited in the early summer when the naturalised rhododendrons fill the woods with colour.

At **Wolferton**, the railway station that used to

bring the Royal family to within 2 miles of their home has now been turned into a museum, whose collection includes Queen Victoria's travelling bed. Alongside, the big church of St Peter has much enjoyable 15th-century woodwork.

In **West Newton**, on the southern fringes of the estate, several neo-Tudor houses dated 1873 are pargeted with Prince of Wales feathers. Half a mile further east, Appleton Farm was once the residence of Queen Maud of Norway. The

Sandringham House

adjacent Italianate turreted water tower, built in 1877, has now been converted to a holiday home by the Landmark Trust.

Anmer, on the eastern edge of the estate, is another Royal residence. Visitors are allowed to visit St Mary's church in the grounds, with its paintings by Sir Noel Paton, given by Queen Mary and dated 1883. The road that skirts the western edge of Anmer Hall provides very fine views: to the east the Hall itself, a handsome late Georgian building, sits well in its naturalistically landscaped grounds, while to the south-west the ground falls gently away to reveal a panorama that extends as far as the Wash.

Saxlingham Nethergate (3/1F)

Seven miles south of Norwich, this delightful village is in two parts. To the north, multi-coloured cottages surround a small green with its brick pavilion sheltering a war memorial. To the south, St Mary's church is partnered by a fine E-plan Elizabethan house, the Old Hall, fronted by topiary yews and the rather sombre yellow-brick Parsonage, designed by Sir John Soane in 1784.

St Mary's is famous for its stained glass, some of the best in Norfolk and of several periods from the 13th to the 15th centuries.

Shotesham, to the north-east, is a parish with four churches. Approaching from Saxlingham, a twist in the road suddenly reveals two of them: the ivy-covered ruin of St Martin, and St Mary's, standing not a hundred yards away. The latter contains an unusual piscina ornamented with heraldic brick panels and two small brasses to Edward Whyte and his wife, who both died in 1528 of 'sweating sickness'. To the north, St Botolph's church is now no more than a few stones in a field.

The best is yet to come for, half a mile to the north-east, All Saints' church stands high above the most picturesque village, on a mound surrounded by a ditch. The church is over-restored and, apart from the unusual tower staircase of iron, the real interest lies in the view from the churchyard. Stretching north-westwards as far as the eye can see is a little marshy stream, a tributary of the River Tas, crossed by a series of white bridges and lined on either side by thatched cottages.

Opposite the church, high on the west bank, is a most handsome Queen Anne house, the former Duke's Head, dated in one of its shapely gables to 1712.

Scole (5/4B) *see* Diss

Sculthorpe (2/1B)

This village lies 1½ miles north-west of Faken-ham. The delightful churchyard of All Saints is a mass of wild primroses in spring and in summer roses flower around the porch. The door, part of the 1847 rebuilding, continues the floral theme, with carved tulips and nightingales singing in an apple bough. The interior is enlivened by more exuberant foliage on the nave capitals, the little 1756 Snetzler organ (originally made for York Assembly Rooms) and the colourful Morris and Burne-Jones glass. Best of all is the square Norman font, carved with the Adoration of the Magi.

The simpler font at St Nicholas, **Shereford**, 1½ miles south, is of a similar date, but the simple church is Saxon, with a Norman doorway fitted within the taller original frame. The

church is prettily situated by the broad River Wensum, along whose marshy valley rare barn owls can sometimes be seen hunting just before dusk.

Sedgeford (1/4B) *see* Heacham

Seething (3/2F) *see* Loddon

Shelton (3/1F)

Shelton lies 6 miles west of Bungay. St Mary's church, which stands alone without any sign of a village, is a monument to the partly realised ambitions of its builder, Sir Ralph Shelton. Begun around 1480, neither the roof nor the chancel were completed and even Shelton's own tomb has only the first hints of the elaborate canopy intended for it.

Even so, enough was built to impress the modern visitor with its grandeur. It is a surprise to discover that the church is built almost entirely of red brick, threaded with a blue-brick diaper pattern. Inside, the upper nave wall between the clerestory windows is ornamented with the most elaborate blank arcading. After this, the shallow pitch roof is a disappointment. The lack of a chancel gives the church an oddly truncated appearance, but there is some compensation in the magnificent east windows, filled with 15th-century glass. Sir Ralph lies below the tomb chest north of the altar. Since his death the church has remained virtually untouched and, stepping outside into the surrounding sheep-grazed meadows, one gives thanks that relative isolation saved it from the hands of those who might have tried to 'improve' it.

Shereford (2/1C) *see* Sculthorpe

Sheringhams, The (2/4A)

Some of the 'Cromer' crabs that are sold locally actually come from **Lower Sheringham**, 4 miles west of Cromer, for here a few fishermen still set their baited pots along the seafront, just as their ancestors did long before the village grew into a holiday resort.

At the entrance to the town is the charming North Norfolk railway station, complete with early W. H. Smith news stand, that made Sheringham an accessible resort when the line opened in 1887. Old steam trains still chug the 5 miles to HOLT on most days in summer.

Much of the town was built in the late 19th

North Norfolk railway station, Lower Sheringham

century, in neo-Tudor style, or else using the abundant supplies of pebbles from the beach. More select developments came in the 1930s to the east, around West Runton, with its golf links and, more recently still, with the Norfolk Shirehorse Centre, which is open in summer.

Perhaps the semi-suburban outer fringes of Sheringham would have spread further had not the National Trust acted to acquire large stretches of the wild and wooded heaths that lie to the south of the town. Geologists know this as the Cromer Ridge, a belt of sand and gravel debris stretching from Cromer to Holt, dumped by melting ice sheets at the end of the last Ice Age. Roman Camp, in the midst of the range, is regarded as the highest point in Norfolk, at 328 feet above sea level.

At the western end of this chain of hills and plateaux, in **Upper Sheringham**, Humphry Repton created what he himself called his favourite park, around Sheringham Hall. When Repton began work in 1812, he found a site already so well wooded and so full of natural scenic delights that he was able to achieve his desired end with minimal change: his principal innovation was to plant newly imported species of rhododendron and azalea, which still bloom in colourful profusion in May and June. The grounds are open all year, the house only by written appointment.

Repton's client was Abbot Upcher, squire of Sheringham, who also donated the circular reservoir that stands on the small village green, in celebration of the *Anno Pacis* – the occupation of Paris in 1814.

Shernborne (1/4B)

This neat Sandringham estate village 2 miles north-east of the House is tucked into a hollow, so you see nothing of it until you arrive. Pairs of farm cottages and a steep-roofed village hall – more in the Sussex than the Norfolk vernacular – surround the church of St Peter and St Paul. This contains one of Norfolk's finest Norman fonts, a mighty piece whose carved feline heads and complex interlace panels are as fine and graceful as those of the famous Anglo-Hibernian illuminated manuscripts, the Books of Kells and Durrow.

The road north-east to **Fring** crosses PEDDARS WAY, striding dead straight across the hills between a double hedgerow. The setting of

Sheringham Hall seen from the temple (National Trust)

Norman font in Shernborne church

Fring's church of All Saints, amid gently rolling chalk hills, is delightful. Below and to the east of the churchyard, Church Farm consists of a group of cart sheds, byres and barns surrounding a courtyard near the source of the River Heacham.

Shipdham (2/2E) *see* East Dereham

Shotesham (3/1F) *see* Saxlingham Nethergate

Shouldham (1/3E) *see* Stradsett

Snettisham (1/3B)

Snettisham village, 3 miles north of Sandringham, is very attractive, despite some unfortunate council houses on the outskirts. Nearly all the houses are of local iron-rich carstone, several with pebble decoration (galleting) in the mortar. Park Farm, opposite the church, is open during the summeråand provides an insight into the workings of a modern commercial farm.

The lovely 17th-century Old Hall with its

Decorated window, west front of Snettisham church

bell-shaped gables, in the centre of the village, is now a Sue Ryder Home for the disabled. Several local businesses (Torc Bookshop, Torc Motors) refer to the hoard of late Iron Age gold torcs, or necklaces, found near by and now displayed in the British Museum.

The character of Snettisham changes markedly westwards towards the sea, past the restored 18th-century watermill. The approach to the beach is dominated by caravan parks and amusement arcades. Beyond this, however, is an extensive R.S.P.B. nature reserve of international importance; the inter-tidal mud flats of the Wash estuary are the feeding ground of numerous birds who migrate south in the autumn and stay until the early spring. (*See* 'Coastal Birds of East Anglia', p. 32.)

The soaring spire of St Mary's church, 175 ft high, is visible from afar and the church lives up to its promise. The splendid west front has an exquisite Decorated window, with tracery forming patterns like tongues of dancing fire, and the interior is tall and airy under a graceful arch-braced roof.

Two miles to the south, at **Dersingham**, St Nicholas's church contains a remarkable ancient chest, of uncertain date. It is carved with naïve and endearing symbols of the Evangelists; that of St Mark, with its pointed snout and wide eyes, looks far more like a fox than a lion. Opposite the church, the step-gabled tithe barn dated 1671 is used by Norfolk County Council as a store for historic building fragments; it belonged to the nearby Hall, which has matching gables, now part of a big housing estate.

Snorings, The (2/2B)

Inevitably, the name of these two attractive villages, 2 and 3 miles north of Fakenham, has been turned into many a pun: 'I can sleep without Snoring', Sir Ralph Shelton is said to have retorted, on hearing that his manor had been sold in 1611.

At **Great Snoring**, St Mary's church is partnered by an outstanding Rectory – not the usual Georgian red-brick house but the original manor house of the Shelton family, built around 1525. Its splendour puts the church into the shade, although there is, above the south door of St Mary's, a boldly painted and rare James II coat of arms, dated 1688.

A mile south, **Little Snoring** stands by the side of the Second World War RAF base. Boards at the rear of St Andrew's church, moved here from the mess, record the results of bombing raids over Germany and Holland.

The church itself is a delightful archaeological jigsaw. The Saxon round tower with its conical cap belongs to a separate church that once stood alongside. The surviving church is Saxon, too, with an extraordinary south door composed of three arches. The lowest one is Saxon, the middle one is Norman, very narrow and pointed but covered in bold zigzag and the outermost is another horseshoe-shaped Norman arch, ornamented with stylised beakheads. Inside the church is another rare James II coat of arms, this time dated 1686.

South Acre (1/5D) *see* Acres, The

South Burlingham (3/2E) *see* Burlinghams, The

South Creake (2/1B) *see* Creakes, The

South Lopham (5/3A) *see* Lophams, The

South Pickenham (2/1E) *see* Swaffham

South Walsham (3/2D) *see* Ranworth

Sparham (2/3D) *see* Lyng

Spixworth (3/1D) *see* Horsham St Faith

Sporle (2/1D) *see* Dunhams, The

Stalham (3/2C)

Five miles south-east of North Walsham, Stalham is both an industrial town and an embarkation point for the Broads. St Mary's church contains a well-preserved font carved with the Baptism of Christ. Sutton Mill, 1½ miles to the south-east, is Britain's tallest windmill: built in 1789 and fully restored, its nine floors now house a museum of Broadlands trades.

Ingham lies 1½ miles to the north-east. The huge and stately church of the Holy Trinity once stood at the centre of a priory, whose ruined cloisters survive along the north aisle. The interior, widely but sensitively restored, retains the base of the stone screen that originally separated the parish church in the nave from the monastic church in the chancel.

Stanfield (2/2C) *see* Brisley

Stiffkey (2/2A)

This tiny village 2½ miles east of Wells-next-the-Sea clings to a ledge above the river of the same name, bedevilled by the busy A road that passes through it. The best place to pull off is by the church of St John the Baptist. From the churchyard there are fine views down the river bottom which gave the village its name: Stiffkey, pronounced 'Stewkey', means island of stumps and probably refers to the appearance of the wide, marshy valley – then, as now, a wilderness of reed and fallen trees, a peat bog in the making and an important wildlife habitat.

From the churchyard, too, the best views are to be had of the spectacular Hall. All that survive are the 1604 gatehouse, adorned with the Bacon family coat of arms, and a wing of the U-shaped flint and brick house built by Nathaniel Bacon in 1578. The ruins of the great Hall have been made into a fine sunken garden and rose terrace, open under the National Gardens Scheme.

North of the village, the Stiffkey Salt Marshes comprise a wild and fascinating National Trust

Overleaf: Ruins of Binham Priory

reserve and source of the rich-tasting Stewkey Blue cockles.

The road to **Cockthorpe**, half a mile south-east, crosses the river, past the Manor and a street of attractive flint cottages, before climbing up through a high-banked sunken lane to the flat top of Cockthorpe Common and its former airbase, now used by glider pilots and light aircraft.

A mile south, **Binham** is a fine agricultural hamlet on top of the chalk downs. The Benedictine Priory was founded in 1091; its church, now the parish church, is an outstanding example of Early English architecture, rare in Norfolk where so many churches were rebuilt with wool money after the 14th century. The west front is one of the country's earliest examples of the Early English style, influenced by Rheims cathedral; although the windows are now blocked, it is still possible to appreciate the quality of the geometric design. The nave is as fine as that of Norwich cathedral and shows clearly the transition from the round-headed Norman arcades of the east end to the pointed arches and richer mouldings of the Early English west end.

After the suppression of the priory in 1540, Edward Paston, of the famous local family, intended to use the masonry to build a new manor house; but a workman was killed during the demolition and to this bad omen we owe the survival of the extensive ruins that surround the church. They are now tended by English Heritage.

Stow Bardolph (1/3E) *see* Runcton Holme

Stradsett (1/3E)

Three miles east of Downham Market, Stradsett now consists of little more than Hall and church. The estate is surrounded by tall shapely thorn hedges. The core of the Hall is Elizabethan, though the rendered façade reveals nothing of its antiquity.

In 1820, the owner of the Hall, Thomas Philip Bagge, acquired some outstanding stained glass which he installed in the east and west windows of St Mary's church. The small window in the tower shows two richly coloured angels, in crimson and gold robes, catching the blood of the crucified Christ in golden chalices. The east window is a complete Nativity scene, rare in any church, made in Augsburg in 1540, with a serene Virgin and ermine-robed Magi realistically portrayed.

The village of **Shouldham**, 3 miles to the north, is so rich in archaeological remains that the great landscape historian W. G. Hoskins was prompted to ask 'just how old is the English village?' Although it has been continuously occupied since Neolithic times, the village has shifted westwards over the centuries, leaving All Saints' church now surrounded by fields that show clearly the sunken lanes and house platforms of the Saxon and medieval settlement. Parishioners still walk across one such field to reach the church, which has a fine double hammerbeam roof.

Strattons, The (3/1F)

Long Stratton is cut through by the A140, on its way to Norwich, 10 miles north, but the long main street of multi-coloured houses struggles to present a neat face and there is much to see in St Mary's church. The famous Sexton's Wheel is displayed in a glass case with an explanation of its purpose – to calculate fast days in honour of the Virgin. St Michael's church half a mile north at **Stratton St Michael** contains rustic benches of massive planks. At some stage, the delicate 17th-century communion rails were sawn up to make fronts for the choir stalls.

At **Wacton**, a mile west of Long Stratton, the windows of All Saints' church have some of the most delightful flowing tracery of the Decorated period in Norfolk.

Strumpshaw (3/2E)

The chief interest of this little village 5 miles east of Norwich is the R.S.P.B. nature reserve in the Strumpshaw Fen. The reserve has a heartening story to tell: once linked to the polluted River Yare, it has since been isolated from the river and damage to the delicate ecology has mercifully been reversed.

From Strumpshaw Hill south of the village there is a magnificent view over the Yare valley, down to the alder carrs – peat bogs in the making – at Buckenham. Unfortunately, the view also includes the huge sugar beet processing factory at Cantley, first built in 1912 and much expanded since.

Descending the hill for a mile the road reaches **Buckenham**, where the church of St Nicholas has a fine 13th-century polygonal tower. The Redundant Churches Fund is restoring the much-vandalised interior.

Swaffham (1/5E)

This elegant small town on the A1065 stands around a triangular market place. On an island at the broad northern end of the market place is

the former Assembly Room, dated 1817, the gathering place of the Norfolk gentry. Several of their handsome townhouses stand near by; to the west is the Swaffham Sixth Form Centre, formerly the Headmaster's House, dated 1736 with, next to it, Oakley House, mid Georgian and heavily rusticated. The focal point of the market place, situated at the apex of the triangle, is the pillared Butter Cross – not a cross at all, but a circular pavilion built by Lord Oxford in 1783 and crowned by a life-sized figure of Ceres.

East of the market place stands the church of St Peter and St Paul. The landmark tower, crowned by a delicate lead and timber spirelet, is ornamented with the crossed keys of St Peter and crossed swords of St Paul. The great surprise of the interior is the stunning double hammerbeam roof, one of the finest in Norfolk, covered all over with so many life-size angels that you expect to hear the beating of their wings. When the sun shines in the clerestory windows, the whole roof glows the golden colour of mellow chestnut and oak.

On the right-hand side of the chancel is the family pew of John Chapman, the famous Pedlar of Swaffham whose fortune was made when he discovered a pot of gold in his back garden.

Oakley House

Chapman appears on the town sign which stands on one side of the market place, carved by a local man, Harry Carter. These signs, found all over Norfolk, are one of the delights of the county; beautifully carved and brightly painted, they summarise the history and legend of each parish. Edward VII is said to have conceived the idea, originally, of erecting signs on the villages of the Sandringham estate, in order to encourage the inhabitants to take an interest in local history. The practice spread throughout Norfolk and many fine signs are still being made at the Queen's Carving School, Sandringham.

Necton lies 3 miles east of Swaffham. All Saints' church is an excellent mixture of ancient and Victorian work. The attractive lantern on top of the tower is framed by the lime tree avenue as you approach the church and was added in 1865. The interior is made sumptuous by the splendid hammerbeam roof, some of whose angels retain their original paint. The pulpit and tester date from 1656 and there is a rood of unusual form, flanked by groups of saints. Several small brasses in the north aisle are excellent for costume details.

Two miles south-east of Necton, at **North Pickenham**, St Andrew's church is much restored, but has good stained glass of 1864, influenced by William Morris. **South Pickenham**, 1½ miles to the south, is an attractive estate village of 18th-century barns and 19th-century flint cottages.

Another 3 miles to the west, postwar plantations surround the pretty hamlet of **Cockley Cley** (pronounced 'cly'), whose origins go back to the Iron Age. The original village was destroyed in about AD 60 following Boudicca's revolt, but a speculative reconstruction has been created in the marshy stream valley south of the present village. The stream has been diverted to form a moat around the timber palisade, within which there are a variety of thatch-roofed huts and long houses. The museum complex includes a delightful streamside nature trail and a collection of agricultural engines and is open daily in summer.

Continuing westwards for 3 miles, St Mary's church at **Beachamwell** is an endearing thatched building with a Saxon round tower. Inside you will find some of the best-preserved medieval graffiti in the country. Scratched into the western column of the south nave arcade are a demon, a lady in a wimple and a record of the quantities of materials supplied to the masons when the church was rebuilt in the mid 14th century.

Just north, bisected by the A1122, is a good stretch of the Devil's Dyke, a linear earthwork which has puzzled archaeologists: some say it was a late Roman defence against invading Anglo-Saxons, others a Saxon boundary demarcating their newly conquered territory.

Swannington (2/4D)

This village, 5 miles south-west of Aylsham, has an enclave of older buildings surrounding the church of St Margaret, including the moated 17th-century Swannington Hall and its contemporary, Swanington [sic] Manor. The Manor gardens are open to the public and are full of unusual plants, sheltered by a 300 year-old box and yew topiary hedge.

The road to nearby **Alderford** passes through wild birch woodland. A pretty stream runs through the hamlet, alongside the castellated 18th-century Bell Inn. The church of St John the Baptist has original 13th-century ironwork on the south door.

Swanton Morley (2/3D)

Numerous narrow lanes converge on this village

2 miles north-east of East Dereham, but none more attractive than the minor road from Worthing, which follows the winding course of the River Wensum. Just north of Swanton, where the lane joins the B1147, it is worth pausing to admire the two triple-arched bridges that cross the river and the early 19th-century mill buildings alongside.

St Mary's church stands high above the river with splendid eastward views. The will of Lord Morley, patron of the church, has enabled historians to date the building to around 1378, which makes this one of the very first Perpendicular churches to be built in Norfolk. The style is already mature and handled with confidence; the massive battlemented tower and the light, elegant interior, lit by a long clerestory, are all hallmarks of a style that quickly spread throughout East Anglia.

The village lies below in a hollow, with the stump of a former windmill high up to the west. Here the Mill Bakery makes and sells Norfolk Nobs and other local specialities.

Two miles east, the hamlet of **Elsing** seems to have changed little since the beautiful Hall was built in 1460. The present owners have created an imaginative garden from the moat and fishponds and the surrounding meadows are a rich tapestry of orchids and fritillaries in spring. The gardens are open under the National Gardens Scheme.

The huge and aisleless church of St Mary contains two treasures: a 14th-century font canopy, one of the oldest in Norfolk, and one of England's finest brasses, commemorating Sir Hugh Hastings, who built the church.

Swardeston (2/4E)

Nurse Edith Cavell, who was executed by the Germans in 1915 for helping Allied prisoners escape from occupied Belgium, was born in the vicarage of this village 3 miles south of Norwich, and is commemorated by a memorial east window in St Mary's church.

Sir William Boleyn, grandfather of Anne Boleyn, was one of several owners of Gowthorpe Manor east of the church, which has changed little since the main part of the house was built between 1530 and 1550. The house is open by appointment.

Intwood Hall, a mile to the north, was rebuilt in 1807; but the gardens, open under the National Gardens Scheme, have a lovely terrace, on which Elizabeth I once played bowls and walls that shelter many varieties of old rose.

A mile south of Swardeston, **Mulbarton** village surrounds the 45-acre green, as vast as the more famous one at OLD BUCKENHAM.

At St Nicholas's church, **Bracon Ash**, 2 miles to the south-west, the most conspicuous feature is the Berney mausoleum, added on to the

Brass to Sir Hugh Hastings, Elsing church
Overleaf: Daffodil crop near the Terrington Marshes

chancel in the 18th century. This must have had an earlier predecessor, because the door to the mausoleum is framed by Renaissance terracotta

panels, identical to those at OXBOROUGH, which are early 16th-century. They add further interest to this beautifully maintained church.

Tacolneston (2/4F) *see* Ashwellthorpe

Tasburgh (3/1F)

The village lies at the foot of a hill 5 miles south-east of Wymondham. The hill once served as an Iron Age encampment and the surrounding banks, no higher than a hedge bank, are visible on the left-hand side of the road that leads north to Rainthorpe Hall. This is one of East Anglia's few 16th-century timber-framed great houses – most of its contemporaries were built in the newly fashionable brick. The lovely gardens, open on Sundays in summer, are threaded by the River Tas. The church of St Mary, up on the hill, has an interesting Saxon tower with two tiers of blind arcading.

The River Tas lends its charm to the village of **Newton Flotman**, a mile north of the Hall; the southern approach to the village crosses a medieval bridge, partnered by a former mill.

Several tributaries of the Tas together form a region of marsh and water meadows to the west, around the hamlet of **Florden**; on the gently rising ground above the hamlet is the handsome red-brick Florden Hall, unchanged since Tudor times.

Terringtons, The (1/2D)

Spalding in Lincolnshire is the bulb-growing capital of England, but the crop has spread eastwards as far as the Terrington Marshes, so that, if you visit in spring, you will find the magnificent church at **Terrington St Clement**, 3½ miles west of King's Lynn, rising above acres of daffodils. Beautiful planting of bulbs and shrubs continues up to the walls of the big detached church tower, used by villagers as a refuge when the sea burst its banks in 1613 and again in 1670.

The sea was not the only threat: the Great Ouse, three miles east, and the River Nene, four miles west, have frequently burst through their retaining dykes to flood thousands of acres of the surrounding land. Just such an event was vividly described in Dorothy L. Sayers's gripping novel *The Nine Tailors*, based in part on this church. The last major flood occurred in 1947; the new sluice gates at DENVER are designed to prevent a similar occurrence today.

The sister village of **Terrington St John** lies 3 miles to the south. The thin west tower of St John's church was once detached but is now linked to the nave by a curious priest's house. A complete set of box pews survives beneath the fine clerestory of circular windows with petal-like quatrefoil tracery.

A mile south-east of Terrington St Clement, just off the A17, the church at **Tilney All Saints** is one of the earliest of the great Marshland churches, with a long Norman nave of solid round pillars and unpointed arches supporting a fine double hammerbeam roof. Most of the woodwork, including the chancel screen, dates from the early 17th century and the handsome font of 1618 is boldly carved with Latin and English inscriptions. The church of **Tilney St Lawrence**, 3 miles further south, was heavily restored in 1846.

Thetford (5/1A)

Forty years ago Thetford, just 2 miles over the Suffolk border on the A11, was a sleepy market town, with a population of under 5,000. In the 1960s it signed an overspill agreement with the London County Council so that today it is five times that size and still growing. Large housing and industrial estates surround the historic core; it was during the development of one of these, Fison's Way estate, that archaeologists discovered a major late Iron Age enclosure in the early 1980s.

The extent and importance of these remains have inevitably led to speculation that Thetford was the tribal capital of the Iceni, the formidable people who, under Boudicca in AD 60, very nearly succeeded in driving the Romans out of Britain. Further Iron Age defences survive to the east of the town, surrounding the 11th-century Norman motte; both these and the motte itself were built to guard the point where the prehistoric Icknield Way crosses the Little Ouse and the River Thet.

At the time of the Norman Conquest Thetford was already a prosperous town, with a mint and a highly productive pottery industry: Thetford ware is found on archaeological sites all over East Anglia. Between 1075 and 1094 Thetford was the seat of the Bishop of East Anglia: the attractive red-brick Grammar School (now Fulmerston School) on Bridge Street stands on the site of the cathedral. Several monastic institutions were established in the town and the ruins of the 12th-century Cluniac priory have survived on the west side of the town, near the

Interior of Terrington St Clement church

railway station. They are now managed by English Heritage and are open to the public.

After the Dissolution of the Monasteries in the mid 16th century Thetford declined; only three of the town's twenty-four medieval churches have survived. Nevertheless, Thetford's many substantial timber-framed and Georgian houses indicate that some inhabitants at least continued to enjoy considerable prosperity.

From the riverside car park off Bridge Street, the route into town crosses the Little Ouse by means of a pretty cast-iron bridge of 1829; from here the road climbs to Minstergate, past the Bell Hotel, an Elizabethan coaching inn. Continuing up the hill, number 21 White Hart Street, the Ancient House, is a beautiful half-timbered building of 1500, with elaborately carved ceilings. It was given to the town in 1921 by the local antiquary, Prince Duleep Singh (see BLO NORTON in Norfolk and ELVEDEN in Suffolk) and converted into an excellent museum.

The house at the top of the street bears a plaque indicating the probable birthplace of Thomas Paine (1737–1809), author of *The Rights of Man* and *The Age of Reason*. An animated statue of Paine by Sir Charles Wheeler stands in front of King's House in King Street, Thetford's principal thoroughfare. King's House, now the district council's offices, was built in the mid 18th century and bears the royal coat of arms on the parapet because an earlier house on the site was built as a hunting lodge for James I.

A 1970s shopping precinct fills most of the centre of Thetford, but the pleasant Market Place further west is surrounded by late Victorian buildings including the cast-iron arcade of 'The Shambles', the 1900 Guildhall and the 1887 Mechanics Institute.

Attractive riverside gardens were laid out to the east of the town in 1818, when Thetford briefly flourished as a spa. The original Pump Room of 1819 stands above the medicinal spring in Spring Walk first discovered in 1746; further west, returning to the town centre, Thetford Mills occupies an island between the two rivers.

Thetford is an ideal centre from which to explore the extensive Breckland heath and forest that surrounds the town. Thetford Forest is the largest lowland forest in Britain, covering an area of 80 square miles and supplying 6% of the timber harvested by the Forestry Commission. Planting began in 1922, by which time the sandy heath had been impoverished by over-grazing. Most of the Forest is under Corsican Pine, but here and there older planting survives; many of

the roads into Thetford are lined with the knarled and wind-blown Scots Pine, planted as early as 1805 in an attempt to reduce erosion, and areas of natural birch-wood forest, rich in fungus species, remain.

One of the most rewarding areas to explore is **East Wretham** Heath, 4 miles north-east of Thetford along the A1075. Nature trail leaflets are available from the site warden. The area consists of a varied habitat of mixed woodland, heath and Breckland meres: these small lakes,

Scots pines, Thetford Forest

overlying pockets of boulder clay, attract a rich birdlife and the woodland is also a sanctuary for red squirrels as well as for four species of deer.

Thompson (2/2F)

College Farm, at the southern end of the village, is a reminder that St Martin's was once the church of a collegiate community, founded in 1349. This helps date the splendid tracery of the chancel and the beautiful rood screen. Brick floors, old benches and a Jacobean triple-decker pulpit add further to the atmosphere of this unspoiled church.

At **Merton**, 1½ miles north, the Hall has twice recently suffered fires, but there is a garden centre in the grounds and the pretty brick lodge house of 1620 has survived. St Peter's church, also in the grounds, has a Saxon round tower and a very fine chancel screen pierced by cusped tracery wheels.

Thornham (1/4A) *see* Holme-next-the-Sea

Thorpe (3/3F) *see* Haddiscoe

Thorpe Market (3/1B)
The village lies 3 miles north of North Walsham. The church of St Margaret is Norfolk's only Gothick church and rather a bizarre and endearing one at that. The plan is symmetrical, with separate porches – one for the priest, one for the congregation – and two spindly screens dividing the church into three.

The church at **Gunton** lies 1 mile to the south-west in Gunton Park. It was rebuilt in 1769 by Robert Adam and is typical of his delicate classical style. From the outside it resembles a temple, with great Tuscan columns fronting the west entrance, while inside there is much fine plasterwork, beautifully restored after the ceiling fell down in 1976. The raised pews of the Sheffield family have splendidly bound prayer books, printed in 1764.

The hall has also been very well restored in recent years, though part of the house which was gutted by a fire in 1882 has been left as a romantic ruin. The earliest, classical, part of the house was built in 1742, and the delightful conservatories and verandas were added by James Wyatt after 1785.

Threxton (2/1E) *see* Saham Toney

Thurning (2/3C) *see* Heydon

Thursford (2/2B) *see* Hindringham

Tilneys, The (1/2D) *see* Terringtons, The

Titchwell (1/4A) *see* Brancaster

Tittleshall (2/1C) *see* Mileham

Tivetshall St Margaret (2/4G) *see* Gissing

Trowse Newton (3/1E) *see* Caistor St Edmund

Trunch (3/1B)
Just within sight of the sea, 2½ miles north of North Walsham, Trunch has greatly expanded since the Second World War, but the core of the old village remains east of the church, around Thatched Hall Farm (formerly the Manor House), a fine Elizabethan building. St Mary's church is rewarding for its splendid woodwork,

including the angel-bearing hammerbeams and the tracery of its magnificent roof.

The stout font canopy is like that at St Peter Mancroft, Norwich, a self-supporting structure standing on six ornately carved legs. The chancel stalls are covered in graffiti, including a sketch of the church dated 1676. A floor slab nearby marks the grave of Horatio Nelson, son of Lord Nelson and Lady Hamilton.

Two miles to the south-east, the isolated church of St Giles, **Bradfield**, is worth seeking for the 14th-century wall painting above the chancel arch depicting Christ in Judgement seated on a rainbow.

Tunstead (3/1C) *see* Worstead

Upper Sheringham (2/4A) *see* Sheringhams, The

Upton (3/2D) *see* Acle

Upwell (1/1E)
Upwell lies on the Cambridgeshire border 5 miles west of Downham Market. One way to approach the village is along the Roman Fen Causeway, which stands slightly raised above the peat-black, rich fen fields, with nothing on the horizon for miles except the occasional pollarded willow or fieldworker's shed. Sometimes the skies can be magnificent, filling the horizon with cloud patterns beloved of watercolour painters; at other times they are a monotonous, cold blue-grey.

Alternatively, you can take the A1122 from Downham Market and stop off to visit the aqueduct at Mullicourt, a mile south-east of Upwell. Here, Well Creek meets the Middle Level Main Drain. Well Creek represents part of the original course of the River Ouse and was an important navigational route from King's Lynn to Wisbech. Thus, when the new drain was dug in 1843, the suggestion that Well Creek should be dammed was rejected: instead, an aqueduct was built to carry the Creek over the Drain and so the Creek continues to flow into Outwell, where it joins the Wisbech Canal.

The church of St Peter at Upwell stands to the east of the Wisbech Canal and is one of the most rewarding churches in Norfolk, principally because the early 19th-century west and north galleries allow visitors to climb into the magnificent roof and study the carvings at close

Font and canopy, St Mary's church, Trunch

quarters. The hammerbeam roof of the nave is covered in splendid angels, with 4ft wing spans, carrying the instruments of Christ's Passion. In the aisle roofs the carpenters allowed their imaginations full play and the wall braces are covered in relief carvings.

Alongside the church, Welle Manor Hall, a fortified house dating back to 1202, is open to the public. Norfolk Punch is made at the Hall, using a medieval recipe and waters from an underground well, and there is a curio museum in the Coach House.

The village of Upwell is made particularly attractive by the Wisbech Canal, dug in 1794, which runs down the middle of the long village green. It also marks the county boundary, for the street on the east bank is in Norfolk, that on the west in Cambridgeshire. A tramway was built alongside the west bank in 1883; although this should have spelt the death knell of the canal, it continued in use, for transporting highway materials only, until 1939.

The canal survives as an open waterway up to the next village of **Outwell**, where the church of St Clement stands almost as an island, surrounded by the canal and the Well Creek. Inside is another splendid hammerbeam roof, carved with angels, and much 16th-century stained glass.

Beyond Outwell the canal has been filled in, but will remain as a transport route since part is being built over as a road to iron out some of the bends and twists in the A1101. This road takes us to **Emneth**, a charmless village of modern housing but whose church of St Edmund has another fine angel roof and an important monument. This was carved by Nicholas Stone, Master Mason to James I, for Thomas Hewer of Oxburgh Hall.

Wacton (2/4F) see Strattons, The

Walpoles, The (1/2D)

Many churches are locally styled the 'Cathedral of the Fens', but St Peter's church at **Walpole St Peter**, 10 miles west of King's Lynn, truly deserves the title.

The pleasures of this massive and enjoyable church begin with the 15th-century porch, which is decorated with religious bosses. The interior is filled with fine woodwork, including a west screen of 1630 and wine-glass pulpit of 1620. Many of the pews and benches have fretwork backs and carved poppy heads. The best are in the chancel, which also retains a rare

and complete set of stone walls with ribbed canopies.

The altar is raised well above the level of the nave and the reason for this becomes clear outside. The east end of the church is built right up against the wall of the neighbouring property and this, effectively, prevented the congregation from processing around the church as part of the Easter Saturday ceremonies. The solution was to build a passage (locally called the 'Bolt Hole') beneath the high altar.

Opposite the church is a fine 17th-century house with a good decorative chimney and original green glass window panes and, behind, an unusual group of single-storey almshouses, dated 1737, with a massive doorcase and Gibbs surround.

The church at **Walpole St Andrew** is currently locked and boarded up, awaiting restoration. It stands on a wide tree-covered green with a pleasing bronze war memorial in the shape of a Celtic cross.

Walsinghams, The (2/2B)

Several ancient pilgrimage routes converge on the little hamlet of **Houghton St Giles**, just south of **Little Walsingham** on the B1105 north of Fakenham and here, by tradition, pilgrims would remove their shoes and walk barefoot the remaining mile to Walsingham's shrine of the Virgin Mary. This, at least, is the story told to account for the name of the Slipper Chapel at Houghton; in fact, however, there is no reference to the name before the 19th century, when the little 14th-century chapel was restored and re-opened as a Roman Catholic pilgrimage centre.

Erasmus, visiting Little Walsingham in 1511, called it 'a town maintained by scarcely anything else but the number of its visitors'. This remains true today; for the shrine, which was once second only in popularity to that of St Thomas à Becket, is once again a pilgrimage centre for Anglicans, Roman Catholics, Orthodox believers and even Methodists.

The first shrine to the Virgin was built in the early part of the 12th century by Richelde of Fervâques, a widow who was transported in a dream to Nazareth, shown the Holy House in which Mary received the news of the coming birth of Christ from the Archangel Gabriel and instructed to build a replica of the house in Walsingham. In about 1153, Geoffrey Fervâques, a relative of Richelde, endowed an Augustinian priory to look after the shrine and thereafter a highly successful pilgrimage industry was established, enhanced by the acquisition of several relics and the discovery of some curative wells.

Several monarchs visited the shrine, including Henry VIII, who early in his reign, walked barefoot from Barsham to place a gold necklace around the neck of the medieval statue of the Virgin. This did not, however, prevent him from suppressing the priory in 1538, when the statue was burned and most of the buildings demolished.

The renaissance of Walsingham as a shrine began with the first annual pilgrimage to the Roman Catholic Slipper Chapel in 1897. In 1921 the Revd Hope Patten was appointed Vicar at Walsingham and organised the first Anglican pilgrimage. Ten years later, the new Anglican shrine was opened, to be greatly extended in 1937 to cope with the volume of visitors, who continue to come in great numbers throughout the summer.

As a consequence Walsingham is today a wholly English town, with much fine medieval and Georgian architecture, but with a Continental atmosphere, for many houses belong to religious orders and many shops are devoted to the sale of religious souvenirs. The shrine of Our Lady of Walsingham, on the corner of Holt Road, is Italianate; the daily devotions, though nominally Anglican, are indistinguishable from the most elaborate Roman Catholic ritual.

West of the shrine, in Common Place, the former Shire Hall is now a museum. A pretty 16th-century brick conduit stands in the middle of the Place, over a medieval well. Leading south from Common Place, the High Street is a delightful sight with its timber-framed houses, many with overhanging upper storeys, the occasional 17th-century brick house with shaped gables and some grander Georgian façades. A little way down on the left, a 15th-century gateway leads to the pleasantly landscaped Abbey Grounds and the remains of the original shrine and Augustinian priory.

At the bottom of the High Street, a right turn leads into Friday Market and to one of the oldest surviving Methodist churches in Norfolk, built 1793–4 in handsome classical style. At the south end of the High Street are the ruins (private) of a friary founded in 1347 and, opposite, the parish church of St Mary and All Saints. This was almost completely destroyed by fire in 1961 but was rebuilt and reconsecrated three years later. The very fine 15th-century Seven Sacraments font survived the fire and remains – despite the decapitation of the figures – one of the finest of

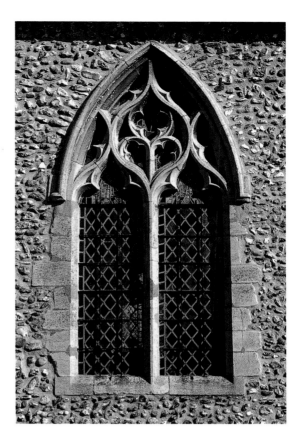

Window in St Peter's church, Great Walsingham

its type in Norfolk, with exquisitely detailed scenes carved in the soft chalk.

Great Walsingham, although less than a mile north, is totally different. We are back in deepest rural Norfolk, away from the crowds, in a pretty village of cottages grouped around a green. St Peter's church stands above the village on an eminence, next to the Tudor Berry Hall; there is a complete, well-preserved 15th-century cross on the approach to the church.

Though St Peter's is now bereft of its chancel and thus presents a truncated appearance, it has lost little of its serene beauty, which derives from the splendid Decorated window tracery, the harmonious warm natural wood colours of the roof and the splendid benches, which are among the best in the county.

Walsoken (1/1D) *see* West Walton

Warhams, The (2/2A)
Warham All Saints is a pretty estate village of almost identical pairs of brick and flint cottages,

Wells harbour at sunset

2 miles south-east of Wells-next-the-Sea. All Saints' church has no less than three fonts: one is carved with an intricate interlace knot and another must once have been as fine as that at BURNHAM DEEPDALE, carved with the Labours of the Months, but sadly mutilated when an attempt was made to cut the square stone into an octagon; the third stands by the lectern, a charming 18th-century baluster font.

The church of St Mary Magdalene at **Warham St Mary** stands at the west end of what is now almost one continuous village with Warham All Saints. Graceful Georgian furnishings, font, chandelier, box pews and unadorned three-decker pulpit give the church the atmosphere of a simple Non-conformist chapel. By contrast, the windows contain much fine and colourful stained glass, the majority of which is part of the same group of 16th-century glass from the cloisters of the Steinfeld monastery in Germany

Waterden (2/1B) *see* Creakes, The

Weasenhams, The (1/5C) *see* Rougham

Weeting (1/4G)

Just north of Brandon and a mile over the Suffolk border, modern Weeting is an unpromising village of 1950s housing estates, but is surrounded by archaeological sites. Weeting Castle lies at the end of a deeply potholed track north of the village and over the border in Norfolk; it consists of an aisled hall with cross wings and the remains of a three-storey tower, originally built around 1180 by Ralph de Plais. The castle is maintained by English Heritage.

Two miles east along the B1108 is another English Heritage site, the Neolithic flint mines at Grimes Graves: a 34-acre network of over 1,700 pits, dug around 2000 BC. Visitors can descend one of the excavated pits to see the complex of tunnels and galleries cut by prehistoric miners in the soft chalk to gain access to the thin veins of top-quality floorstone flint. A small museum on the site exhibits objects found during the excavations.

The size of the mine complex indicates a considerable demand for flint tools, which were used primarily for forest clearance. Some 4,000 years later the surrounding Breckland is once again under forest, most of it planted between 1922 and 1937, largely in order to stabilise the thin sandy soil of the region. The heath around Grimes Graves has been left free of trees and has been designated a Site of Special Scientific interest for its rich bird life.

Much of the Breckland to the north and east of Grimes Graves (the Stanford Battle Area) is used for military training and access is prohibited to the general public.

Wells-next-the-Sea (2/2A)

Wells is a most enjoyable coastal town that has retained the atmosphere of a working harbour while developing as a popular resort. Vessels from as far away as Malta still moor at the quayside, unloading timber, grain and fertiliser in front of the 19th-century Maltings with its gantry and cranes. Little boys fish for crabs along the harbour wall and the muddy creeks are dotted with small boats in search of shrimps, whelks, crabs and sprats.

Visitors come here to walk, as much as to swim, out along the mile-long 'Bank', thrown up in 1859 to straighten the channel and provide access to the sea through the muddy silt that

that is found, among other places, at KIMBERLEY and HEVINGHAM.

Immediately south of the Warhams, on the bank of the River Stiffkey, is Norfolk's best-preserved Iron Age hill fort. Recent excavations found substantial quantities of Romano-British pottery, suggesting a pre-Roman date.

Half a mile south again, **Wighton**, another attractive village of farm buildings and Georgian houses surrounded by flint garden walls, clings to the hillside above the river.

threatened to close the harbour. Having worked up an appetite, they return to the shellfish stalls and fish-and-chip shops of the quay; in summer months the sea wall is packed with contented *al fresco* diners.

South from the quay, a series of narrow lanes, known as yards, runs up to the centre of the town; the finest of these, Staithe Street, has many surviving Victorian and Edwardian shop fronts. The southern end of Wells has a different character again: a broad rectangular green, called 'The Buttlands' because it was once used for archery practice, is lined with grand late Georgian and Victorian houses. The nearby church of St Nicholas, patron saint of sailors, was rebuilt after a fire in 1879.

Just east of the town, on the A149, enthusiasts have created the Wells and Walsingham Steam Railway, building a 10¼ inch gauge track along the course of the old Great Eastern line, a pretty route noted for its wild flowers and butterflies.

Welney (1/3E) *see* Downham Market

West Acre (1/4D) *see* Acres, The

West Barsham (2/2B) *see* Barshams, The

West Dereham (1/3E) *see* Barton Bendish

West Lexham (2/1D) *see* Lexhams, The

West Newton (1/3C) *see* Sandringham

Weston Longville (2/4D)
This village 6 miles east of East Dereham was once the home of Parson James Woodforde (1740–1803) whose amusing *Diary of a Country Parson* (published 1924–31 in 5 volumes by Oxford University Press) is a minor classic of English literature. All Saints' church is well worth a visit for the 14th-century *Tree of Jesse* wall painting in the north aisle.

The next-door village of **Ringland**, a mile south-east, has a fanciful group of 18th-century estate cottages south of the church, aspiring to grandeur with their pedimented windows and stepped gables. St Peter's church has a graceful roof, whose hammerbeams are encased in a delicate fan-vaulted coving, a sumptuous form of enrichment that it shares in East Anglia only with St Peter Mancroft, in NORWICH and St Michael, FRAMLINGHAM, Suffolk. The clerestory windows contain an exceptional set of mid 15th-century glass panels.

West Somerton (3/3D) *see* Hemsby

West Walton (1/1D)
West Walton is 2 miles north of Wisbech, Cambridgeshire, in flat fenland countryside: any piece of ground more than five feet high is called a hill and on these, wisely, the older farmhouses are built.

St Mary's church is a splendid example of Early English architecture – a rarity in an area of mainly Perpendicular work. Almost dwarfing the church is the huge detached tower, open at ground level and rising through three stages of blank arcading and pointed lancets. The splendid little south porch is an ambitious, though not fully realised, conception: very narrow side arcades are uncomfortably squeezed into the corner angles. The ceremonial west front, modelled on Lincoln Cathedral, has two doors divided by multiple shafts with bolt stiff leaf capitals. More gorgeous capitals rise from the Purbeck marble shafts of the nave arcade and the nave walls have paintings of 1240–5, contemporary with the building of the church, designed to resemble tapestry wall hangings.

Two miles south, **Walsoken** is a dull suburb of Wisbech. The church of All Saints is a matter of feet away from the Cambridgeshire border. Like West Walton, the splendid Early English west tower was inspired by Lincoln, but the body of the church is a little earlier, representing the last flowering of late Norman: all seven bays of the nave arcade, and the pointed chancel arch, are covered in deep horizontal zig-zag mouldings.

Weybourne (2/4A)
The shingle beach, known as Weybourne Hope, 2½ miles west of Sheringham, is backed by low cliffs of soft, easily eroded yellow-orange sandy gravels. Behind lies a stretch of similar glacial debris, pushed along by the advancing ice front in the last Ice Age and now covered in bracken. The beach here shelves so steeply that deep-draught boats can come to within yards of the shore and in 1939 fear of invasion led to the establishment of an army camp. This is now a museum, the Muckleburgh Collection, of military equipment from battlefields all over the world.

Salthouse, 3 miles further west, was once a thriving port linked to the sea by the Mayne Channel. The canal was blocked as part of a land reclamation scheme of 1638, destroying the livelihood of many a fisherman and sailor. Now the salt and freshwater lagoons of the Salthouse Marshes support a host of breeding birdlife.

Wheatacre (3/3F) *see* Burgh St Peter

Wickhampton (3/3E)
Wickhampton is separated from Great Yarmouth by 5 miles of fields, dykes and windmills. The splendid but remote church of St Andrew is well worth seeking out for the tombs of Sir William Gerbygge (d. 1270) and his wife, two of Norfolk's earliest effigies and the outstanding 14th-century wall paintings. These comprise one of the most complete and best-preserved depictions of the popular *memento mori* theme, The Three Quick and The Three Dead.

From both Wickhampton and Halvergate, a mile to the north, it is possible to follow footpaths for two miles or so across the marshes to Berney Arms High Mill, one of the best and tallest of the county's windmills, which is run by English Heritage. Alternatively, it is accessible by boat, or by railway from Great Yarmouth or Reedham, for there is a little station, as well as a pub, near by. The present mill was built about 1865 to grind cement and converted to a

Interior of St Mary's church, West Walton

pumping mill shortly afterwards. The vast expanse of Breydon Water begins a quarter of a mile north of the mill; the footpath which skirts the northern edge of the estuary is ideal for bird-watching (*see* 'Coastal Birds of East Anglia', p. 32).

Wiggenhalls, The (1/2D)
Wiggenhall St Germans, 4 miles south-west of King's Lynn, stands by the Great Ouse, whose great retaining banks reach almost as high as the church roof.

Wiggenhall St Peter's church is now a roof-less ruin, romantically surrounded by wild flowers blooming in the churchyard, which has reverted to pasture.

Wiggenhall St Mary Magdalene is 2 miles further south and the church stands next to the folly-like Old Rectory. Here, some 14th- and 15th-century stained glass has been gathered together in the north aisle windows, illustrating over 40 saints.

Bench ends at Wiggenhall St Mary the Virgin

The church at **Wiggenhall St Mary the Virgin** is the best of the group; tucked into the angle between two fen drainage channels, it stands close to St Mary's Hall, which has a Tudor stable block and gatehouse: the rest of the house is 19th century but in the same warm red brick and higgledy-piggledy arrangements of battlements and ornate chimneys. The church is reached by walking through the garden of Wiggenhall House, past an orchard full of hens and geese. Now maintained by the Redundant Churches Fund, St Mary's contains another superb set of benches which have survived in a remarkably good condition.

Wighton (2/2B) *see* Warhams, The

Wilby (2/3F)
Three miles south of Attleborough, the road first passes Wilby Hall, a fine moated Elizabethan

E-shaped house. In Wilby, the main interest of the pretty church of All Saints is the woodwork, replaced after a fire in 1633.

Quidenham, 2 miles south, is an attractive farming hamlet with picturesque Victorian estate cottages. St Andrew's church is made rather gloomy by the dark Victorian glass, but under the Saxon tower arch is the original 16th-century chancel screen moved when the church was restored, elaborately carved with pelicans and angels.

Beyond the church is a group of open-fronted cart sheds. Next to these are the entrance to Quidenham Hall, a Carmelite convent and then a prominent tumulus, known locally as the 'Viking mound'. Legend has it that this is the burial place of Boudicca, but it is more likely to be a Norman motte.

A mile further south, **Kenninghall** is a delightful village: the oldest houses lie on the back road to the church, high up above a wide raised walkway; they include the late medieval Church Farm House, with its oversailing upper floor, and the 18th-century Baptist church, now a pottery, which retains its panelled gallery. St Mary's church has a solid Norman door and a splendid kingpost roof, as well as a rare and delightfully rustic painted coat of arms of Elizabeth I.

Winbotsham (1/3E) *see* Runcton Holme

Winterton-on-Sea (3/3D) *see* Hemsby

Witchinghams, The (2/4D)
Little Witchingham is a farming hamlet 2 miles south-east of Reepham. The church of St Faith, has recently been brought back into use after standing roofless for 30 years. Extensive areas of 14th-century wall paintings were discovered during the restoration.

Great Witchingham, half a mile west, is another farming hamlet, where St Mary's church stands by a duck pond surrounded by agricultural buildings. The Seven Sacraments font is carved, on the eighth side, with a bold depiction of the *Assumption of the Virgin* – a rare scene, paralleled in Norfolk only at BRIDGHAM.

The Norfolk Wildlife Park, by the A1067 south of the Witchinghams, specialises in rare species of British and European fauna, exhibited in large natural enclosures set in 40 acres of parkland.

Witton (3/2B) *see* North Walsham

Wolferton (1/3C) *see* Sandringham

Woodbastwick (3/2D) *see* Salhouse

Woodton (3/1F)
Woodton, 3 miles north-west of Bungay, is a featureless village of modern housing. The church of All Saints, to the north of the village, has a tall round tower and long low nave and the south aisle has a fine traceried roof.

Bedingham is half a mile to the south as the crow flies, three times as far by road. The church of St Andrew contains much to enjoy: a fine 13th-century chancel, box pews, a garlanded 17th-century pulpit and much stained glass, including representations of St Stephen and St Paul from King's College, Cambridge, the patron of the living. Priory Farm next door is a fine old house with shaped gables and big brick chimney clusters.

Worstead (3/1C)
As you approach this surprising village, 2½ miles south of North Walsham, the noble church tower rises high above the surrounding buildings. The spacious Plain in front of the church is partly enclosed by large Jacobean houses and partly open to the countryside. In the narrow side streets brick-built weavers' cottages survive, for Worstead was once a prosperous centre for the manufacture of high-quality worsted cloth, introduced by Flemish émigrés and made of tightly twisted yarn. The church of St Mary is a legacy of Worstead's former wealth. In recent years a newer industrial suburb has developed to the south-west, around the railway station which opened in the 1870s.

A mile south of this, St Bartholomew's church at Stoley contains one of the best-preserved Seven Sacrament fonts in Norfolk. A mile south again, the magnificent church of St Mary's, **Tunstead** is another product of wool wealth. The aisles are filled with fine large Decorated windows and above, instead of a clerestory, the upper nave is decorated with flint flushwork panels. The door has a splendid 14th-century ornamental boss surrounded by scrolling foliage. Behind the altar is a unique raised stone platform, with a chamber below, perhaps formerly used to store and exhibit the church's holy relics.

Worthing (2/2D) *see* North Elmham

The Norfolk Broads

CHRISTOPHER SOMERVILLE

The swampy, narrow footpath emerges from a tangle of alder trees to arrive at a tumbledown wooden boathouse, its ancient thatch sprouting grass and moss. You find a perch on a fallen branch and stretch out your legs, all mud from the knees down. Behind you through the trees there's a glimpse of a flat landscape of grassy marshes rolling away to the horizon, where a round flint church tower points up into an enormous sky. A dark crimson sail inches across the marshes; the river that carries the boat winds out of sight in its channel below the level of the land, marked by the armless brick stump of a derelict wind-pump that once drained the marsh. In front of you opens out one of Norfolk's secret broads, a wide stretch of water fringed with rustling reed beds from which an unseen grass-hopper warbler is clicking away – the only sound to be heard, apart from the gentle sucking of water against the bank. Beyond the reeds a long

line of woodland seems to be floating on the surface of the water. No one else is in sight or sound. Broadland is casting its familiar spell, that deliciously slow, relaxed mixture of water, woodland and wildlife. You are sunk deep, buried and rooted in a mesmerising landscape. Impossible to tear yourself free, for the rest of this timeless afternoon at any rate.

The Norfolk broads themselves are justly famous for their tranquil beauty, but they form only part of the large area of eastern Norfolk known as Broadland. The spell of Broadland, ever more compelling the further and deeper you explore, is a subtle one. Water, woodland, fen, marsh and sky all play their part, blending harmoniously in a landscape in which flint church towers, brick wind-pumps, weatherboarded mills and hump-back medieval bridges all seem part of the natural order of things – unsurprisingly, since the landscape shaped by these different elements is almost entirely a manmade one. Rivers form the watery framework from which the body of

Langley Marshes, from Burgh Castle

Broadland grows, radiating eastwards from Norwich and spreading as they approach the sea, draining two-thirds of Norfolk and a good deal of northern Suffolk. Providing 125 miles of navigable waterway in a countryside predominantly flat, Broadland's rivers dominate the scene.

From Norwich the River Yare flows east for some 20 miles to meet the River Waveney straggling up from the Suffolk borders. In a great plain of dyke-drained marshland near the coast they meet the River Bure on its winding course down from north of Norwich, to empty all together into the long, muddy tidal basin of Breydon Water on the outskirts of Great Yarmouth. The upper reaches of the Waveney and Yare bring the water off wide, shallow valleys of arable farmland, while the Bure threads its way through many miles of dense, wet woodland, where the views are compressed among the branches and leaves of alder and willow. Further north and east, cradled by the long curve of the Norfolk coastline, flow the Ant and the Thurne, tributaries of the Bure which run in the more open, flatter landscape of marshland. And along the Broadland rivers, like beads on a wriggling

Boats on the River Bure at Horning

string, lie the unique inland lakes of the broads themselves.

Until the middle years of this century the broads were thought to be ancient arms of the sea, trapped and left isolated as land nearer the coast was reclaimed. Then the truth gradually became clear: the broads were flooded pits, nearly fifty of them, excavated in medieval times by peat-diggers, varying in size from small holes to great craters 2 or 3 miles across. Peat digging in Norfolk started on this huge scale soon after the Norman Conquest in response to the insatiable need for fuel of the fast-expanding city of Norwich and its surrounding monasteries. Millions upon millions of peat turves were dug out in the following two centuries, until the rising sea level of this eastern coast brought water inland to flood the workings and create the broads. The pits were joined to each other and to the nearby rivers by channels dug by subsequent generations of Norfolk wildfowlers and fishermen, and by thatchers cutting reeds and sedge. A landscape of open lakes and channels of water was created, haunt of spoonbills, avocets, ruffs and bitterns, butterflies, fish and otters – a naturalist's paradise, if any had been there to appreciate it. In the marshlands nearer the coast the marshmen cut an intricate web of drainage dykes and grazed their sheep and cows on the rich pasture. Broadland was in being, a delicately balanced, intimate world of water and wildlife in which people lived in much the same way down the generations, in small villages or isolated farmsteads and cottages, unnoticed by the outside world for centuries until Victorian sailing enthusiasts began to arrive in the district in search of somewhere remote and new.

The string of broads that fringes the River Bure a few miles north-east of Norwich is a powerful magnet for today's visitors. On summer weekends, and especially on Bank Holidays, the twin riverside villages of Wroxham and Hoveton, and their sister village of Horning a few miles downstream, are packed with people intent on lunch in one of the willow-shaded pub gardens by the Bure, followed by a trip on a crowded boat down the river and round its broads. Wroxham Broad's long sheet of water is dotted with sailing boats racing or just pottering about. On nearby Salhouse Broad the children get a taste for life on the water as they career around in uncapsizable dinghies, or paddle on the sandy margins by the picnic spot. At Ranworth Broad a little further down the river there's a nature trail across the fen and under the trees. The river that connects these broads is crammed with boaters of all sorts, from parties of riotous youths in hired motor boats to smart, experienced sailors with rising blood pressure as the amateurs swing nonchalantly under their shiny bows. The best vantage point from which to view all this activity is the top of the church tower at Ranworth, a breathless spiral climb to a superb vista over the Bure, its broads and surrounding farmland.

Further east, where the Ant and Thurne snake down to join the Bure, the crowds thin out as the landscape flattens. Much of this area lies below sea level, threatened and occasionally overwhelmed by freak sea surges breaking through the sand dune sea defences knitted together with planted marram grass. Pollarded willows line the long, straight roads that pass tightly huddled groups of farm buildings, their enormous thatched barns of brick and flint redundant these days, many in decay. Though the farms boast gigantic modern ploughing, sowing and spraying machines,

River Ant and Turf Fen at sunset

Horsey windpump (National Trust)

this is a countryside very little changed by the 20th century, visibly at any rate. Even the outdated wind-pumps, no longer draining the maze of dykes, retain their old sail arms.

Hereabouts the broads are fringed deeply with Norfolk reeds. A broad, left to nature's slow processes, reverts from an open sheet of water to fen, a thick mass of reeds and sedge; then to carr woodland in which grow thickets of water-loving trees such as alder and willow; finally to dry woodland, usually of oak. About half of Norfolk's original broads have reverted in this way. Out here in the River Thurne's flatlands, Hickling Broad and Horsey Mere are two of the broads where the reeds are regularly cut back to stave off reversion. Reeds go to make the main body of the

thatched roof, while sedge is used to top it off. Managing the broads in this way leaves them clear for sailing boats; and, more importantly, it encourages a spectacular variety of wildlife. At Hickling Broad, for example, the bird list includes reed bunting; long-tailed, bearded and marsh tit; willow, sedge, reed and grasshopper warbler; redpoll and spotted flycatcher; redshank, sand-piper and snipe; kestrel and marsh harrier; and the rare bittern, whose booming voice is occasion-ally heard sounding off among the reed beds. Swallowtail butterflies, startlingly yellow and large, can be seen at Horsey Mere, where visitors are sternly – and quite rightly – directed to keep to their appointed paths and let the waders, the ducks and geese, songbirds and butterflies have the space they need. A hot summer's afternoon along these northern broads, binoculars and bird book to hand, is a treat to savour, a rare taste of lonely delight.

Down in the great green tableland of marshes behind Great Yarmouth, Broadland wears yet another of its guises. Here the views lead like arrows for miles in all directions, with nothing but church and pumping towers, stands of trees and pylons to catch the eye. Farmhouses and shepherds' cottages stand where they have stood for hundreds of years, some more than a mile from any surfaced road, sheltered by tattered belts of overgrown willows. Swans lie at ease among the cows, sensing no threat from the few humans who walk these bare, windy grasslands with their thousands of vein-like drainage dykes. Villages perch on the edge of the marshes at the feet of almost imperceptible swells in the land – remote places like Wickhampton and Halvergate where people switch off tractor engines and motor mowers when they see the stranger coming and set themselves comfortably for a good long chat.

The Broadland that those eager Victorian amateur sailors and landscape-hunters found was a unique and fragile blend, a jigsaw puzzle in which each piece played its part – dry woodland, carr woodland, reedswamp, fen and open broad, dyke, marsh and river – each complementing and completing all the others, each with its own variety of wildlife and human livelihood. The railways were only just beginning to penetrate the heart of Broadland and the roads were few and rough. Most traffic went up and down the rivers on the Norfolk wherries, wooden-hulled boats with large black sails that had to be lowered and raised again each time they passed under a bridge. The wherries moved slowly across a slow landscape, picking up and setting down their loads of beet, coal, thatch, beer, bricks and corn at the numerous 'staithes' or jetties that jutted into the rivers at every village and waterside farm. The water of the broads, dykes and rivers was clear, showing a low growth of green aquatic plant life at the bottom of every watercourse. The first outsiders to sail tentatively into Broadland may have brought new money and new ways with them, but until the early years of this century they represented only one extra piece in the complex jigsaw of the area. Then the puzzle began to show signs of coming apart and the picture of blurring, at first gradually and then with noticeable and frightening speed, as things started to go wrong. Today the Norfolk broads and their surrounding landscape face a bewildering range of threats from over-crowding, pollution and poor management that have until recently looked like breaking up the perfectly balanced jigsaw for ever.

The very characteristics which make Broadland so attractive – its many miles of obstruction-free waterway, its wildlife, its pretty villages and sail-dotted broads, its air of remoteness – bring in the visitors in numbers that would have staggered those early adventurers under sail. Nearly a quarter of a million people every year take a boat-hire cruising holiday on the broads. About half as many keep or bring their own private boats here. Several hundred thousand come for the pubs, the waterside strolls and the atmosphere, and never venture on to the water at all. Those that do all contribute, in greater or lesser degree, to pollution of the rivers and broads by their engine oil and to erosion of the banks by the wash their boats create. Speed limits of five miles an hour or so are supposed to be kept to, but a few minutes' observation will show you just how few boats comply. A motor boat full of happy jaunters, ploughing past at ten miles an hour, leaves a rush of wavelets sucking for a minute or more at the fringe of reeds. As the reeds lose their hold and die off, so the banks, deprived of their binding mass of reed roots, slip away into the water. In many places trees can be seen apparently growing in mid-broad, their supporting banks having been entirely eroded away. The old wherrymen, passing a tree on the edge of a river, would lassoo it with a rope and whip it out; trees cut off their vital flow of wind. But these little acts of vandalism were mere fleabites in comparison with the gobbling of river and broad bank that the power boats' propeller wash achieves. Parts of the River Bure are widening by several yards every year. And all that mud, sucked from the edges and stirred up from the bottom, is gradually filling in the broads and the rivers. Barton Broad on the River Ant, unless the erosion is checked, will be filled right to the brim with mud by the year 2025, claim the conservationists.

Erosion is only one of the problems besetting Broadland. Recent relaxation of green belt laws protecting the countryside has had its effect here, with a rash of new housing going up along the river banks in redundant boatyards, some of it tastefully designed and carefully blended with its neighbouring traditional building styles, most of it not. The flat acres of the marshlands have been threatened, too, by the dereliction of the old wind-pumps and consequent silting up of drainage dykes. Some farmers, seduced by dreams of EEC grants, have ploughed up their marshes for crops, releasing the natural sulphates infused in the soil by sea flooding in times past. These in their turn produce ochre, a metallically stinking orange sludge which seeps into dykes to kill off the plant life there. Many of the marshland swans have bright orange heads and necks, stained as they search through the ochre for food. The worst problems of all, however, are caused by a process known as 'enrichment', a term that sounds positively beneficial at first hearing.

Algae love both phosphates and nitrates. They get them in abundance in Broadland: phosphates from the outfall of sewage treatment plants, nitrates from the modern chemical fertilisers that have made these East Anglian farmlands so productive. The algae thrive, turning the waters of rivers, dykes and broads into a murky pea soup, thick and impenetrable to sunlight. The aquatic plants that should be growing low on the bottom of clear water at first shoot up in leafy profusion, then wither and die as their light is blocked out and their oxygen is stolen by the algae. Salhouse Broad, covered in water lilies when today's Broadland grandparents were children, is now a barren sheet of water.

The algae, meanwhile, floating on the surface of the water, fatten at the expense of other wildlife. As they warm up the water, bacteria begin to breed – botulism that kills water birds, for example. Some strains of algae poison the fish, too; local anglers will tell you how slim the pickings are these days. Enrichment has cut a wide swathe through the wildlife of Broadland. Before 1900 almost every broad was full of clear water. By the 1940s most were full of luxuriant plant growth, stimulated by the chemical input. Nowadays only four of the broads are clear, another six or so full of plants. The rest, thirty or more, are sterile, algal soups.

Remedies are at hand, however; some already effective, others experimental. Three National Nature Reserves have been created, at Hickling Broad, Bure Marshes and Ludham Marshes –

Somerleyton Marshes and Herringfleet Smock Mill

over 4,500 acres in all. The Norfolk Naturalists' Trust owns and manages parts of these and carries out experiments that act as guiding lights – for example, encouraging uncommon water plants such as water soldier to grow in an unpolluted side channel of the horribly adulterated Barton Broad. The National Trust owns Horsey Mere. The Royal Society for the Protection of Birds manages other reserves in Broadland. Over twenty Sites of Special Scientific Interest have been declared. Polluted mud is pumped out of sterile broads, and new plant life encouraged. Traditional management of fen and swamp has helped to restore some of the disappearing wildlife. Most important of all, the public at large is beginning to get involved.

These days it's impossible to spend time on the broads without having your nose rubbed in their problems. The Broads Authority was set up in 1978 with a brief to combat the degeneration of Broadland, and it is doing an excellent job with its information centre at Hoveton, its activities for children – nature trails, walks, boat trips, work parties and fun weekends – and its juggling of the interests of nature lovers, sailors, local people and holidaymakers with those of the farmers and water authorities. Crops must be sown, and sewage got rid of, after all. Public education is the watch-word, by whatever means is most effective: a quiet word in the ear of a sceptical farmer, a pushbutton display in the Information Centre showing an arid arable prairie taking over from a teeming marsh, a 'Hunt The Bogbean' expedition, a speaking map, a duckboard trail like the one at Ranworth Broad where visitors are led down the reversion process from mature woodland to open water, ending up at a floating exhibition centre.

One suggestion for keeping that delicate Broadland jigsaw intact has been to ban all boats except those under sail. Another is the excavation of new broads, properly managed from the outset. But the Broads Authority needs more power to its elbow, more legal teeth and better funding. There's hope ahead at last with Broadland's recent designation as a National Park – a step that should have been taken 40 years ago when Dartmoor, Pembrokeshire, Yorkshire, the Lake District and the others were being set up. Broadland in all its diversity, its richness of wildlife and its spellbinding peacefulness, is a national asset far too precious to be eroded and polluted out of existence.

Berney Arms Mill on the River Yare at dusk

Wroxham (3/1D)

Wroxham, half a mile south of Hoveton, is the unofficial 'capital' of the Broads. The marina is the starting point for excursions by paddleboat or motor launch through the adjacent broads and the whole village is extremely busy in the summer (see 'The Norfolk Broads', p. 124).

St Mary's church, well away from all this, has one of Norfolk's few Norman doorcases – a splendid and impressive work with ornamental motifs strung around the mouldings like beads on a necklace and a series of grotesque figures.

On a by-road north of the village, Wroxham Barns is a rural craft centre occupying a collection of 18th-century farm buildings, set in 10 acres of parkland. A mile to the west, St Peter's church at **Belaugh** is worth visiting if only for its position, high on a bank that drops sheer to the River Bure and for the peaceful river views from the churchyard.

Horning, 3 miles east, is another village dedicated to the pleasures of the Broads. Here there is much interesting riverside architecture to enjoy: thatched and half-timbered Edwardian houses, with moorings and thatched boathouses alongside. St Benedict's church stands alone on a hill, well to the west of the village. Few people visit the church at **Barton Turf**, 3 miles northeast of Wroxham – not, perhaps surprisingly, for near by is an army signals station, bristling with aerials and patrolled by soldiers. Its screen, however, is one of the best in Norfolk: mid-15th century and painted with the heavenly hierarchy of angels and three saintly kings, Edmund, Edward the Confessor and Henry VI.

Beeston Hall, a mile south-west, was built in 1786 in the Gothick style. As well as furniture and family portraits, it contains objects collected by a former owner, Sir Thomas Preston, who was British Consul at Ekaterinburg in 1918, at the time of the murder of the Russian Tsar and the imperial family. The house is open to the public in summer.

Wymondham (2/4E)

Pronounced 'Wyndham', this busy working town on the A11, 7 miles south-west of Norwich, is full of simple, functional houses, few of them striking in themselves, but attractive in their overall homogeneity.

The town centre is marked by a raised octagonal market cross of 1617. Running south, Bridewell Street is lined with close-studded timber-framed buildings and terminates in the Georgian Old Gaol, or Bridewell, which retains

Doorway in St Mary's church, Wroxham

some barred windows. Market Street runs downhill to the north and, at the bottom of this hill, Damgate is a long winding street lined entirely by simple two-storeyed cottages. These well illustrate the development of terraced housing over several centuries: medieval timber frame gives way to 18th-century brick, Victorian and finally modern, but all of the same compact dimensions.

The scene changes on the western side of the town. Here, around the church, are the grander houses; in Middleton Street and Vicar Street, these are of Georgian red brick and, less aesthetically pleasing, of Regency and Victorian yellow brick. Church Street begins with the 14th-century chapel of St Thomas à Becket and next to it the pretty timber-framed Green Dragon Inn.

As Church Street bends round to the north, the two famous towers of Wymondham Abbey come into view, one now a cavernous yawning ruin. The towers resulted from a rivalry between the townspeople and the Benedictine monks,

Wymondham Abbey looks down on marshy meadows

which grew so fierce that in 1249 Pope Innocent IV had to intervene. In many towns abbey and church were quite separate from each other, but here the Norman founder of the Abbey, William d'Albini, intended the monks and parishioners to share the one building. The dispute was over the amount of the church that each was to enjoy; the matter was finally settled by the erection of a physical division – a solid wall – separating the parish at the west end from the Abbey at the east.

The now-ruined monastic tower seems to have been built in about 1400, slightly to the west of the original Norman crossing tower. The parishioners responded with their own west tower, begun about 1448. Neither has the slightest pretensions to elegance, but their sheer height and mass are impressive. Both lack parapets or battlements and look unfinished.

No doubt the Dissolution of the Monasteries in the mid 16th century gave private satisfaction to the townspeople and little now remains of the Abbey's east end except the tower and a few walls, surrounded by gaunt and ancient Scots Pine trees. The townspeople, meanwhile, continued to embellish their church, giving it a majestic clerestory and angel-covered hammer-beam roof, which soars above the stout Norman nave columns and triforium. The blocked east wall, symbol of strife, was turned into a moving memorial to a greater battle, when Sir Ninian Comper provided the rich golden reredos as a First World War memorial.

Wymondham Abbey today soars above open countryside on the edge of the town, looking down on to the marshy meadows on either side of the River Tiffey. How long this view will remain open and green is uncertain: already housing estates are beginning to nibble at the edges of the meadows which were left to the town by a 17th-century benefactor.

Nearby **Ketteringham**, 3 miles to the east, is an estate village with lovely neo-Tudor cottages and a fine Jacobean farmhouse. The church of St Peter contains an unusually large number of very fine monuments.

Suffolk Gazetteer

Acton (4/4E) *see* Waldingfields, The

Aldeburgh (6/4D)

For the view of Aldeburgh that inspired Benjamin Britten for so many years, enter Aldeburgh from the north and ignore the town for a moment. Along the shingle seafront, half a dozen fishermen at most sell fish, caught that day, from wooden shacks. Their small, multi-coloured fishing boats stand near by, drawn up on the beach amid fishing nets laid out to dry, lobster pots and rusting anchors.

The fishermen are young, continuing a tradition that has brought them and their forebears just enough to live on for generations. Their catch lies in plastic bakers' trays – big, ugly-faced fish, with velvety grey skins, such as cod, rock eel, skate and bass. There is nothing commercialised about this and nothing here for the tourist who wants ready-made amusements; just a long beach, fronted by whitewashed houses, and a little basin for sailing toy yachts, alongside the 16th-century Moot Hall, still used as an office by the parish clerk and with a museum on the ground floor.

Not much has changed here since Britten (born in Lowestoft) moved into the neighbourhood. The house in which he lived between 1947 and 1957 lies just south-west of the beach, next to the red-brick Jubilee Hall, scene of many early performances of his work.

Crabbe Street, leading into the High Street, commemorates another Aldeburgh artist, George Crabbe (1754–1832), whose poetic portrait of the town (*The Borough*, 1810) provided the libretto for *Peter Grimes*. Crabbe claimed that he hated the place and called its people

> . . . a wild amphibious race,
> With sullen woe displayed in every face;
> Who far from civil arts and social fly,
> And scowl at strangers with suspicious eye.

Not so any more, for the annual June festival, started in 1948, has made Aldeburgh an internationally renowned centre for the arts, and the strangers who visit all year round to savour the town's unspoilt beauty are warmly welcomed.

16th-century Moot Hall, Aldeburgh

The Festival has created a mini-industry; such a major undertaking requires professional administration, and the former East Suffolk Hotel in the High Street, with its bold Tuscan porch, is now the permanent headquarters of the organisers (*see* 'East Anglian Festivals', p. 138).

South of the High Street is the 'downtown' end, or Slaughden, where once there stood a major fishing and ship building centre, destroyed (like DUNWICH) by the sea. Here a lookout tower reminds us that local people once made a living from the grim business of salvage, taking what they could from ships wrecked off the shore. Here too is an eccentric group of beach houses, one built by R. A. Briggs around 1903 and resembling a windmill. Beyond is a Martello tower, built in 1810 against a feared Napoleonic invasion; it is the largest and the northernmost of a chain that stretches up the south-east coast. After that, there is nothing for 5 miles but the wild shingle bank of the Orford Ness nature reserve.

Returning northwards again, anyone interested in Victorian, Edwardian and 1920s architecture should wander through the residential streets that run parallel to the sea on the terraces above the High Street. Long before Britten arrived discerning and wealthy holidaymakers – including the Marquess of Salisbury – built splendid villas and summer residences here.

The church of St Peter and St Paul at the northern end of the town is big and airy, thanks to its wide aisles, almost square in plan, and seems almost purpose-built for theatricals. Lord Leicester's players certainly performed here in 1573 and Shakespeare may also have paid a visit in 1595, when his company performed in Ipswich. Ronald Blythe has also discovered that ship auctions were formerly held in the nave, so Britten's use of this marvellous church for recitals and musical drama followed a well-established tradition. The building fell into decay in the 19th century, however, and today's pristine church owes much to recent restoration, which has included the replacement of the roof. Among the fine memorials are a bust of George Crabbe and John Piper's stained glass window commemorating Benjamin Britten (d. 1976). Both Britten and his life-long friend, the singer

Romantic ruins of Knettishall church

Peter Pears, are buried in the churchyard.

Snape lies 4 miles to the west. There is a fine walk across the marshes, woods and warrens to the place which Britten made his home before moving to Aldeburgh. Just before the entrance to the village a tumulus on the left, by the road to Rookery Farm, is one of a group excavated in 1840–63 and found to contain ship burials contemporary with those of SUTTON HOO.

Snape Maltings was built by Newson Garrett (1812–93), one of the LEISTON family who were both pioneering industrialists and leading intel-lectuals of the late 19th century. He was the father of both Elizabeth Garrett Anderson (1836–1917), the first woman doctor, and Dame Millicent Garrett Fawcett (1847–1919), suffragette and one of the founders of Newnham College, Cambridge. The Maltings is familiar to many from news and magazine pictures, but the first-time visitor may not be prepared for the sheer size of the complex. Photographers often choose an angle that shows only the concert hall, brilliantly restored between 1969 and 1970 by Arup Associates after a fire and crouching amongst reed-fringed marshes. Behind this is a vast conglomeration of quayside warehouses and

industrial buildings, many of which have been converted to conference and exhibition rooms, restaurants, shops and galleries. This has been achieved without spoiling the essential character of the complex: functional and dour, but in the Suffolk tradition of brick and weatherboarding under steep pitched roofs.

On the opposite side of the road, a footpath leads to Abbey Farm, a splendid aisled barn, awaiting restoration, whose date of about 1300 makes it Suffolk's oldest. On the hillside above is the stump of a windmill, dating from 1668 and again possibly the oldest in the county. Here, in this windmill, from 1937 until his move to

Aldeburgh 10 years later, Britten lived and composed some of his greatest masterpieces.

Aldringham (6/3C) *see* Thorpeness

Ampton (4/4B) *see* Ixworth

Assington (5/2F) *see* Bures

Bacton (5/3C) *see* Finningham

Badingham (6/2C) *see* Worlingworth

Badley (5/3D) *see* Needham Market

Badwell Ash (5/2C) *see* Walsham le Willows

Bardwell (5/2B)
The lanes of this peaceful village, 2 miles north of Ixworth, form a rectangle, with one core of older thatched cottages around a green to the east and another group overlooking the Black Bourn river further west, by the church of St Peter and St Paul.

The arms of Sir William Bredewell (d. 1434) appear on the fine tall porch which he paid for, and his portrait is among the lovely mixture of old and new stained glass in the north nave. The chancel is made gloomy by bad Victorian glass, but there is a lively monument to Thomas Read, dated 1652, and original vine scroll painting survives in the pleasing 16th-century roof.

Bardwell Windmill, on the north side of the village, has been fully restored and is producing stoneground flour. It is open on Tuesdays, Fridays and Sundays all year round.

At **Barningham**, 3 miles north-east, pretty thatched cottages face a modern housing estate. St Andrew's church is enriched by the complete set of 15th-century benches, with poppyheads, blind tracery and figures on the armrests, including a camel and an owl.

Two miles north of Barningham, Knettishall Heath Country Park is the official starting point of PEDDARS WAY (*see* Norfolk Gazetteer). On the eastern edge of the marshy heath, the abandoned ruin of All Saints church stands in romantic isolation.

St Peter's church at **Hepworth**, 2 miles south-east of Barningham, was rebuilt after a fire in 1898, but the curious, massive font cover was rescued. The lower stage is a castle in miniature, bristling with battlemented towers and doorways, at which tiny figures in military dress keep guard.

East Anglian Festivals

PAUL JENNINGS

If you were asked to guess how long a computer print-out of festivals in East Anglia would be, would you say 8 inches, 3 feet, 7 feet? Well the one I have here won't spread out flat in any room in the house. It is 23 feet long. For people who don't know East Anglia, that puts rather a different complexion on this Noël Coward-flat, sugar-beet-and-wheat-prairie, remote, Nato airfield-dotted, wind-from-the-Urals region, does it not?

In fact East Anglia comes nearer than any other part of Britain to providing an answer to the question classically posed in Thomas Love Peacock's *Nightmare Abbey*:

'I distinguish the picturesque and the beautiful, and I add to them, in the laying out of grounds, a third and distinct character, which I call *unexpectedness.*'

'Pray, sir,' said Mr Milestone, 'by what name do you distinguish this character, when a person walks round the grounds for the second time?'

You would perhaps need a room 23 feet long to get a full conspectus of East Anglia's remarkable ability to surprise you, to go on surprising you, in the matter of festivals – since the old ones are forever developing and changing and new ones are starting. But could it be that there are three converging causes?

First, there is of course the always gratifying unexpectedness of the marvellously snug, self-contained village or town with its warm life suddenly come upon in – yes, let us admit, if not indeed boast – lonely, open, windswept country, often still pitch-dark at night even in these days of universal orange street lights. Now we're here, bor, let's celebrate, even if it's only pub quoits or dwile-flonking (throwing wet flannels). Every glorious sun-sparkling, colour-changing flint church standing up on a low ridge or among windblown reed-beds is a permanent visual festival in itself.

Second, there is that in the character of true, native-born East Anglians – so dour on superficial acquaintance, so oak-true and full of humour when you know them, with jokes springing out of some ordinary deadpan encounter – which corresponds with new-born festivals springing unexpectedly from self-contained, sober little towns. A lady visiting us overshot the house, in spite of the careful directions we had given her. She lowered her window and said to the splendid Suffolk man who stopped to help, 'I'm looking for 25 High Street, Orford; what have I done wrong?' 'Well, ma'am, I don't think I've known yew long enough to tell yew,' he said – before walking her to our front door.

Third, there is the extraordinary marriage, hastened by post-war mobility and the new accessibility of East Anglia, between this strong local culture and the general, highest-standard, professional culture which in earlier days would simply have had to be described as metropolitan, indeed international. Long before the Snape Maltings concert hall was built – with some of the best acoustics and surely the most idyllically pastoral surroundings in the world – a friend was present at a performance of Britten's *Let's Make An Opera* in that original home of many epoch-making first performances, the 300-seat (if you really squash them in) Jubilee Hall in Aldeburgh, the kind of red brick Victorian building with the date in a stone diamond you can find in a thousand English towns and villages. As Brittenites will know, in this work the audience are given song sheets and required variously to imitate the sounds of such creatures as the raven or the chaffinch. Being in the raven section he was amazed to hear behind him a *kaa-ah-ah* in a tremendous female voice. It was only Kirsten Flagstad, the greatest Wagnerian soprano in the world.

As a matter of fact all these three elements could be illustrated by a conversation I overheard in an Aldeburgh pub. In 1950, long before (well, six years before) I dreamt I should come to live in Suffolk, I was covering the third Festival for the *Observer*. It was the first time I had heard the inimitable East Anglian accent (I have yet to hear it spoken convincingly in Wesker's *Roots*, for example; the mummers always come up with some sort of stage Mummerset). Three old boys were slowly sipping their Adnam's at the bar.

'What dew yew think to these 'ere flowers o' culture, then, Cecil?' asked one.

'That's no good to arsk '*im*, bor. On'y flowers he's int'rested in is his cauliflowers down his allotmint.'

Among other events, such as Edith Sitwell

Snape Maltings

speaking her own verse in *Façade* and my first hearing of the immortal Alfred Deller (later to become a lifelong friend) with the Purcell Singers, there was E. M. Forster lecturing drily in the Baptist Chapel on John Skelton, tutor of Henry VIII, 'King's Orator' – precursor of Poet Laureate – and rector of that crossword-clue Norfolk town, Diss. It was, of course, hearing in America a broadcast by Forster on the Aldeburgh poet Crabbe that in 1942 determined Britten and his lifelong collaborator and supreme interpreter, Peter Pears, to return to England from 'a weekend that turned out to last three years' in America. (Britten was a Suffolk man, born in Lowestoft.) Here again, you don't need mere jollity for a festival. Forster quoted Crabbe:

> Where gaping mussels, left upon the mud,
> Slope their slow passage to the fallen flood

'How quiet this writing is: you might say how dreary. Yet how sure its touch; and how vivid that estuary near Aldeburgh.'

Aldeburgh is, of course, the setting of the opera which rocketed Britten to enduring world fame, *Peter Grimes*, already commissioned by Koussevitsky and in his mind as they crossed the wartime Atlantic.

The Aldeburgh Festival has come a long way since Peter Pears suggested it to his friends Britten and Eric Crozier when they were all on their way to Lucerne in 1947 to present *Albert Herring* (libretto by Crozier) and *The Rape of Lucretia* – having been unable to win support for them in London, Manchester and Edinburgh. It started from a local meeting in the Jubilee Hall raising initial guarantees of £200 and has grown ever since, to something much greater than the famous June fortnight which had long since made it Britain's best-known home-grown festival, with many of the world's greatest artists honoured to accept invitations. As a humble chorus member in a 'semi-staged' performance of Britten's *Paul Bunyan*, a kind of youthfully joyous (it is an early work) Radio Three *Oklahoma*, I was surprised and moved, as were many locals, to find that the brilliant American soloists from Minnesota, who made the Virgin recording such a resounding success, were almost awed by Aldeburgh, as if on holy ground.

'Is it fanciful to look forward, through a series of annual Festivals, to Aldeburgh as the centre of arts in East Suffolk?' wrote Crozier in 1948. He need not have worried. Never mind East Suffolk, visitors as well as artists and composers come from all over the world. Rostropovich, the great Russian cellist, permanently grateful for the support from Britten and Pears in his troubled pre-*perestroika* days, has a house in Aldeburgh and presides over a unique autumn Rostropovich festival whenever his globe-trotting schedules permit. His wife, the equally famous Vishnevskaya, teaches at the Britten–Pears School for Advanced Musical Studies, for which top young professionals compete to get into master classes, conducted by

Blythburgh, the 'cathedral of the marshes'

the likes of Hans Hotter, Suzanne Danco, Murray Perahia, Hugues Cuenod – and of course Nancy Evans, wife of Eric Crozier.

Not only can the public often see the results from a school which was a 'centre of excellence' before that phrase became common property; the Festival spreads in other ways through the year as well as from its heart at the beautiful Snape Maltings. It uses buildings with other and older beauty, particularly the wonderful East Anglian churches: Ely Cathedral, Blythburgh, the noble 'cathedral of the marshes', Orford, the great seamark church which saw the first performances of *Noyes Fludde* and the church operas, glorious Long Melford and several others. There are Christmas and Easter series. Seats are removed for the Maltings Proms in August, when you are likely to hear anything from brilliant chamber orchestras, through Gershwin and Sondheim, to top brass bands and, of course, something for which the Maltings have also made themselves a name – jazz.

Such well-known groups as the Jazz Warriors (also heard at Snape) are visitors to the Jazz Festival (usually October) organised by the extremely active and enterprising Norwich Arts Centre; indeed well over half its mailing list of regular attenders live outside the city. Its other main events are a Mime Festival early in the year and a Children's Festival in later autumn. But throughout the year there is a continuous round of recitals, exhibitions and one-man shows from the kind of unusual performer whom you can afterwards boast of having seen before his (or her) TV fame.

This is part of the continuing tradition of artistic vitality in this elegant metropolis of East Anglia, with its noble cathedral and castle and over thirty wonderfully-named medieval churches (St John Maddermarket, St Miles-in-Coslany, St James in Pockthorpe – even if this one became a puppet theatre – St Michael-at-Plea).

All other festivals are of course johnny-come-latelies compared with the famous Norwich Triennial, the oldest non-peripatetic festival in the country. After some run-up trials in 1788 it got going as the Triennial in 1824, when only the Three Choirs Festival, based on Gloucester, Worcester and Hereford, pre-dated it (by exactly 100 years), and it has been a major event in the English musical calendar ever since. It saw the première of Elgar's *Sea Pictures* in 1899, of Janáček's amazing *Glagolitic Mass* – as well as that of Bliss's *Morning Heroes* and Vaughan Williams's *Suite for Orchestra* – in 1930, evidently a vintage year. In 1947, the year Aldeburgh was just a gleam in Britten's eye, it celebrated its post-war rebirth with the glorious voice of Ferrier in *Gerontius*.

As a result of recent re-thinking, the Triennial may coalesce with the Norfolk and Norwich Festival, losing 'Triennial' from the title. As well as the traditional 900-seat St Andrew's Hall (once the nave of a vast Dominican church) for the big orchestral-choral events, there are venues such as the increasingly prestigious Sainsbury Centre for major art exhibitions, the castle and Holkham Hall – Norfolk's, indeed one of England's, greatest Palladian mansions, its apotheosis of aristocratic, artistic life the more delightful for the proximity of the lonely northern coastline at Wells-next-the-Sea.

Follow the coast anti-clockwise and you will come to King's Lynn, Norfolk's understated answer to Venice, a water-town still, with its beautiful Tuesday Market Square, elegant Caroline Customs House, dark-brick old Hanseatic warehouses, reminding you that in the 14th century it was England's third largest port. Its very remoteness has somehow ensured that its Festival,

started in 1950 and centred on a delightfully sociable waterside art-centre-cum-club, had a unique atmosphere of friendly intimacy. The visitor is likely to come across anything from Sir Michael Tippett to a famous flamenco dancer, from one-man shows and quartets to the Philharmonia and other great orchestras (in the church of St Nicholas which, while perfectly large enough, is only a 'chapel-at-ease'; but then you should see the size of St Margaret's, where Burney was once organist). A developing feature is called 'Cross-Over', in which classical, folk or jazz audiences and performers make creative efforts to share cultures.

Considering that Bury St Edmunds possesses a cathedral, a splendid open space – Angel Hill opposite the remaining gatehouse of the abbey, once the greatest shrine in England – *and* the most enchanting bijou Georgian theatre, restored to its former glory after long use as a beer store, where no seat is more than 25 feet from the stage, it may seem surprising that its Festival, in May, should only have started in 1986. But it is clearly able already to attract performers of the calibre of the BBC Symphony Orchestra and the London Mozart Players, not to mention Beating the Retreat from the band of the Royal Marines. (What a chance to see Angel Hill with *anything* other than cars on it, let alone one of the best military spectacles in a country notoriously good at such things!)

We have seen already that enterprising festivals such as those at Aldeburgh or Norwich have quickly spread out from their home bases into great houses or churches. They are not alone in this: half a dozen chamber concerts or recitals are dotted throughout the year at the great house of Felbrigg Hall near Cromer, for instance. But the centre of East Anglia's most spread-out festival is Wingfield College. Wingfield Arts and Music derives its name from a medieval college of priests, which suffered the usual Reformation fate and, now a private house, was Georgianised in the 18th century. The original medieval structure with its superb timber-aisled great hall was restored by the present owner, artist Ian Chance, who now runs an amazing range of events throughout the year with the enthusiastic support of five local authorities, Eastern Arts and other sponsors such as Shell.

Performers such as Emma Kirkby and Anthony Rooley (respectively soprano – and what a soprano! – and lute) or a top international quartet may be performing in Wingfield College's hall, or Wingfield Church. Or there might be jazz from the Ronnie Scott Quintet in Diss Corn Hall; or Grimethorpe Colliery Band in Beccles Church; or The Taverner Consort; or the Moscow String

Wingfield College
Opposite: Customs House, King's Lynn

Quartet; or the English Sinfonia. And, Ian Chance being an artist, exhibitors have included Elizabeth Frink, Victor Pasmore, Eduardo Paolozzi and Edward Ardizzone.

I heard a marvellous Wingfield concert, with the English Sinfonia and the amazing young Danish recorder virtuoso Nicola Petri (also known at Aldeburgh) at another of its local venues, the splendid church at Eye. This was not part of Eye's own Festival, which dates from only 1987 but is already going strong, with a *ceilidh*, street theatre, a kite festival and the South Norfolk Youth Symphony Orchestra.

Drawing perhaps a little more on local talent (and there's a great deal of it in East Anglia), Beccles and Bungay also now have festivals. In fact it's becoming quite hard to think of an East Anglian town that doesn't have something happening. Sometimes you just strike lucky. You might be around for the Snape Maltings Proms in August and find the Aldeburgh Carnival in the middle of it and, leaning against a sea wall, see a spectacular firework display along the shore. In my own village, Orford (which in its great pre-silted-up medieval port days was a borough), they have an end-of-summer Fun Day. Some purse their lips at this title. But you should see the floats, the judging down on the sunny quay, the free open-air circus, the jolly bands – and above all the torchlight procession, with hundreds if not thousands of Chinese lanterns, from the Jolly Sailor up to the castle where, for a joyous but innocent family crowd (lots of children on shoulders) there are absolutely the most marvellous fireworks I have ever seen (and I've seen the fireworks at Elche, on Spain's firework-mad Mediterranean coast, for their glorious Assumption Festival on 15 August). Orford saves up all the year for it. That's why East Anglian festivals really are fun. And, by now, not entirely unexpected.

Tower of St Michael's church, Beccles

Barham (5/4D) *see* Coddenham

Barking (5/3D) *see* Needham Market

Barningham (5/2B) *see* Bardwell

Barsham (6/2A) *see* Beccles

Bawdsey (6/2E) *see* Sutton

Beccles (3/3F)

The best view of this town, on the far north-eastern border with Norfolk, is from the north-western approach along the A146, for this prospect has been protected, whereas the eastern perimeter is fringed by industrial estates. The view takes in mellow red-brick houses rising above the Gillingham Marshes on the steep eastern bank of the River Waveney. Leisure boats moor in the river where once there was a busy port and St Michael's church, with its 97-foot high detached bell tower, provides the focal point of the scene.

Narrow lanes, or 'scores', run up from the river to the church. St Michael's was damaged by several fires that swept through the town in the 17th century, but Victorian restorers did an excellent job of providing new furnishings; the lovely chancel and parclose screens are designed in a real 15th-century spirit. The glory of the church is its much-decorated south-west porch, built around 1455.

South-east of the church, on an island, is the old Town Hall, a low octagon of red brick which resembles a Non-conformist chapel. Beyond is the New Market, where the creeper-clad King's Head Hotel is everyone's idea of a typical coaching inn. Begun in the 17th century, it grew to fill a whole block in the town centre, a fine jumble of red-brick extensions around a central courtyard. Just to the east, in Newgate behind the Post Office, there is a small museum of rural life.

Leaving the town by the A1116 Bungay road you pass the Roman Catholic church of St Benet, built in 1889, an imposing and accomplished Romanesque-style building. Further out is the handsome red-brick Roos Hall (open by appointment), built in 1593 by Sir John Suckling and still owned by his descendants.

A mile further west is **Barsham** and the highly rewarding church of Holy Trinity, reached down a green lane and surrounded by a wilderness of a churchyard, left as a wildlife sanctuary. Much of the detail was added this century: the stuccoed chancel ceiling of 1906 with its roses and lilies, the colourful rood canopy of 1919, and John Fisher's exuberant stained glass of 1903, with its angels and baroque swags of wild flowers. The terracotta tomb chest of Sir Edward Eckingham (d. 1527) was made from the same set of moulds as those of the Bedingfeld monuments at OXBOROUGH (Norfolk). The eastern exterior wall of the church should not be missed; it is covered entirely in flushwork diamonds, a theme picked up and continued by the window tracery. The design was probably the work of Joseph Fleming, rector from 1617 to 1636.

There are several fine gardens in the Beccles neighbourhood. Two miles south-west, Redisham Hall is a Georgian house with a large kitchen garden that produces fruit and vegetables for the Hall and for sale in local shops. The 200-acre estate is planted with splendid specimen trees. The gardens are open under the National Gardens Scheme.

Sotterley Hall, 3 miles to the south-east is not open but the long footpath to St Margaret's church passes through the beautiful oak-filled parkland, past the lake and close to the house itself.

At **North Cove**, 2 miles east of Beccles, the five-acre Hall gardens, open under the National Gardens Scheme, were planted in 1760; the surviving trees have now reached a considerable height. The Norman church of St Botolph contains numerous 14th-century wall paintings, including scenes from the Passion, which were touched up when they were discovered in 1874.

Benacre (6/4A) *see* Covehithe

Bildeston (5/2E) *see* Chelsworth

Blaxhall (6/2D) *see* Orford

Blythburgh (6/3B)
Suffolk offers few more surprising sights than the wild marshes of the silted-up River Blyth and the magnificent church of the Holy Trinity, which seems to rise straight out of the reed beds.

Blythburgh once a port but now a tiny village 3 miles south-west of Southwold, is tucked away to the east of the church so that nothing stands between the noble 83-foot tower and the tidal waters that lap almost at its feet. Nearly all the huge airy and uncluttered church is mid 15th-century work, including the roof with its angels bearing the shields of numerous benefactors. The lovely bench ends are quite unlike anything else in Suffolk, except for some Victorian copies, and depict the Labours of the Months and the Seven Deadly Sins. Because they are not idolatrous, they escaped iconoclastic destruction and survive in a remarkably complete state (though Lust has been censored).

To the north of the church The Priory, a timber-framed house with handsome oriels, stands on the site of the Augustinian priory. The fine early brick White Horse Inn on the main road was once the village courthouse.

East of the village, the tidal River Blyth was once contained within banks, some stretches of which remain. The river burst its banks in the 1920s and the flooded area, never reclaimed, is now a bird reserve.

A path leading off from the White Horse Inn follows the course of a disused railway track, round the rim of the estuary and over heathland to Walberswick, a distance of 3 miles. The old railway bridge, a mile north of Walberswick, can also be used by pedestrians to cross the river to SOUTHWOLD on the opposite bank; cars must travel 8 miles round by road.

Walberswick is a long village which went into decline as a port as early as the 16th century and the majestic church of St Andrew was partly dismantled in 1695 because the parish was too poor to maintain it. Even in its semi-ruined state, it is possible to sketch in the details in one's mind and reconstruct what must have been as splendid a building as that at Blythburgh. From the church, The Street spreads eastward to The Greens, lined with neat houses, trim gardens and the pubs and teashops on which Walberswick's survival now depends. The village stops abruptly at the small riverside harbour, bright with colourful fishing boats and offering views across the marshes to Southwold.

Angel on the cambered tiebeam roof, Blythburgh

South of the village, the Walberswick National Nature Reserve stretches for 3 miles to DUNWICH. Although rich in bird life for the whole of the year, it is best visited in winter for the sake of the shy and elusive snow buntings, the marsh and hen harriers, the merlins and the rough-legged buzzards (*see* 'Coastal Birds of East Anglia', p. 32).

Botesdale (5/3B)
The A143 links Botesdale, 4 miles south-west of Diss, and its two neighbours, Rickinghall Superior and Inferior, into one long continuous ribbon settlement. It is a busy but most attractive thoroughfare. Approaching from the east, you will find St Botolph's chapel on the left; originally a chantry built in about 1500, it was absorbed into the Free School established in 1576.

Next door is a beautiful Georgian house called The Priory, one of several houses which have bow-fronted additions on their west-facing gable ends, facing downhill to enjoy the views of multi-coloured timber-framed and early brick houses. Half way down the hill, Chilvers flower and garden shop has a fine broad-fronted Victor-

ian shop window. Climbing up the other side of the hill, Hamblyn House has an ornate Dutch gable. Over the crest of the hill the Rickinghalls begin, slightly less pretty because numerous new houses have infilled the spaces between the pleasing thatched cottages.

At the end of the village of **Rickinghall Inferior** St Mary's church is fronted by a stream and has much flushwork on the 14th-century upper stage of its tower. The inventive tracery of the nave windows is reflected in the ornate carving of the font. St Mary's at **Rickinghall Superior** is set apart from the village, to the south. A typical north Suffolk church, it is rich in flushwork and boasts a two-storeyed vaulted porch and delightful Decorated tracery.

Boxford (5/2E) *see* Polstead

Boxted (4/4D) *see* Denston

Bradfields, The (4/5D)
Bradfield Woods, 5 miles south-east of Bury St Edmunds and on the eastern edge of the parish of **Bradfield St George**, is an outstanding nature reserve, managed by the Suffolk Trust for Nature Conservation and saved by the local people from threatened destruction in the 1960s.

The two woods, Monkspark and Felshamhall, have been coppiced since 1252 and are still managed in the same way: poles grown from the stools of pollarded trees are coppiced on a 10-year cycle and used by local woodworkers to make fences, posts, rakes and scythe handles. Few places anywhere in England are as rich in wildlife; here is a veritable Noah's Ark amid a sea of open, soulless farmland.

One wonders whether Arthur Young (1741–1820) would have approved; throughout his life, as a prolific writer on social, economic and agricultural subjects, Young campaigned against the medieval open-field system and was a strong supporter of both enclosure and the ploughing up of grazing lands in order, to use his own words, to 'turn sand to gold'. He lies buried in the churchyard of All Saints, **Bradfield Combust**, under a simple casket-shaped tomb chest, whose inscription invites every patriot to shed a tear for his lost genius.

Two miles north-west of Combust, at **Hawstead**, is one of those big sweeps of common land that Young wanted to see used more productively. The little church of All Saints, standing in an overgrown churchyard fringed with big box hedges, contains many important monuments, including one to Sir Robert Drury (d. 1615). When his daughter, Elizabeth, died in 1609 aged 14, John Donne composed the poem later called *A Funerall Elegie* to comfort her grieving parents. Donne may also have composed the epitaph on her tomb, which portrays the young Elizabeth, intended as the Prince of Wales's bride, smiling enigmatically.

Nearby Church House is an early Tudor guild hall; scores of these fascinating and little-studied buildings survive in East Anglia, often unrecognised. There is another splendid example at **Cockfield**, 4 miles south-east, presenting an ornate frontage to St Peter's churchyard. Now a cottage, it was once used for parish council meetings, festivals and marriage feasts.

Bramfield (6/2B)

Three miles south of Halesworth, St Andrew's church faces the undulating crinkle-crankle wall of the Tudor brick Bramfield Hall. A detached Norman round tower stands south-west of the church suggesting, perhaps, that today's thatched church was rebuilt slightly north of a predecessor. Inside is a delightful coved chancel screen, with much of its original colouring, and one of Suffolk's best monuments, to Sir Arthur

Coke monument, St Andrew's church, Bramfield

(d. 1629) and Dame Elizabeth Coke (d. 1627), former occupants of the Hall, carved by Nicholas Stone. Look, too, for the ledger slab commemorating Bridget Applewhite; in all England there are few more amusing epitaphs than hers.

Just under 2 miles to the east, the ornate Saxo-Norman round tower of St Peter's at **Thorington** looks perfect in its sylvan setting. Inside, a bench curves all round the interior of the tower to frame the 13th-century font which stands on an 15th-century pedestal carved with lions.

Bramford (5/4E) *see* Coddenham

Brandeston (6/1C) *see* Easton

Brent Eleigh (5/2E) *see* Eleighs, The

Brightwell (6/1E)

This hamlet lies 5 miles south-west of Woodbridge; with a new road system to the north, the old A1093 has reverted to a quiet leafy lane above which sits the church of St John the Baptist. So few people stop to see this rewarding church that any visitor will surprise scores of rabbits that have invaded the churchyard from the adjoining sandy heath.

The history of the church is very much linked to that of the Hall and tells a melancholy tale which M.R. James might have turned into a moving story. A family called Essington settled here in the mid 17th century and built a magnificent mansion. They also rebuilt the church, completing it around 1656; the lovely brick tower is supported inside not by the usual pointed arch but by two great Tuscan columns. Two unusual and beautiful monuments commemorate a son and daughter of the family, both of whom died in childhood. In 1760 the Hall was demolished and now the only reminders of what was once here are the daffodils planted in the garden which reappear every spring.

If you travel north from this romantic spot, you return with a jolt to the 20th century. Martlesham Heath, once an important experimental air station and Second World War aerodrome, is now a large and growing high-tech industrial estate, dominated by British Telecom's research station.

Bungay (6/2A)

This quiet town on the north-eastern border with Norfolk has blossomed since being by-passed: buildings once blighted by heavy traffic are being cleaned up and opened as speciality shops. Townspeople no longer risk injury if they step off the pavements of the narrow winding streets that focus on the small triangular Market Place. Here, the lead-covered Butter Cross was erected in 1689, the year after a great fire destroyed much of the town. The fine lead statue of Justice on the top was added in 1754.

Tucked away to the west of the Market Place are the substantial remains of the great keep erected by Earl Bigod in 1165. The massive walls, as thick as those of any castle in England, were undermined during a siege in 1174; fortunately the occupants surrendered before the final *coup de grâce*, so both the walls and the mining gallery have survived.

The town has two churches, both north of the Market Place. The smaller, Holy Trinity, is Saxon with a round tower and herringbone masonry, and has a fine pulpit of 1558 ornamented with arabesques. This was the parish church

until the 15th century, for nearby St Mary's was built as a conventual church, serving a community of Benedictine nuns. All remains of the nunnery and the chancel of the church were lost in the 1688 fire and for the same reason the interior of St Mary's is rather stark; it does, however, have a splendid 90-foot tower, begun around 1470.

One of the few buildings to escape the fire lies immediately south-west of this church: above the modern supermarket façade are three oriel windows with carved sills, belonging to a merchant's house of around 1500. The houses on either side, with their Georgian doorcases and red-brick façades, speak of the town's 18th-century prosperity. At that time the River Waveney was navigable to Bungay and there was a wharf to the east of the town – now, with its neighbouring mill, surrounded by modern housing. On the northern edge of the town close to the by-pass are the premises of Richard Clay & Son (The Chaucer Press), the well-known printer whose business was established here in 1876.

There is another castle just under 2 miles to the east at **Mettingham**, built around 1344 by Sir John de Norwich and used from 1394 as a college of priests. The gatehouse, standing to full height, and the curtain wall have survived, while the interior is filled with 19th-century farm buildings. All Saints' church, a mile to the north, is a simple building with a Norman doorcase; its boldly carved font has a stone stopper which is a miniature version of the font itself.

Bures (5/2F)

Five miles south of Sudbury, Bures lies on either side of the River Stour which forms the county boundary with Essex. On the Suffolk side, modest brick and half-timbered houses tumble down the steep hillside to a small market place and the church of St Mary, with its unusual 16th-century brick south porch.

St Stephen's chapel, a mile to the north-east, was dedicated in 1218 to commemorate the spot on which St Edmund was crowned King of East Anglia on Christmas Day, AD 855. Now beautifully restored, it contains three magnificent 14th-century monuments to the de Veres, Earls of Oxford, whose descendants, 150 years later, contributed to the building of the church at LAVENHAM.

Cathedral and rose garden, Bury St Edmunds

Assington, 3 miles north-east of Bures, was the setting for an early successful attempt at co-operative farming by the Quaker, John Gurdon, in the 1830s. Several of his Puritan ancestors are commemorated in a series of accomplished monuments and brasses in St Edmund's church. This stands in open, sheep-grazed meadows next to the turreted ruins of the Gurdon's family home, gutted by fire in 1957.

Burstall (5/3E) *see* Copdock

Bury St Edmunds (5/1C)
Bury, as the town is known locally, is a rare example of an unspoiled English town, whose rich character is the result of evolution over a period of several centuries untouched by large-scale modern developments. The rectangular grid of streets, following the 11th-century layout, offers long vistas of delightfully varied façades and rooflines, pleasing as a townscape and rewarding to explore in detail. The town has no less than 980 buildings considered worthy of preservation. Now that the A45 bypass has brought relief to Bury, it is a peaceful, civilised place – though plans to double the population to 40,000 have provoked doubts as to how long it will remain so.

The town's motto encapsulates its history; 'Shrine of a King; Cradle of the Law'. The king buried here was St Edmund, for long the patron saint of England, and his shrine made Bury a prosperous early medieval pilgrimage centre. On St Edmund's Day (20 November) in 1214, a group of 25 powerful barons met here, together with Stephen Langton, Archbishop of Canterbury, and swore on the martyr's shrine to force King John to ratify the Magna Carta. They succeeded in their objective the following year and Victorian antiquarians therefore dubbed Bury the 'birthplace of our natural rights'.

The first monastery at Bury was founded in about AD 630, at the confluence of the town's two rivers, the little Linnet and the larger Lark. When Edmund, King of East Anglia, was slain by Danish marauders in AD 870, he was buried first at HOXNE, site of his martyrdom. Miracles attributed to him, however, soon led to his canonisation, after which his remains were brought here. After the Danish King Canute conquered England in 1016, he was converted to Christianity and gave substantial gifts of land to the monastery at Bury in atonement for the crimes and devastation wrought by his forebears. From that time on, the newly created Benedictine

abbey flourished, particularly under Baldwin, who became abbot in 1065. As a Norman, he was not replaced after the Conquest; he stayed at the helm until his death in 1097 and was largely responsible for the shape and layout of the town, which was renamed St Edmundsbury under his administration. He made the abbey the focal point of the grid-iron pattern of streets that was created in open fields to the west of the precinct wall.

This street plan has survived, though the

Icknield Way path and oak, near Bury St Edmunds

abbey and its great church remain only in the form of massive rubble walls, robbed of their facing stone. These ruins lie within the extensive perimeter wall which sweeps down to the River Lark and to Abbot's Bridge, an attractive survivor of the abbey's dissolution in 1539. The abbey grounds are now planted with a great variety of trees and shrubs, as well as with formal flower beds, a magnificent example of municipal park design at its very best.

Churchgate Street, though no longer the principal throughfare, was originally planned as a ceremonial route to St Edmund's shrine, aligned on the west door of the abbey church. Here we find a magnificent group of buildings erected under Abbot Anselm. The massive Norman Gate, which resembles the tower of Norwich cathedral, was begun in about 1121 as a belfry.

Anselm founded the two great churches that

stand near by. Both have been rebuilt since the 12th century. St James's became the cathedral of the diocese of St Edmundsbury and Ipswich in 1914. The lofty and elegant nave is attributed to John Wastell, the 15th-century architect of the fan-vaulting in King's College Chapel, Cambridge. Sir George Gilbert Scott provided a new hammerbeam roof in 1862. In this century the chancel has been rebuilt and all the roofs painted in splendid colours. The planned central tower and spire are yet to be completed. St Mary's church, further south, is reached through a large and beautiful tree-shaded churchyard. Rebuilt many times, its outstanding feature is the impressive 15th-century oak roof.

From St Mary's church, Crown Street, Chequer Square and Angel Hill form a continuous broad thoroughfare immediately west of the abbey walls. These open spaces have served at various times as a market place and site of the annual Bury Fair. At the southern end is the Greene King brewery and the Theatre Royal, built in 1819 and a fine example of a late Georgian playhouse. It is still used as a working theatre.

The Athenaeum in Angel Square is an even older cultural centre, a Georgian Assembly Room built in 1789 with an Adam-style ballroom. The Athenaeum Literary Institute acquired the building in 1854, and Charles Dickens gave two of his celebrated public readings here. Dickens also immortalised the nearby Angel Hotel by making it the setting for one of Mr Pickwick's adventures.

The west and north sides of the broad square called Angel Hill are lined with handsome Georgian and Regency houses, as well as the neo-Georgian Borough Offices built in 1938. Among them, but set back a little, is the delightful Queen Anne house called Angel Corner, used to house the Gershom-Parkington collection of 'time measurement instruments', ranging from portable sundials and tavern clocks to the most elegant and intricate of time pieces. A popular time to visit is at noon, for the sweet music of scores of chiming clocks.

Abbeygate Street heads westwards up the hill, and must be one of the most handsome and varied shopping streets in all England. At ground level many old shop fronts survive and as the eye rises to the upper storeys the slightly tilted gables and lack of true alignment betray timber framing that has moved as the woodwork has become seasoned over several centuries. Much of Bury was rebuilt after a great fire in 1608. Whereas in London the post-fire buildings had by law to be built in fireproof stone or brick, here in Bury the builders simply continued with the traditional timber-framing techniques. This led the writer Celia Fiennes, visiting the town in 1698, to comment that 'there are no good houses, but only what are old and rambling'.

Near the top of Abbeygate Street we encounter one of Bury's more recent buildings; the 1861 Corn Exchange has an imposing colonnade and a weighty pediment ornamented with the figure of Ceres and a portrait of Queen Victoria. The area behind the Corn Exchange and bounded by Butter Market and Cornhill was once a large open space, but gradually the market stalls became permanent buildings. Thus Skinner Street and The Traverse represent late medieval encroachment into the market area, the only part of the town in which the strict rectilinear grid gives way to narrow winding alleys.

Further north up The Traverse, the handsome Cupola House was nearly built when Celia Fiennes visited in 1698 and the only house that she singled out for praise. Just beyond, facing into Cornmarket, is the Market Cross, originally built to the design of Robert Adam as a combined market hall and theatre, hence the masks of tragedy and comedy that decorate the façade. The upper floor is now used as an art gallery. Opposite, in Cornhill, is a delightful and exuberant neo-Jacobean shop, purpose-built at the end of the 19th century as a shop for Boots the Chemist. Four lifesize statues in niches and the bold stucco work that covers the façade all illustrate people and incidents associated with the history of the town. The building was saved from demolition by local preservationists a few years ago.

The most recent development in Bury is tucked away north of Cornhill in Brentgovel Street. The Cornhill Shopping Centre is a modest post-modernist greenhouse, with the merit of being well hidden. Ironically, it stands alongside Bury's oldest surviving building, Moyses Hall, a well-preserved 12th-century merchant's house, with living quarters above a vaulted undercroft. In its long history, Moyses Hall has been the town goal, a workhouse and a police station. Now it is a museum and a most enjoyable one at that. Like Bury itself, the museum has escaped 'improvement' and is a glorious jumble of eccentric curiosities.

Carlton Colville (3/4F) *see* Lowestoft

Cavendish (5/1E)

On the A1092, 6 miles north-west of Sudbury, Cavendish is popular for the pub on its broad green, where customers can sit and look down on the charming cottages, colour-washed and thatched. One of the best groups, twice restored since 1956, nestles at the foot of the church tower on 'Hyde Park Corner'.

The chancel of St Mary's church was built under the will of Sir John Cavendish (d. 1381), who was beheaded by followers of Wat Tyler. The splendid brass eagle lectern is 16th-century, and there is a fine Flemish altarpiece of the same date (though over-painted in the 19th century) depicting the Crucifixion.

Nether Hall Manor, north of the church, is a well-restored 16th-century farmhouse at the centre of the famous Cavendish vineyards, both of which are open daily. The Old Rectory, down in the village, is another fine timber-framed Tudor house, now owned by the Sue Ryder Foundation and used to explain its work for the sick and disabled. It too is open daily.

Charsfield (6/1D)

The village lies 3 miles west of Wickham Market

'Suffolk pink' cottages at Cavendish

and is best described in the words of Ronald Blythe:

> It is not a particularly striking place and says little at first meeting . . . it is doubtful if any preservationist society would launch an appeal to save it. It is not that kind of village . . . [it is] a little arable kingdom where flints are the jewels and where existence is sharp-edged.

These quotations are taken from *Akenfield* (1967), the absorbing study of the people of an East Anglian village which Ronald Blythe wrote in an attempt to capture the real meaning of rural life: an antidote to the romantic view of the good life and yet an elegy for lost knowledge, instincts and emotions. The book was partly based on Charsfield and at least one villager has capitalised on the fame which has followed its publication. The owners of number 1 Park Lane have named their semi-detached council house 'Akenfield'; their half-acre garden, packed with colourful flowers and neat rows of vegetables, is open daily in summer.

Apart from St Peter's church with its 16th-century brick tower and unusual flushwork, there is little else for the visitor to see: yet Mr Blythe has revealed just what invisible riches even such a humble place can yield.

Chelmondiston (6/1F)

Five miles south of Ipswich, Chelmondiston (sometimes pronounced 'Chempton') is an excellent starting point for walks along the peaceful banks of the River Orwell. North of the village, leafy Pin Mill Lane leads to a car park and the start of a 6-mile waymarked path to Woolverstone.

At Pin Mill itself, the Butt and Oyster pub dates to the 17th century and is associated with the stories of Arthur Ransome. Moored nearby are a number of restored Thames barges, surviving examples of once-important trading vessels. Enthusiastic owners take part in an annual race up the Orwell. Pin Mill Cliff, owned by the National Trust, is an ancient alder and oak coppice; the mudflats below are an important breeding area for oystercatchers, turnstones, pintails, shovellers and redshank.

Woolverstone, 2 miles to the north-west, is a planned village of 19th-century estate workers' cottages laid out around Woolverstone Hall, a Palladian-style house set in fine parkland which is now a boys' boarding school. The waterfront is used as a marina by the Royal Harwich Yacht Club. Woolverstone House in Mannings Lane is an essay by Sir Edwin Lutyens more in the Surrey than the Suffolk vernacular style.

Two miles north at **Freston**, the B1456 descends right to the water's edge; the north-westward view is dominated by the Ipswich docks, the power station and the new Orwell road bridge. In the opposite direction, south-eastwards, the view is delightfully rural and the river is alive with small boats, just like a Devon creek. Visible only from the water is the six-storey red-brick look-out tower built in about 1553 by Thomas Gooding, an Ipswich merchant; it may have served a practical function, but many prefer to see it as a pure folly, the oldest surviving example in England.

Chelsworth (5/2E)

The River Brett is as pretty as the more famous River Stour into which it flows and its marshy banks, bright with buttercups and marigolds, form the first view as you enter Chelsworth from the east. The river flows within feet of All Saints' church, beautifully sited next to the

pargeted Grange, dated 1694 on the porch but probably much older and standing on the edge of the open parkland of Chelsworth Hall.

The church is rendered – the only intrusive element in the scene – but a flint pinnacled projection to the north hints at something splendid within: a remarkable tomb canopy, covered in ballflower and foliage carving.

After flowing through the grounds of Chelsworth Hall, the river re-emerges in the centre of the immaculate village, passing beneath two brick hump-backed bridges. This is a spot in which to linger and enjoy the village landscape, all timber-framed and thatched houses with colourful gardens grouped around the Peacock Inn.

One mile north, at **Bildeston**, the long, winding High Street is lined with timber-framed houses that were built in the 16th century when the town was famous for its blue cloth – a trade later lost to the water-driven mills of the Cotswolds. Later buildings and the squat clock tower in the Market Square are built of local red and yellow Woolpit brick.

A twisting steep lane leads to St Mary's church, high on the hill west of the town. Less handsome since the collapse of the tower in 1975, the interior nevertheless conveys a sense of grandeur, with its airy clerestory and sweeping roof.

At **Hitcham**, a further mile north, All Saints' church sits in a spacious, well-gardened churchyard; the Old House, by the church gate, was once the parish guild hall. The interior is memorable for the splendid nave roof and raised chancel.

Chevington (4/3C) *see* Saxhams, The

Clare (4/3E)

Place-name scholars speculate that this town, 8 miles east of Haverhill, was so called because of the brightness and clarity of the River Stour that flows to the south, now forming the county boundary with Essex. The river is not visible from the town but it makes an attractive feature of the Country Park just off the High Street. Swans now nest here, and kingfishers flash along the bankside, where the town's railway station once stood, cutting a swathe through the inner bailey of Clare Castle. The great motte survives, thrown up by the Normans, and is crowned by the remains of a 13th-century keep. The riverside footpath leads west to the remains of the Austin Friars priory, the first of this order to be

Ancient House, Clare

founded in England, in 1248 and now once again used by the Augustinian order. More earthworks lie to the north of the town. Surrounded now by housing estates, they remain impressive, with high ramparts surviving from an Iron Age hill-fort.

In between these two groups of monuments lies the handsome town, with its noble church of St Peter and St Paul set on an island on Market Hill. The chancel was rebuilt in 1617, but you would never know, so true is the rebuilding to the Perpendicular style of the nave and aisles. Fine 17th-century woodwork includes ornate choir stalls and a gallery projecting from the porch into the nave, like the singing galleries in the churches of Tuscany.

Several houses around the church are pargeted: one particularly fine specimen of bold plaster-work foliage decorates the 15th-century Priest's House, south of the churchyard, now used as the town museum.

The neighbouring village of **Stoke by Clare**, just over a mile to the west, has a charming group of cottages around a tiny green, shaded by ancient oak trees.

Cockfield (4/5D) *see* Bradfields, The

Coddenham (5/4D)

An up-to-date map is essential for navigating the villages north of Ipswich since, as the city has expanded, a completely new network of roads has been established. The benefit is that many villages, once on busy main roads, are now by-passed, though landfill sites, multiple pylons and gravel works occasionally mar the landscape.

Coddenham, 7 miles north of Ipswich, is far enough away to have retained its rural charm intact. Timber-framed and jettied houses painted Suffolk pink cling to the steep hillside above the River Gipping and the water-meadows in the valley below are a sheet of dazzling buttercup yellow in early summer. Masses of wild flowers also fill St Mary's churchyard, where the steepness of the slope dictated that the tower be built to the north of the nave rather than to the west.

Two miles south at **Barham**, the church of St Mary now also serves the much-enlarged Ipswich suburb of Claydon and Henry Moore's *Madonna*, originally commissioned as a war memorial and formerly at Claydon, has been moved here. St Mary's vestry is fitted with an unusual and delicate window of terracotta, covered in Italian

Renaissance ornament. This was cast from the same moulds as the windows of nearby Shrubland Hall – now a health clinic – dating originally from around 1525 but rebuilt by Gandy in the last century, whose magnificent Italianate gardens were laid out in 1848–52 by Sir Charles Barry.

At **Little Blakenham**, 2 miles to the west, Lord Blakenham's delightful wooded garden is open on certain afternoons in summer and enwraps the whole village in leafy beauty. The 5-acre bluebell wood is densely planted with camellias, azaleas, rhododendrons, roses and hydrangeas, which fill the shady grove with colour for much of the year.

Bramford, 2 miles south, is the closest to Ipswich and most difficult to find, but worth the effort for its streets lined with 16th- and 17th-century cottages and St Mary's, a small but decorative church with a delicate 16th-century font cover.

Combs (5/3D) *see* Needham Market

Copdock (5/4E)

Just 3 miles south-west of Ipswich, Copdock has so far remained rural and only pylons betray the proximity if the city. St Peter's church stands beside a beautiful 16th-century red-brick barn; though comprehensively restored in 1901, its west gallery incorporates five carved Elizabethan panels, one of which is said to represent Edward VI on horseback.

Burstall, 3 miles to the north, has a lovely complete 14th-century church, one of few in the county that escaped rebuilding in the Perpendicular style. It is small, but the delicate window tracery and arcade piers will delight anyone who prefers the curvaceous Decorated style to the more linear Perpendicular.

Hintlesham, a mile further west, is famous for the Hall, beautifully restored as a restaurant and hotel by Robert Carrier, though now under different ownership, still maintaining the highest culinary standards. The only way to see the magnificent Elizabethan plasterwork ceilings is to book a table; but the neo-Palladian façade, added 1725–40, can be viewed from the public footpath that passes through the beautiful wooded grounds.

Cotton (5/3C) *see* Finningham

Covehithe (6/4A)

This coastal village lies 4 miles north of South-

Blakenham Woodland Garden, Little Blakenham

wold. John Sell Cotman captured the ruined beauty of Covehithe's church in watercolour when he came to stay here at the house of his wealthy patron, Dawson Turner, in 1804. The church, St Andrew's, was left a ruin after the Civil War and a tiny thatched church was built within the walls of the former nave, dwarfed by the massive tower which Cromwell's agents left standing as a navigational aid – a poignant symbol of mutability. All that now survives of the once-thriving port is a couple of houses and a farmyard close to the cliff tops.

Two miles to the north, across sparsely populated farming country, is the church of St Michael at **Benacre**, restored in 1769 and given a lovely set of box pews. Accessible only by footpaths, Benacre Broad is delightful and unspoiled; no boats intrude and nature is allowed her own way. By contrast, **Kessingland**, 2 miles further up the coast, is a sprawling resort, but with an excellent Rare Breeds and Wildlife Park, which is open daily in summer.

Cowlinge (4/3D)

The village lies 7 miles north-east of Haverhill. St Margaret's is a lovely rustic church with a red-brick tower, brick floors and a high crown-post roof. At the rear of the church, a set of benches is dated to 1618 by an inscription that declares they are 'for the use of the Keeper of the Correction House in Cowlinge and the prisoners therein'. The correction house, 2 miles south, is still in use as a prison.

At **Wickhambrook**, 2 miles to the south-east, All Saints' church contains another notable monument, by Nicholas Stone, carved with the recumbent figure of Sir Thomas Heigham (d. 1630) and a long inscription that gives a full account of his exploits as a man-at-arms in Ireland. An earlier Heigham built Gifford's Hall, a mile further south-east, in about 1485. Its moated grounds perfectly complement this many gabled, timber-framed house. They are open under the National Gardens Scheme.

Cratfield (6/2B) *see* Laxfield

Crowfield (5/4D) *see* Stonhams, The

Culford (4/4B) *see* Icklingham

Debenham (5/4C)

Numerous rivulets meet at this attractive village, 12 miles north of Ipswich, to form the River Deben, and water flows alongside several of its

Covehithe new church within the ruins of the old

numerous back lanes. The main street, once the primary route between Ipswich and Norwich, rises to a ridge and then falls away the other side. On this ridge stands St Mary's church, the ancient origins of which are indicated by the Saxon long and short-work quoins of the west tower. The massive simple round arch within belongs to the Saxo-Norman overlap, the years just before the rich repertoire of Norman archi-

tectural motifs began to have an impact on England. Opposite the church, the row of fine Tudor houses has several cart entrances leading to long back alleys where rush weavers once worked. Interrupting this fine prospect is the massive hall of the Ancient Order of Foresters, built originally as a Non-conformist chapel but given its handsome classical façade in 1905.

As the village street falls away to the north, you find a maze of narrow streets and the little market hall, built in the early 17th century and

descendants still produce organic apple juice, cider and vinegar on the farm and the original 18th-century wood and granite press is still used on occasions.

Two miles south of Debenham, at Boundary Farm, **Framsden**, the Fox Fritillary Meadow is one of a handful of sites in England where the elegant snakeshead fritillary still flowers in abundance in the wild. The meadow, a protected reserve, is open for one weekend a year, generally in early May.

Dennington (6/1C) *see* Worlingworth

Denston (4/3D)

Denston lies 7 miles north-east of Haverhill. The stately Perpendicular church of St Nicholas, with its fan-vaulted porch, was built as a collegiate church in 1474. Having been the subject of an energetic restoration campaign since the beginning of the 1980s, it is now in pristine condition. Some of the outstanding brasses have lost their inscriptions, and we do not know the identity of the two shrouded figures; it would be nice to think that they were John Denston and Katherine, his wife, who founded the college. The glass in the east window is a modern rendering of the life of St Nicholas, designed by Martin Travers in 1932 when the church was last restored.

From Denston, the lanes eastwards to **Boxted** weave up and down the valley of the River Glem, through sunken lanes and a patchwork of small, high-hedged fields: scenery that was common in Suffolk until 20 years ago when, in the words of landscape historian Richard Muir, the great 'theft of the countryside' began and hedges were removed to create 'featureless grain factories'. The church of All Saints at Boxted, stands on the boundary of two estates and the southward view is of massive fields, scores of acres in extent, robbed of the hedges which gave England her unique landscape.

Dunwich (6/3B)

Every schoolboy and girl knows that Dunwich, 4 miles down the coast from Southwold, fell into the sea, but it requires a visit to realise just how completely this major medieval port and city has been wiped from the map. Nothing survives except for the ruins of the friary, founded on the spot where St Felix is supposed to have landed early in the 7th century from Burgundy, via Canterbury, to bring Christianity back to East Anglia.

later used as Hitchans School. Opposite, the Debenham Gallery occupies the ornately timbered former Guildhall.

A mile or so north of Debenham is the charming 17th-century Aspall Hall, surrounded by a moat which forms a lush water garden. The Cyder House (open daily except weekends) is 16th-century; it was converted in 1728 by C. B. Chevallier, who brought a Normandy cider press with him when he emigrated to this apple-producing corner of Suffolk. Chevallier's

Local fishermen sell their catch from timber huts on the beach and a token village of Victorian terraced houses stands well back from the still-crumbling cliffs. One of the cottages contains a small museum of relics dug from the shore: a dangerous practice now forbidden. Further west still the Victorian church, replacing the nine that the sea has destroyed, stands alongside the ruins of a Norman lepers' chapel, surviving only because it was sited well outside the town walls.

To the south lies the haunted coast that features in M.R. James's masterly ghost stories and some nature reserves of national importance. Dunwich Common, owned by the National Trust, and the great sweep of Westleton Heath are both relics of the sandy heathland, once grazed by sheep, that made Suffolk a wealthy wool-producing county. Heather and gorse provide a blaze of colour in their flowering seasons, and sand martens nest in the Dunwich and Minsmere Cliffs. Further south still, the R.S.P.B. Minsmere Reserve is one of the last remaining homes of the nightjar (*see* 'Coastal Birds of East Anglia', p. 32).

Earl Soham (6/1C) *see* Sohams, The

Earl Stonham (5/4D) *see* Stonhams, The

East Bergholt (5/3F)

Midway between Colchester and Ipswich, East Bergholt is famous as the birthplace of John Constable. The house in which he was born in 1776 no longer exists but its successor, on the east side of Church Street, is called, inevitably, Constables. The artist's parents are buried in the north-east corner of St Mary's churchyard, but he would have been appalled by the dreadful memorial window of 1897 in the church, with its garish colour and cartoon-like figures.

The unusual bell house in the churchyard is a real crowd-puller, for here, at 9.30 am every Sunday and at 6.00 pm in summer, local ringers peal the bells by grasping the shoulder stocks: thirsty work for which they are rewarded by the donations of intrigued onlookers. The timber-framed bell cage, resembling a dovecote or granary, was built in 1531 when work stopped on the ambitious west tower, which now survives only as a stump.

Constable's father owned the mill at **Flatford** and, a mile south of the village, we can still walk the leafy lane down to the River Stour which father and son trod daily.

Carefully preserved to look just as it does in

Constable's famous painting, the mill is now a Field Study Centre and is not open to the public. The National Trust has, however, waymarked several footpaths which follow the banks of the Stour and offer many a tree-framed view of the lock, weir and mill. Willy Lott's cottage, subject of another famous Constable picture, *The Hay Wain*, stands a little further downstream.

Constable claimed to know and love 'every stile and stump, and every lane' around his home village, and he made several sketches in

his early 20s of the church, houses and water meadows at **Stratford St Mary**, 2 miles west of East Bergholt. It was here, too, that Henry Williamson, auther of *Tarka the Otter*, as a boy came face to face with his first otter. The watery views remain; sadly, however, tranquillity has been lost as traffic thunders through the village on the elevated A12 trunk road linking Colchester and Ipswich. St Mary's church was given a highly idiosyncratic porch in 1876 by the accomplished Victorian architect Henry Woodyer, and the

Dunwich clifftop churchyard has almost entirely disappeared

angels of the lovely nave roof may well be his work too.

Easton (6/1D)

Two miles north-west of Wickham Market, Easton stands among the lush meadows of the River Deben; the whole village resembles an outsize cottage garden.

Separate timber bell-tower, East Bergholt

Easton Park, on the western side of the village, is surrounded in its entirety by a crinkle-crankle wall, over 2 miles long in its total length. Where the wall meets the small village green it is planted on the public side, with a profusion of roses, irises and hardy perennials.

Flowers spill from the gardens of heavily timbered neo-Tudor estate cottages and line the walk up to All Saints' church, where we can learn something of the families who stamped their character on this most attractive village. The first owners of the manor were the Wingfields, commemorated in a remarkable series of brasses. Their family pews, installed about 1650, are extraordinary; the cage-like structures carved with cherubs are positioned on either side of the altar and within the area delimited by handsome 17th-century communion rails. From the Wingfields, the estate passed to William Henry Zuylestein who came to England with his cousin William of Orange, later William III. The last of his descendants, the 5th and last Earl of Rochford (d. 1830), is commemorated in a monument that begins with a catalogue of his many titles, ending, as if the sculptor grew tired, with a laconic 'etc, etc'.

Of the Rochfords' house nothing remains – the crinkle-crankle wall now encloses modern bungalows – but a dovecote, several *cottages ornés* and the Easton Harriers Hunt Kennels all survive. Moreover, Easton Park Farm, open daily in summer, is still run on model principles; the Victorian dairy is kept in immaculate condition alongside the modern milking unit, and the farm has pioneered the conservation of rare breeds.

Neighbouring **Letheringham** lies less than a mile to the west, along the lovely unpolluted River Deben. Parallel with the river, several monastic fish ponds indicate the extent of an Augustinian priory, founded here around 1200. All that survives of the priory is a low 15th-century gatehouse and some Norman masonry in St Mary's church, reached by negotiating an untidy farmyard. Inside the church is one of Suffolk's finest brasses: Sir John Wingfield (d. 1389), armoured and at prayer.

At **Brandeston**, 2 miles to the north-west, the 16th-century Hall, largely rebuilt in 1845 after a fire, is now a school. The Lords of the Manor, the Revett family, made their views on the divorce of Henry VIII and Katherine of Aragon quite plain; three small panes of stained glass in All Saints' church show Katherine's pomegranate badge, the crown of Henry and a quotation from the marriage service: 'Whom God hath joined together, let no man put asunder'.

Edwardstone (5/2E) *see* Polstead

Eleighs, The (5/2E)

The Eleighs, 5 miles north-west of Hadleigh, are thought to be named after Illa, the leader of a group of Saxons who chose a delightful part of Suffolk in which to make their settlement, on the wooded banks of the River Brett.

Woods, brimming with wild flowers in early summer, reach right up to the door of St Mary's church, **Brent Eleigh**, remarkable not just for its 14th-century traceried south door but also for a beautifully expressive painting of the Crucifixion, said to date from around 1300 and perhaps the only medieval reredos surviving undamaged in its original position. The painting is of the highest quality, comparable to the best work of the Norwich School and is flanked by later wall paintings of unusual clarity.

The lovely William and Mary Hall next door was modified internally by Lutyens in 1933.

The village, to the south, is dominated by a fine 15th-century house, enhanced by Edwardian additions in the same style – timber-framed with brick nogging.

Monks Eleigh, 2 miles downstream, consists of colour-washed thatched houses around a triangular green. Beautifully sited at the apex of the green is St Mary's church, with its striking flushwork tower, a view so harmonious that it used to be used on railway posters promoting the charms of Suffolk.

Elmswell (5/2C) *see* Stowmarket

Elveden (4/4A)

Good neo-Tudor houses line the short main street of this estate village 3 miles south-west of Thetford, which receives a merciless battering from the heavy traffic that thunders between Newmarket and Norwich.

Elveden Hall is a sad but romantic place: sad because it has been empty for many years and faces an uncertain future; romantic because it was once the home of the deposed ruler of the

Stratford St Mary

Punjab Prince Duleep Singh and beneath its classical exterior is a ravishingly rich Moghul palace. Deposed in 1848 by the Treaty of Lahore, the boy prince came to London, where Queen Victoria was enchanted by his pretty manners and gave him an *entrée* into upper-class English life. Granted a substantial pension (but forced to hand over the Koh-i-Noor diamond), he bought Elveden and employed John Norton as architect to transform it into a palace, modelled on those of Lahore and Delhi. The cost contributed to his eventual bankruptcy and the house was sold on his death. (His son settled to a quiet life as a scholar of local history – see BLO NORTON, Norfolk.)

The new owner, Lord Iveagh, rebuilt the village and the church of St Andrew and St Patrick in 1904–6. The ornate Art Nouveau Gothic style delights some visitors but is too rich for the taste of others. Hidden from the road, on the south side of the church, is a bell tower built in memory of Lady Iveagh, connected to the church by a cloister walk designed to commemorate the dead of the First World War. There are views of the house from the tower.

The present Earl of Iveagh sold the house contents in 1984 and lives in a cottage on the estate when he comes over from Ireland. According to *The Guinness Book of Records* Elveden is the largest arable farm in England; 11,246 acres are farmed but the total extent of the estate is 22,916 acres.

Erwarton (6/1F) *see* Shotley

Euston (5/1B)

Broad avenues of noble trees signal the work of Capability Brown well before you arrive at Euston itself, and everywhere on this 8,000-acre estate there is evidence of benign management by the Dukes of Grafton over three centuries. The village, 3 miles south-east of Thetford, is little more than a pretty row of cottages, standing just outside the gates that lead to the church and the Hall, which is open on Thursdays in summer.

The Hall was built in 1666–67, rebuilt in 1902 after a fire and partly demolished in 1951. One principal attraction is the series of family portraits dating back to the reign of James I, including works by Stubbs, Van Dyck, Kneller and Lely. The other is the garden, created in recent years by the present Duke, which is full of colour throughout the summer.

The church, dedicated to St Genevieve, dates mainly from a remodelling of 1676. The delicacy and richness of the wood carving, especially around the reredos and pulpit, might well be due to the hand of Grinling Gibbons and the ceiling above the family pew is prettily ornamented in stucco.

Eye (5/4B)

Eye is a town 3 miles south of Diss. As you approach from the east, along the B1117, there is a splendid view of the church of St Peter and St Paul with its 101-foot tower rising above water meadows. The church stands on the extreme eastern edge of the town alongside the castle, both of them overlooking the River Waveney which was once navigable from Great Yarmouth to this point deep in the heart of Suffolk.

William Malet, one of William the Conqueror's supporters, is credited with founding the town sometime before his death in 1071. He built the castle on high dry ground among the marshes. Malet's castle mound survives opposite the church, though the circular keep on top is a folly added in 1845.

The town seems to have been a commercial success from the start, for Domesday records that by 1086 the market at Eye had ruined the trade at nearby Hoxne. Some four centuries later, local people contributed £40 to the building of the splendid church tower, one of East Anglia's finest examples of flushwork. The west face is covered, from base to battlements, in thin vertical panels of blind arcading, drawing the eye upwards and serving to emphasise the tower's great height. Inside, successive restorations have enhanced the beauty of the lofty nave and chancel. Incorporated into Sir Ninian Comper's chancel screen of 1925 are the painted panels of its 1480 predecessor. Three depict monarchs: St Edmund, St Edward the Confessor and Henry VI, who was never canonised but was renowned for his sanctity. Another illustrates St Ursula with a great number of little figures sheltering within the folds of her cloak. According to early sources, Ursula was martyred with eleven companions but a clerical error in the 10th century increased the number to 11,000.

Just outside the church is the heavily restored timber-framed guild hall, with the Archangel Gabriel carved on a corner post. Leading up towards the town centre, Church Street is lined with the houses of prosperous 16th-century burgesses, its serpentine form reflecting the line of the outer bailey of the Norman castle.

15th-century panels in Eye's rood screen

The original market place is now largely filled in with 18th- and 19th-century buildings, notably the extraordinary Town Hall of 1857, a cross between a Byzantine church and seaside pebble palace and a most exotic intrusion into what is, in all other respects, a handsome Suffolk market town.

Two miles west is **Yaxley**, where the beautiful church of St Mary is famous for its iron Sexton's Wheel, used for calculating fast days and one of only two that have survived. (The other is in Norfolk, at LONG STRETTON.) It is displayed above the south door, together with some of the carved wooden angels that once adorned the roof wall-plate. Even without its angels, the roof is very graceful and retains its original paintwork. The 1635 pulpit has been called the best in Suffolk and few anywhere in England are as richly carved.

Eyke (6/2D) *see* Woodbridge

Felixstowe (6/2F)
Sited at the southern tip of the peninsula formed by the Rivers Orwell and Deben, Felixstowe is really two entities. To the west is the container port, linked by newly built trunk roads to the Midlands and the north of England. A ferry carries foot passengers from here over the busy harbour to Harwich, but otherwise no tourist would ever want to visit this district.

To the east, however, is the most attractive Edwardian seaside town, which is far more delightful for the range and inventiveness of its architecture than for the beach, which is rather cold and stony, broken up by numerous breakwaters and groins and battered by bracing easterly winds: excellent for beachcombing but offering few temptations to the bather.

Perhaps that is the reason why Felixstowe has gone into genteel decline. Once, steamers pulled up at the pier bringing passengers from Yarmouth, Walton and Clacton, even as far away as London. Now it is a place to which Ipswich people come on a Bank Holiday; but few stay more than a day and alternative uses have been found for the big hotels and guest houses, marvellous Queen Anne-style villas with ornate balconies, big gables and sea-view turrets. Grand hotels such as the Felix (now called Harvest House) have been converted to offices and many smaller establishments have become homes for the elderly.

A worthwhile day in Felixstowe would begin

at the southern tip of the peninsula at Landguard Point nature reserve where the shingle beaches support those strange plant species that thrive only in saline, impoverished sandy soil. Landguard Fort, by the docks, can be visited on Sunday and Wednesday afternoons in summer. The impressive structure was built in 1718 to guard the entrance to Harwich harbour.

Walking north along the promenade, the steep terraces cut into the cliffside are bright throughout the summer, with hanging gardens and vivacious municipal planting. Beyond Old Felixstowe, the landscape becomes more open and less hilly. Walton Castle, a submerged Roman fort, lies just offshore. The scant remains are visible only at exceptionally low tides. Beyond lies the golf course and an attractive walk to Felixstowe Ferry, past two Martello towers, built in 1810–12 against the threat of invasion by Napoleonic troops. They were modelled on the Torre della Martella in Corsica and many survive at roughly one-mile intervals all the way up the Suffolk coast.

Mid way between Felixstowe and Ipswich is the village of **Levington**. The name is familiar to all gardeners as that of a potting compost developed at the Fisons research centre here in the 1950s. The north of the village is really 'Fisonstown', but to the south is a separate peaceful farming hamlet perched above the River Orwell. Fields of contented Guernsey cows feed in the flowery meadows around St Peter's church, much rebuilt in the early 17th century and full of good woodwork of the same date.

Finningham (5/3C)

Finningham village lies 6 miles north of Stowmarket. Around St Bartholomew's church is a small enclave of thatched houses, including Yew Tree House whose façade is decorated by handsome pargeting of fig trees and vines. The church has an unusual font cover, with its pulley system intact.

Westhorpe, a hamlet to the west, was once the home of Mary Tudor, sister of Henry VIII, who lived here after the death of her first husband, Louis XII of France, and her romantic marriage to Charles Brandon, the first Duke of Suffolk. The beautiful little church of St Margaret, with its floor of medieval tiles, bricks and ledger stones, is unspoiled and atmospheric. The Barrow chapel of the north aisle was built in the 17th century for the large monument, dated 1666, of Maurice Barrow, a splendid corpulent figure flanked by equally overweight cherubs.

At Bacton, a mile to the south, St Mary's church has a lovely double hammerbeam roof while in neighbouring Cotton, a mile east, is the fascinating Mechanical Music Museum, an extensive collection of novelty music boxes, organs and gramophones which is open on Sundays in summer.

The chapel of St Nicholas, 2 miles south at **Gipping**, is the most curious and fascinating church in this part of Suffolk. It was built as a private chantry chapel in about 1484 by the Tyrell family, whose family emblem, the Tyrell knot, is carved all over the buttresses and on the family pew inside. The whole design is most idiosyncratic, but pleasing. Huge windows admit a flood of light and the east window contains much original glass. Best of all is the little room off the chancel, which might have been a priest's house for it contains a fireplace. Externally, the chimney is disguised as an oriel window, with flushwork panels in place of glass.

Flatford Mill (5/3F) *see* East Bergholt

Fornham St Martin (5/4C) *see* Hengrave

Framlingham (6/1C)

Nine miles north of Woodbridge, Framlingham is a flourishing small town which, while a major tourist centre, also supports numerous rural enterprises: in it you will find saddle and violin makers as well as thriving horticultural and agricultural supply companies.

The castle on the northern edge of the town was begun in the 12th century by Hugh Bigod, first Earl of Norfolk, but what we see today, rising handsomely from its complex of earthen baileys, is an early 13th-century fortification. The extensive curtain wall, with its thirteen towers, was based on late Roman and Byzantine defensive systems which English crusaders had encountered, and failed to destroy, in the Near East. The castle is today maintained by English Heritage.

Framlingham remained the stronghold of the Howards, Dukes of Norfolk, until 1635, when they sold the estate and moved to Arundel in Sussex. Thomas, 3rd Duke of Norfolk, rebuilt the chancel of St Michael's church in 1540, the same year that his unfortunate niece, Catherine Howard, was secretly married to Henry VIII. The 3rd Duke had intended to convert Thetford Priory into a college and make it the family mausoleum, but in the end he transferred his ancestors' monuments here.

Two monuments, commissioned after the chancel was completed, are outstanding works of art, comparable with the finest in Europe. On the left-hand side of the altar, the tomb of Henry Fitzroy (d. 1536), the natural son of Henry VIII by Elizabeth Talboys, is carved with scenes from Genesis and Exodus; their remarkable state of preservation is nothing short of miraculous, given that the iconoclast William Dowsing (see LAXFIELD) wrought such destruction hereabouts. Equally pristine is the tomb of the 3rd Duke himself (d. 1554), carved with marvellously humane and realistic figures of the Apostles, each one standing in a shell niche. He was condemned to death for treason in 1547 and was only saved by the death of Henry VIII the night before the sentence was due to be carried out. Less fortunate was his son, Henry Howard, Earl of Surrey, poet and soldier, who was beheaded

Tomb of Thomas Howard, 3rd Duke of Norfolk

in 1547. His gorgeously painted tomb was not erected until 1614.

The Howards sold their estate to Sir Robert Hitcham (d. 1636) who, not to be outdone, has a lovely memorial carried by four kneeling angels. Hitcham bequeathed the estate to Pembroke College, Cambridge, which gave the gorgeous organ to the church. Built in 1674, it is one of very few Carolean organs still in use.

Framsden (5/4D) *see* Debenham

Fressingfield (6/1B) *see* Wingfield

Freston (5/4F) *see* Chelmondiston

Gipping (5/3C) *see* Finningham

Glemhams, The (6/2D)

Four miles south-west of Saxmundham, the Hall at **Little Glemham** has delightful gardens, though the architecture of the house is rather severe. The plain façade was added by the North family when they acquired the Elizabethan house early in the 18th century and there are several good monuments to the Norths in their mausoleum, attached to St Andrew's church, in the Hall grounds. The Hall is open occasionally in summer.

At **Great Glemham**, 2 miles to the north, All Saints' church has a fine arch-braced roof with pendant bosses and a lively Seven Sacraments font.

Great Ashfield (5/2C) *see* Walsham le Willows

Great Glemham (6/2D) *see* Glemhams, The

Great Saxham (4/3C) *see* Saxhams, The

Great Thurlow (4/2D) *see* Thurlows, The

Great Waldingfield (5/2E) *see* Waldingfields, The

Great Wratting (4/2E) *see* Kedington

Grundisburgh (6/1D)

Three miles north-west of Woodbridge, St Mary's church at Grundisburgh (pronounced 'Grundsbra') stands beside a green, the warm red-brick of its south-west tower a handsome sight, framed by 17th-century cottages. The lovely roof inside is one of Suffolk's best, with carved angels soaring among the hammerbeams, a fine font, gilded chancel screen and bold wall painting of St Christopher. The ornate south chapel was built by Thomas Walle, a man who made his fortune from salt and who married Alice, daughter of Henry VII's master cook. Their excellent timber-framed house, built in 1520, stands east of the church and is named, aptly, Basts.

Two miles south is **Playford**, set in the steep-sided valley of the River Fynn. St Mary's church, with its outstanding brass to Sir George Felbrigg (d. 1400), stands on the hilltop.

Hadleigh (5/3E)

Even with so many other contenders for the title, Hadleigh, half way between Sudbury and Ipswich, deserves to be singled out as one of Suffolk's finest towns. Whereas Lavenham is all timber, Hadleigh is a patchwork quilt in which every variety of Suffolk vernacular architecture is represented, together with more cosmopolitan Regency and flamboyant Victorian, along both sides of its mile-long High Street.

All deserve attention, but two buildings stand out: number 62–6 has a splendid Carolean upper storey, dated 1676 in the leadwork of the central window. Opposite, number 45 has a Victorian shop front, with pegs still attached for hanging out displays of produce. Church Street leads west off the High Street and terminates in a broad green, resembling a miniature cathedral close.

St Mary's church was badly served by Victorian restorers and contains little of interest. It is the glorious broach spire, rising to 135 feet above a 14th-century tower, that lends such dignity to the scene, crowning the town's roofscape. The red-brick Deanery Tower is the perfect companion, a smaller version of the gatehouse at OXBURGH HALL (Norfolk), built in 1495 to form a grand entrance to the palatial Deanery of Archdeacon Pykenham; the Deanery has since been rebuilt in neo-Tudor style.

Opposite the church, the Guildhall is still used for parish functions and is well worth entering on these occasions for a sight of the massive moulded timbers of the Long Room. Described as newly built in a deed of 1438, the Guildhall has scarcely been altered, except for the addition of chimneys, and one can easily imagine the wealthy wool merchants of the town meeting here to regulate prices and wages and to discuss measures for the benefit of the sick and poor of the parish.

In a remarkable example of continuity of function on the same site, the Town Hall of 1851 backs on to the Guildhall, facing into the now filled-in Market Place and next door to the 1813 Corn Exchange.

The next lane south, Duke Street, leads down to a medieval brick bridge over the River Brett; beyond lies the house called 'Holbecks', set in several acres of early 19th-century terraced and walled gardens which are open under the National Gardens Scheme.

Two miles east of the town, Wolves Wood is an R.S.P.B. nature reserve, renowned for its spring orchids and early summer nightingales.

Equally rich in small birds and colourful wild flowers is the Hadleigh Railway Walk south of the town, which follows the course of the old

Double hammerbeam roof in St Mary's church, Grundisburgh

Ipswich branch line down as far as **Little Wenham**, a distance of 5 miles. If you want to visit the church here, take the precaution first of obtaining the key from the Rectory, for All Saints lies at the end of a long pot-holed track. The journey is definitely worthwhile for the setting is perfect; we have John Keeble, founder of the Oxford Movement, to thank for its preservation, for he successfully resisted demolition proposals in the mid 19th century. Inside, 14th-century wall paintings of the Virgin and Child, angels and saints survive in astonishingly fresh colour. Outside, the church forms part of an outstanding group of buildings, including 16th-century barns and the best-preserved 13th-century Hall in England (private), built in pink and yellow brick made on the site from the clay dug to form the moat.

Halesworth (6/2B)

Few houses in this small town, 6 miles inland from Southwold, are outstanding, but the narrow winding lanes are attractive enough – or would be, but for the heavy traffic. The Market Place contains a rather neglected but substantial Elizabethan timber-framed house. It has a more ornate counterpart in The Thoroughfare, east of the church, late Tudor with a little oriel window and ornate Jacobean porch. From here, Steeple End runs up to the church and contains a Dutch-style row of almshouses, built in 1686, now converted to a library and art gallery.

Brewery House, north of the village, was the home of the founders of Kew Gardens, London, Sir William Hooker and his son Joseph. To reach it, you continue up The Thoroughfare, past a shop with a huge carved beam like a fireplace bressumer, over the River Blyth and then right on to the B1123. Brewery House is the first building on the right. It is surrounded by modern housing, where the riverside maltings and the quay once were. The garden of the Hookers has gone, but a park is planned to commemorate them along the riverside.

Continuing along the B1124, **Westhall** is 3 miles north-east. The little rural church of St Andrew is dwarfed by fine trees. The tower hides a surprising Norman portal, the original west front wildly carved with grimacing faces on unfinished beakheads.

Harkstead (5/4F) *see* Shotley

The soaring spire of St Mary's church and the red-brick Deanery Tower at Hadleigh

Haughley (5/3C) *see* Stowmarket

Hawstead (4/5D) *see* Bradfields, The

Helmingham (5/4D)

Eight miles north of Ipswich, Helmingham Hall is the family seat of the Tollemache family, who have been here since about 1485. Their genealogy is gloriously illustrated in the monuments inside St Mary's church, all of which are splendid. Beer lovers owe the family a debt of gratitude for founding the Tolly Cobbold brewery in Ipswich in 1886. The Queen comes here once a year on a shooting weekend; when she attends morning service, the church is too small to contain all the onlookers.

Next door to the church, Helmingham Hall is completely surrounded by a moat and the drawbridge is still drawn up every night. Begun in about 1500, it was remodelled on four occasions, the last time in 1841 by Salvin, but retains its early Tudor courtyard plan. The gardens, renowned for their herbaceous borders and old roses, are open to the public in summer and herds of red and fallow deer and Highland cattle roam in the park.

Two miles south-east at **Otley**, the smaller but equally ancient moated Hall is open at weekends in summer. The mellow 15th-century timber-framed house was once the home of Bartholomew Gosnold (d. 1607), the explorer who discovered Cape Cod and founded Jamestown, Virginia. St Mary's church contains excellent Jacobean woodwork; the chancel roof, with its bold scrolly decoration, also looks typical of the early 17th century but was in fact created in the 19th. There is a rare mid 17th-century total immersion font preserved beneath the floorboards of the vestry.

Hengrave (4/4C)

Three miles north-west of Bury St Edmunds, Hengrave Hall (now a religious retreat centre) and the church of St John Lateran make a lovely group, side by side in extensive parkland. The Hall, which is open by appointment, was built in 1535–38 by Sir Thomas Kytson, partly of Northamptonshire limestone and partly of yellow brick, deliberately chosen to match the colour of the stonework and a very early example of the use of this material. In 1578, Elizabeth I and the entire court visited the Hall; they were treated to an entertainment 'representing the fayries'. The tiny church, set in a beautifully planted churchyard, is so filled with monuments that there is scarcely room for the altar.

Helmingham Hall

Two miles to the south-east, **Fornham St Martin** is, despite its attractive name, a village of post-war housing estates. The church is worth a stop, however, for the misericord, reused as a lectern, which depicts St Martin of Tours dividing his cloak and giving half to a beggar.

Hepworth (5/2B) *see* Bardwell

Herringfleet (3/3F) *see* Somerleyton

Hessett (5/2C)

Hessett lies 5 miles south-east of Bury St Edmunds. The church is dedicated to St Ethelbert, the East Anglian king slain by Offa, king of the Mercians, at Hereford in 794 and later eclipsed in popularity by the 9th-century king and martyr, St Edmund. A remarkably clear set of wall paintings has survived, as well as some lovely glass dating from the 16th century. In the

surviving tumulus of a group of four which stands besides a stretch of Roman road a mile to the west. Despite its prehistoric appearance, excavators found Roman burials when they dug in 1843.

Rushbrooke, another mile to the west, is a highly unusual estate village, consisting of houses built in the 1950s and 1960s by Lord Rothschild. The whitewashed bungalows with single pitch slate roofs are excellent. They cluster around older thatched and weatherboarded farm buildings, the angle of the roof pitch exactly matching that of the barns.

St Nicholas's church is delightfully eccentric. A former Lord of the Manor, Colonel Rushbrooke (1779–1845), stripped the Hall (since destroyed) of its panelling and spent his nights as a carpenter, building a set of stalls that face each other across the nave, like a college chapel. The tympanum between nave and chancel bears a splendid Henry VIII coat of arms flanked by a portcullis and Tudor double rose. Described as 'unique', there is now more than a suspicion that it was fabricated by the Colonel.

Heveningham (6/2B) *see* Huntingfield

Hintlesham (5/3E) *see* Copdock

Hitcham (5/2D) *see* Chelsworth

Holbrook (5/4F) *see* Tattingstone

Hollesley (6/2E) *see* Sutton

Horham (6/1B) *see* Wingfield

Hoxne (5/4B)

Hoxne (pronounced 'Hoxen') lies 3 miles northeast of Eye, close to the Norfolk border. At the beginning of the 12th century, Bishop Herbert of Norwich declared Hoxne to be the place in which St Edmund, the 9th-century king of East Anglia, was killed by the Danes. No doubt he hoped that pilgrims to the martyr's shrine at BURY ST EDMUNDS would add Hoxne to their itinerary. Abbey Farmhouse, a 16th-century timber-framed building south of the village, stands on the site of the Benedictine priory founded to commemorate the martyr.

Today Hoxne is a charming little village of thatched cottages, built around a green in the valley of the River Goldbrook, which joins the

east window of the south aisle, St Nicholas blesses four children, one of whom is holding a hockey stick.

A mile to the west, at **Rougham**, the church stands well to the north of the village: in 1349 the parishioners burned their houses and started again half a mile south in an attempt to eradicate the plague. They continued, though, to lavish money on All Saints, which was considerably enlarged in the 15th century.

Eastlow Hill, much overgrown, is the sole

Overleaf: Oaks at Fornham

Waveney a mile to the north. Excavations in 1978 revealed a Palaeolithic (Old Stone Age) settlement on the river terrace and some of the finds are displayed in the north aisle of the church of St Peter and St Paul. The church also houses an oak screen carved with scenes from the life of St Edmund. The wood came from a tree which collapsed in 1848; according to local legend, it was the same tree on which St Edmund died, transfixed with arrows for refusing to renounce his Christianity.

Huntingfield (6/2B)

This valley village is 5 miles south-west of Halesworth. In 1859–66, an artistic rector's wife, Mrs Holland, painted the roof in the most gorgeous colours and added figures of saints in 14th-century style between the rafters. As a memorial to Mrs Holland the soaring Victorian font cover was made in 1878.

At **Heveningham** (pronounced 'He'ningham'), just over a mile south, St Margaret's church stands in a beautiful wooded valley. The Tudor clerestory windows are of rose-covered brick, and, despite Victorianisation, the fine roof and Jacobean fretwork benches in the north chapel are still pleasing.

To the east, the B1117 skirts the parklands and lake, landscaped by Capability Brown, that front the imposing Georgian façade of Heveningham Hall. Once used for public concerts, recent changes of ownership and a disasterous fire mean that it is no longer visitable; should the situation change, however, it is well worth going to see James Wyatt's magnificent Adam-style interiors.

Icklingham (4/3B)

Icklingham, 4 miles south-east of Mildenhall, sits on the edge of the Breckland. It is not clear whether the name derives from the settlement here of the Iceni tribe in the Iron Age, or from the Latin 'ecclesia', a church, which would suggest that there was a physical church building here as early as the 4th century. The excavation of a Roman villa at Weatherhill Farm, just south of the village, uncovered a lead cistern bearing the Chi-Rho monogram, which may have been used as a font, and the baptismal spoons of the famous MILDENHALL treasure in the British Museum provide further evidence of a local group of Christian converts.

The thatched church of All Saints, maintained by the Redundant Churches Fund, is simple, atmospheric and unspoilt; medieval floor tiles

cover the chancel; it dates to the 1360s when the Norman church was heightened and given its Decorated windows. A very fine chest of the same date, covered in wrought-iron foliage, was moved to the church of St James at the northern end of the village, which was comprehensively restored in the 1860s and remains in use by the parish.

Two miles to the south-east, on the sandy soils of the Breckland, is the reconstructed Saxon village of **West Stow**. This was one of England's

West Stow reconstructed Saxon village

earliest examples of 'experimental archaeology': having excavated the remains of a substantial village dating from between AD 400 and 650, archaeologists decided that they could learn even more about Saxon building techniques and the quality of life at the time by reconstructing some of the huts. The result is now an integral part of the West Stow Country Park, which is open daily with an excellent visitor centre. The Saxon village is also the starting point for a 5-mile Nature Trail which passes through wood-

land, marshes and Breckland heath with a rich and varied birdlife.

Modern West Stow is a neat estate village surrounded by tall and ancient deciduous trees, through which you can glimpse the early 16th-century hall with its remarkable brick gate-house.

A mile further east, St Mary's church at Culford can only be reached by a footpath,

The rotunda, Ickworth House (National Trust)

which passes through the grounds of Culford Hall, now a school. The church was all but rebuilt in 1856.

Ickworth (4/4C)

Ickworth House, 2 miles south-west of Bury St Edmunds and now in the care of the National Trust, is a most unusual building, quite unlike any other in England, with its central rotunda and gracefully curving wings. It was begun in 1795 by Frederick, 4th Earl of Bristol and Bishop of Derry (1730–1803). A passionate collector, his extensive travels on the Continent led to numerous Bristol Hotels being named after him. Ickworth was, like his other houses in Ireland, intended primarily as a gallery for his works of art, but these were seized by Napoleon in 1798 and never reached England. Instead of antique statuary, therefore, the house now contains neo-classical work by the highly accom-

furnishings, which reflect early 19th-century taste. His successor, the 3rd Marquess of Bristol, went back to Roman antecedents for the so-called Pompeian Room; the beautiful frescoes were, in fact, copied from wall paintings discovered in 1777 at the Villa Negroni, in Rome.

The gardens, begun in the 1820s, are planted with evergreens in semi-formal Italian style. They enclose the house in such a way that it is impossible to see the full extent, over 600 feet in length, of the sweeping side arms. Such planting was perhaps necessary to screen the house from bitter north-easterly winds and has the pleasing effect of reducing the house to a more intimate scale, glimpsed in sections framed between stands of mature holm oak, yew and cypress trees.

Iken (6/3D) *see* Orford

Ipswich (5/4E)

The people of Ipswich are fortunate to live in a town that, for all its recent growth, retains the compactness and intimacy of a market town. The historic core lies within the egg-shaped area defined by late Saxon ramparts, still traceable in the street plan.

To the north, Christchurch Park is a beautifully wooded public space, bigger in area than the whole of the town centre. To the south, the working docks stand on the Orwell estuary, a broad channel which brought successive waves of Saxon invaders deep into the heart of Suffolk. Some stayed on and founded the settlement of 'Gipeswic' at the point where the freshwater River Gipping becomes the tidal Orwell.

Victorian developers, in a determined effort to keep Ipswich thriving and modern, swept away much of the old town, whose appearance survives now only in Clevely's painted panorama in the Christchurch Mansion Museum. Even so Cornhill, with its flamboyant neo-classical, Italianate and mock Jacobean buildings, perpetuates the site of the first Saxon market place.

Buttermarket, one street south, contains the most famous building in Ipswich, the Ancient House, also known as Sparrowe's House after the merchant family that lived in it for 200 years. The house is 15th-century, but the bold pargeting was added in about 1670 and depicts, in allegorical form, the continents of Europe, Africa, America and Asia. The windows, too, are highly unusual; handsome oriels with two side casements and a central arch. This motif recurs in several of the oldest timber-framed

plished sculptor, John Flaxman (1755–1826). His work includes the two Homeric low relief friezes which run round the outside of the rotunda, and the dramatic group *The Fury of Athamas* which fills the staircase well, lit by the skylight in the dome.

After the death of the 4th Earl, his son first considered demolishing the house which was most impractical for everyday living. Fortunately, he changed his mind and finished the work, providing the majority of the splendid

Pargeting on the Ancient House, Ipswich

houses of Ipswich and was also widely copied by the Victorians.

Just to the west, in Friars Street, the Unitarian Meeting House, erected in 1699, is one of the oldest Non-conformist chapels in the country. Its existence reflects close links with the free-thinking Low Countries; the lovely brass chandelier is Dutch, while the pillars that hold up the ceiling may have been cut down from ship's masts. Next door, the 1974 Willis Faber building, designed by Norman Foster, is clad entirely in black glass. By reflecting all the surrounding buildings it continues, despite its bulk, to blend into the environment rather better than one might expect. South of Friars Street, St Nicholas and St Peter Street is one winding road of timber-framed houses and back courtyards, inevitably now an area of restaurants, wine bars and antique shops.

Those prepared to brave the busy roads and gaunt industrial buildings at the southern edge of the town will find Wolsey's Gate, on an island between Star Lane and College Street. The brick gateway is all that survives of a college founded by Cardinal Wolsey, a native of Ipswich, in 1527. The ambitious scheme was scarcely begun before the Cardinal fell from grace.

Over another busy road and down narrow alleys between towering granaries, you find the pleasing muddle of the Ipswich Wet Dock, the largest in Europe when it was opened in 1845. Today, brick warehouses that have been converted to waterside offices stand alongside working grain silos and the whole area has the distinct aroma of malt and barley. Plump pigeons pick the spilled grain from beneath the abandoned railway tracks while restored tall-masted ships, as well as cargo vessels, moor in the basin. In the middle of the long quayside, the Custom House of 1843 is a handsome classical building of red and yellow brick.

Back in the centre of Ipswich, Lower and Upper Brook Streets contain a number of good Georgian houses. They lead to Northgate Street and the Great White Horse Inn, setting for an episode in Dickens's *Pickwick Papers*. Next, the 15th-century former Royal Oak Inn has a corner post carved with a blacksmith working at his anvil. The alley, alongside Oak House, frames a view of St Mary-le-Tower church, rebuilt in 1850 and now the town's principal church.

A little further north, the bold Bethesda Chapel with its polished granite pillars, built in 1913, stands squarely on St Margaret's Plain; eastward, up Soane Street, lies the finest church in Ipswich, St Margaret's. The side of the nave facing towards the town was designed for spectacular effect and is covered in lavish flushwork from the base of the close-set clerestory windows to the tip of the battlements. Inside, the magnificent double hammerbeam roof was painted in baroque style during the reign of William III.

Immediately to the west is the entrance to Christchurch Park, a great asset to the town for it provides a large leafy oasis within minutes of the central shopping district. The Elizabethan mansion, in which the Queen herself stayed in 1561, was built on the site of an Augustinian priory and the remodelling of the front, with its red-brick Dutch gables and blue brick diapery, occurred after a fire in 1674. The interior has handsome woodwork of the same date. Part is now used as a museum, packed with fascinating furnishings from demolished Ipswich houses. Another part forms the Wolsey Art Gallery, used to display paintings by Constable, Gainsborough and Sir Alfred Munnings, one of this century's most popular horse painters.

There is a second museum in the High Street, on the north-western edge of the town centre, with replicas of the Sutton Hoo and Mildenhall treasures, an excellent Roman gallery and a large ethnographic collection.

Ixworth (5/2B)
This lovely small town, 5 miles north-east of Bury St Edmunds just off the A143, is full of houses of all periods, timber-framed and multi-coloured as well as Georgian brick. One old house at the south end of the village has a few surviving ornamented ridge tiles, with a standing figure and a dog.

St Mary's church lies west of the main street and has a fine porch decorated with a frieze of lions' heads. Tiny brass effigies to Richard Codington (d. 1567) and his wife are set above a fine Renaissance tomb chest; the inscription records that Richard was given the manor here by Henry VIII in return for Codington Manor in Surrey – which Henry rebuilt and named Nonesuch. A path west of the church leads past a striking house called 'The Abbey', Georgian in external appearance but incorporating sub-stantial remains of an Augustinian priory founded in 1170.

At **Ixworth Thorpe**, 2 miles north, All Saints is a delightful example of a church rescued from neglect and restored by the local community, in 1972. Thatched roof, Tudor brick south porch and a set of bench ends carved with a mermaid, animals and figures, make it a charming and atmospheric church.

There are two mills, both still working, in **Pakenham** parish, although they are only just to the south of Ixworth. The 18th-century water-mill, alongside the Black Bourn, produces stone-ground flour and is open at weekends in summer. The tower windmill is a little further west, near Fulmer Bridge – a corruption of 'fowl mere', the old name for Pakenham Fen. This extensive stretch of undrained marsh is used for the production of thatcher's reed. Pakenham village displays some fine examples of both thatched and pargeted cottages. St Mary's church stands high above the village, its impres-sive size and Saxo–Norman doorways reflecting the patronage of the abbey at Bury St Edmunds. Four monks sit around the base of the fine Perpendicular font, carved with symbols of the Evangelists.

Troston lies 3 miles north-west of Ixworth. St Mary's is a neat church with an ornate porch and an unusual quantity of well-preserved wall paintings. West again, the road to Ampton skirts the now ploughed-up grounds of Livermere Park, though the big serpentine mere, renamed Ampton Water, survives as a sanctuary for waterfowl and herons.

Ampton is a mini-estate, backing on to the larger one. Lovely wrought-iron gates survive from the old Ampton Hall, built in the 17th century, burnt down in 1885 but rebuilt soon after in convincing neo-Jacobean style.

St Peter's church is squeezed between the almshouses of 1693 and the Bluecoat School of 1705 (now cottages), and is scarcely taller than either. All were built by the Calthorpe family, whose numerous monuments fill the church.

Kedington (4/3E)
This village 2 miles north-east of Haverhill, and its near neighbours, suffer from their proximity to that ever-expanding town, designated a London overspill town in the 1950s. Even so,

Perpendicular font at Pakenham

the old core of the village is made pretty by the infant River Stour, and the church of St Peter and St Paul, set on a hilltop, is the most interesting in this south-western corner of Suffolk. The interior, though something of an incoherent muddle, has some fascinating elements; the pews, warped with age, standing on floorboards which lift to reveal the foundations of a Roman building; a lovely bow-fronted 18th-century west gallery, complete with hat pegs; a false hammerbeam roof lit by Victorian skylights; and an ingenious triple-decker pulpit of 1610. The fine communion table and railings were given by Samuel Barnardistan (d. 1707), a leading Puritan whose cropped hairstyle gave rise to the nickname 'Roundhead'.

Neighbouring Great and Little Wratting, to the north-west, have nothing so rich to offer, but both are associated with men who founded substantial commercial enterprises. John Sainsbury lived at **Little Wratting**, where Holy Trinity church has a shingled oak-framed steeple, strayed across the border from Essex where such turrets are relatively common. **Great Wratting** received the largesse of W. H. Smith, who paid for the comprehensive restoration of St Mary's church in 1887. The churchyard is bordered by amusing topiary: the yew and box have been clipped into the shapes of a church, a cross and a large padded armchair.

Two miles further west, **Withersfield** is a long village of open greens and houses clinging to the undulating valley side, grouped around the lovely Old Rectory of 1720. In the valley bottom, alongside a tributary of the River Stour, St Mary's church contains an excellent set of poppyheads.

Kelsale (6/2C) *see* Saxmundham

Kersey (5/3E)

Suffolk's prettiest village, 2 miles north-west of Lavenham, is invisible until you arrive, hidden in the steep-sided valley of a small tributary of the River Brett. At the centre of the village is a ford and cart wash and, as you look down on the village from the hilltop churchyard, the view is filled with the mellow, litchen-patched red roofs of weavers' cottages. Sometimes, in the still of a summer afternoon, you think you can almost hear the clack of looms, but it is now several centuries since the village ceased to be the industrious production centre for hard-wearing Kersey broadcloth.

The sheer size of St Mary's church shows how

prosperous the village was and, despite ruthless mutilation by iconoclasts, the headless angels and battered fragments of an alabaster reredos bear witness to former splendour. Facing away from the village, the south porch is covered in ornate flushwork.

Two miles to the north-west, the scattered hamlet of **Lindsey** was once famous for Lindsey Wolsey cloth, a good, plain, hard-wearing fabric that kept the chill off the back of many a medieval yeoman farmer. Unlike its neighbour

Kersey, it has preserved little to evoke its former prosperity. St Peter's church is of the simplest type, now lacking even a west tower; that was pulled down in 1836. St James's, south of the village, is merely the shell and beaten earth floor of a 13th-century chapel, maintained today by English Heritage. It may have served the nearby castle, whose great mound was thrown up during the troubled reign of King Stephen.

Kessingland (6/4A) *see* Covehithe

Guildhall, Lavenham (National Trust)

Knodishall (6/3C) *see* Leiston

Lakenheath (4/3A) *see* Mildenhall

Lavenham (5/2E)

Five miles north-east of Sudbury, Lavenham is so well known, so often photographed, that the very name conjures up an instant picture of timber-framed houses, running up and down steep lanes in unbroken succession, with glimpses of open fields at the margins. There is not a single true vertical or horizontal line in this town of timber; massive close-set studs and jetty beams lean this way and that; roof ridges and gable ends curve and tilt in the exact antithesis of the mathematical precision of brick or stone.

The sheer quantity of timber demonstrates the wealth of Lavenham's wool merchants in the 15th century, for mature timber was then already scarce and expensive; only the rich could afford to use such prodigious quantities for decorative effect, far more wood than was necessary for structural stability.

Lavenham appears timeless, but subtle changes have taken place, even in the last decade or two. Our notion that timber-framed buildings were all black and white, an idea inherited from Edwardian neo-Tudor architects, has changed. Many houses have been cleaned up, the timber limewashed to a silvery grey and the panels between the studs painted pink in imitation of the old practice of mixing pigments – ox blood or sloe juice – into the plaster coat. Telegraph poles have been removed and cables buried underground, television aerials hidden in lofts, all to enhance the authentic appearance of this unique town; if only coaches and traffic could be banned from the Market Place, there would be little to intrude on a townscape that has scarcely changed in four centuries.

The Guildhall in the Market Place is the most substantial building in Lavenham, after the church, and is now owned by the National Trust. It was built sometime after 1529, when the Guild of Corpus Christi, a trade organisation that regulated local wool production, received its charter. It is consequently a relatively late building, dating from a time when the local wool industry, begun by refugee Flemish weavers in the 14th century, was already beginning to decline. The Guildhall gathers together all the architectural themes that are repeated in endless variation throughout the surrounding streets: heavy studwork, a lovely porch whose corner posts are carved with the rampant lion emblem of the guild, oriel windows with timber mullions, gable ends facing on to the street and flat-arched Tudor-style doorheads. The interior has been altered considerably during its long and chequered history and now houses a display depicting seven centuries of the cloth trade.

Shilling Street, the easternmost of three lanes that run downhill from the Market Place, contains Shilling Grange, built by John Schylling

in the 15th century. Shilling Street leads to Water Street: the river now runs underground but once supplied the water for wool washing and dyeing processes. At its western end is the priory, founded by the Benedictines and recently opened to the public after an admirable 10-year restoration campaign which has uncovered Elizabethan wall paintings.

Ironically, while so many of Lavenham's secular buildings have been maintained under the best principles of conservative repair, the front of the great south porch of the church of St Peter and St Paul has been painted in the most ill-advised manner. Instead of natural stone, we are greeted by sickly cream, a disappointment after the clipped box spheres that line the approach to this hilltop church with its massive tower. The church was built in the late 15th and early 16th centuries, principally out of the wealth, and for the greater glory, of two families, the Springs and the de Veres, Earls of Oxford. Inside, both families have chantry chapels which are the chief attraction of the church, especially the parclose screen that surrounds the tomb of Thomas Spring (d. 1523).

Laxfield (6/1B)

Laxfield lies 8 miles south-west of Halesworth. The church of All Saints stands broadside on to the wide main street, its magnificent flushwork-covered tower facing the Guildhall, built in 1516–20 and now an informative small museum. The vast church has a barn-like scissor-braced roof and a jumble of box pews which were made in the 18th century. The carpenters reused beautiful 16th-century panels from an earlier set of benches, scattering them at random around the nave, so that some exhibit the most accomplished Renaissance carving of dragons, foliage and caricature portraits; some of this pre-dominantly secular carving might have come from Laxfield House.

At **Cratfield**, 3 miles to the north-east, the beautiful font in St Mary's church was so severely defaced by 17th-century iconoclasts that it now requires a strong imagination to reconstruct the appearance of what has been described as 'the most beautiful font in the kingdom'. As well as detailed Seven Sacraments tableaux around the bowl, the stem is carved with saints under canopies and seated figures.

Leiston (6/3C)

This bustling Suffolk town is 3 miles north of Aldeburgh. When Richard Garrett's engineering firm closed in the late 1970s, many people feared that it would be the death of Leiston (pronounced 'Layston'), the majority of whose inhabitants worked for the firm. A decade on, the worst predictions have proved groundless and the town is buoyant; former employees have established specialist engineering companies and Sizewell nuclear power station, 2 miles to the east, has filled the employment vacuum. The town is immaculately maintained by people with a strong sense of community, and the principal buildings of the Richard Garrett Works have been turned into a fascinating museum, exhibiting the products, from seed drills to traction engines and trolley buses, once manufactured here.

The church of St Margaret, to the west of the town, is a brilliant exception to the usual academic and derivative work of Victorian church architects. Built in 1853 to the design of Edward Lamb, it grew out of his pioneering studies of domestic timber-framed architecture and is nearly all roof, carried on low walls. The splendid roof timbers, all joining at the big open central crossing, remind us of a Scandinavian stave church. The piers of the chancel arch are prettily painted with a frieze of vines and barley and there are several examples of the Arts and Crafts designs of Dorothy and Ellen Mary Rope.

The famous Summerhill school of A. S. Neill stands to the north of the town; a mile out are the extensive remains of Leiston Abbey, used in part by the Pro Cordia Trust which holds summer schools here for gifted young musicians.

The Abbey (open all year) was founded in 1182. Its heyday was in the 14th century when Premonstratensian Canons moved here from their unhealthy swampy site at MINSMERE (now an important R.S.P.B. nature reserve) 2 miles to the north. The Canons reused Norman mansonry from their original abbey, so that Leiston exhibits a range of architectural styles from the 12th to the 15th centuries.

A mile west of Leiston, almost under the forest of pylons that marches across the fields from Sizewell, is the little church of St Mary at **Knodishall**. Hanging above the Jacobean pulpit is a fresh and endearing painting of Jacob and Rachael. It was painted by William Dyce in 1851; Dyce, who painted the frescoes of the House of Lords, is the almost forgotten artist whose *Madonna and Child* (1828) originated the Pre-Raphaelite style of painting in England.

Letheringham (6/1D) *see* Easton

Levington (6/1F) *see* Felixstowe

Lindsey (5/2E) *see* Kersey

Little Blakenham (5/4E) *see* Coddenham

Little Bradley (4/2D) *see* Thurlows, The

Little Glemham (6/2D) *see* Glemhams, The

Little Saxham (4/3C) *see* Saxhams, The

Little Stonham (5/4C) *see* Stonhams, The

Little Thurlow (4/2D) *see* Thurlows, The

Little Waldingfield (5/2E) *see* Waldingfields, The

Little Wenham (5/3F) *see* Hadleigh

Little Wratting (4/2E) *see* Kedington

Long Melford (5/1E)
This appropriately named town, 3 miles north of Sudbury, has a 3-mile long main street whose grand effect is best experienced by entering from the south. At first the road is lined by relatively recent buildings, but it then opens out into a mile-long High Street of considerable width, lined with timber-framed and Georgian houses, none remarkable, but pleasing in their variety.

The best lies beyond, for, just as the High Street closes in again to cross the Chad Brook (site of the mill ford which gave the town part of its name), it debouches into a magnificent, wide green, bounded by the walls of Melford Hall on one side and rising to the almost hidden hilltop church.

Surrounded by the 16th-century almshouses of Trinity Hospital and by urbane red-brick houses, the true magnificence of Holy Trinity church is not revealed until you enter the churchyard up a narrow lane. Then you see the spectacular nave, with its flushwork battlements recording the names of all the townspeople who contributed to the building, and its windows, so numerous that it seems all glass, a triumph of 15th-century architectural bravura. Contemporary with nearby LAVENHAM, it is far better proportioned, far more graceful. There, the church was a product of the wealth of two families; here it speaks of the spirit and communal endeavours of a much larger number of people and the many donors are depicted in

Kentwell Hall, Long Melford

stained glass of outstanding quality in the north aisle. At the eastern end of this same aisle is a lovely alabaster relief of the *Adoration of the Magi*, dating to 1350 and found beneath the chancel floor in the 18th century. Near by is the entrance to the Clopton Chantry Chapel, with its most beautiful Lily Crucifix window symbolising the shared suffering of Christ and his mother.

The Lady Chapel is a separate and curious structure to the east of the church, built in 1496 in the form of a completely enclosed cloister. The ambulatory, with its fine Tudor ceiling, may have been used as a processional way, surrounding the central chapel (*see* p. 93).

Melford Hall was built by William Cordell in the 1570s on land that, before the Dissolution of the Monasteries, was the country retreat and deer park of the abbots of Bury St Edmunds. The distinctive pepperpot turrets survive from that date, but much of the house reflects the

work carried out by the Parker family, who have lived here since they acquired the Hall in the 18th century. The rooms are remarkable for their ornate walnut furniture and there is a small display of water colours by Beatrix Potter, a relative of the family. The house is owned by the National Trust and is open in spring and summer.

Kentwell Hall lies to the north of the village, at the end of a mile-long drive planted with lime trees in 1678 which frame the distant view of the mellow red-brick Tudor manor house. The present moated hall was begun in the 1550s, and the owners mount regular 'historical recreations', using actors and musicians, in order to raise money for the extensive restoration work under way. Other attractions include the handsome brickwork maze, in the form of a Tudor rose, that fills the courtyard and a rare breeds farm. The house is open in summer.

Lound (3/4F) *see* Somerleyton

Lowestoft (3/4F)

Some imagination is required to picture Lowestoft, in far north-east Suffolk, as it was before the Second World War bombing and post-war development despatched most of the medieval town. Large-scale development began as early as 1847 when the arrival of the railway put Lowestoft within reach of London consumers, boosting the small-scale fishing activity into a major industry.

The best way to make sense of modern Lowestoft is to dissect it into its different parts. The harbour, with its twin lighthouses, was built in 1827–31 at the mouth of Lake Lothing. The lake itself was dug, like the Broads, for peat extraction and a cut was made linking it to the sea as part of the 19th-century harbour development. The harbour is now a yacht basin used by the Royal Lowestoft Yacht Club. The commercial port is further inland along the banks of the lake and is used principally by grain and timber ships and for boatbuilding.

South Town is the chief holiday resort and was developed as such from 1847 onwards. North of the harbour, the streets are pedestrianised and form one large shopping complex which runs uphill to the point where it meets the old fishing town. Further north still is the North Beach and Lowestoft Denes, an esplanade constructed around 1900 as a rival to the southern resort but never a success; for that reason it is now a pleasantly quiet area of the town, with excellent walks along the seafront.

The old town is architecturally the most rewarding, for the High Street has a good run of Georgian houses, including number 55, with its Venetian windows and richly ornamented doorcase. Running east of the High Street are numerous alleys, called 'scores', which were once lined with the pebble-built cottages of herring fishermen, with smokehouses attached. Most were bombed; instead of a view of the beach you now see, framed at the end of the

Lowestoft harbour

alleys, the huge Birds Eye factory. The best surviving scores are at the north end of the High Street around Upper Lighthouse (open in summer). This stands on the site of Britain's first ever lighthouse, powered originally by a coal fire.

To fill in the picture sketched by these scant remains it is best to visit the Maritime Museum in Whapload Road, with its models of boats and displays of fishing gear, or to take a guided harbour tour in a trawler (details from the Tourist Information Centre).

St Margaret's church is so far out of the town (on the B1074 to Oulton) that it scarcely seems to belong to it. The great dignity of the long church, with its 120-foot high spire, is compromised by the housing estates that sprawl all around its feet. Nave and chancel are full of impressive monuments to naval commanders; the stained glass windows were designed in 1819

the newly-established East Anglia Transport Museum, last resting place of the charabancs that once brought trippers on their annual summer outings, as well as trams, railway engines and steam rollers.

Mendlesham (5/4C)

Five miles north-east of Stowmarket, Mendlesham is a quiet village of mellow brick houses with an imposing church. Heraldic lions and wodehoses – wild, hairy men – mount guard on the pinnacles of the tall two-storey porch, and the upper storey contains a remarkable collection of armour, dating from 1470 to 1630, surviving from an age in which every village had an armoury and yeoman farmers were trained to resist the threat of invasion. The very accomplished architectural font cover and pulpit were made in 1630 by John Turner, one of a line of carpenters that once made the village famous for its chair-making industry. Now the name of Mendlesham is familiar because of the 1,000-foot-high transmitter that stands to the south-east of the village, erected in 1959 by the Independent Broadcasting Authority.

A mile and a half to the north-east, **Wetheringsett** is a lovely tree-shaded village with a stream running round the edge of a churchyard and, underneath, a curious thatched cottage built on stilts. All Saints is a handsome church with tall clerestory windows deep set between buttresses and a stately 13th-century nave.

Mettingham (3/2F) *see* Bungay

Mildenhall (1/3B)

The famous Mildenhall Treasure was discovered here, in the far north-west of the county, in 1946 and is now displayed in the British Museum. The splendid late Roman embossed dishes and goblets and the silver baptismal spoons, indicate the substantial wealth that a 4th-century estate owner enjoyed; no wonder then that Saxon raiders crossed the North Sea to strike deep into the heart of East Anglia. Many treasures of equal quality must have been lost but here at Mildenhall the owners buried it in the sandy Breckland soil, from which it was turned up by a ploughman some 1600 years on.

The people of modern Mildenhall enjoy one of Suffolk's finest churches, dedicated to St Mary and St Andrew and renowned for its series of spectacular 15th-century roofs. Iconoclastic Puritans fired off volleys of buckshot in an

by Robert Allen, a designer at the celebrated Lowestoft Porcelain factory.

Some of the products of that factory are displayed in the museum at **Oulton Broad**, 2 miles west of Lowestoft, together with exhibits on local history and archaeology. The Broad itself is the southernmost of the Broadlands network, linked to the Norfolk Broads by the River Waveney. It is a popular summer holiday resort with a lively water carnival in August.

Two miles to the south, at **Carlton Colville**, is

attempt to destroy it, but they failed and only the heads of the angels suffered any substantial damage. The best carving is in the north aisle, where monstrous dragons crouch on the hammerbeams above Biblical scenes.

It is instructive to compare these roofs with the sumptuous work at St Mary's church, **Lakenheath**, 5 miles further north, perhaps by the same carpenters. The benches down below are also carved with many a lively figure, including acrobats, leaping fish and a tigress looking at her reflection in a mirror.

Both Lakenheath and Mildenhall stand on the edge of huge U.S. Air Force bases and the combination of American accents and huge automobiles give these fen-edge towns a unique trans-Atlantic atmosphere.

Brandon, 5 miles north-east, is a major thoroughfare town for travellers heading towards north Norfolk, and has been for several centuries, as the large Georgian houses around the railway station, built as coaching inns, testify. South of the town, Brandon Country Park consists of 30 acres of landscaped grounds and woodland laid out around 1826 when the stucco-fronted Brandon Park House was built.

Monks Eleigh (5/2E) *see* Eleighs, The

Monk Soham (6/1C) *see* Sohams, The

Nayland (5/2F)

The best way to approach this pretty village 5 miles west of East Bergholt is along the narrow lane which climbs up Clicket Hill east of BURES, and follows the crest of a river terrace high above the River Stour. From this twisting, switchback road, every bend reveals a new view of Constable country, of lush green pastures dotted with ancient moated houses.

Just before reaching Nayland, it is well worth visiting the delightful church of St Mary which, with the Hall alongside, is all that remains of **Wissington**, a mile to the west of the village. Victorian restorers rebuilt the collapsed apse on its original foundations, but otherwise St Mary's is a rare and wholly unspoiled early Norman church. The nave walls are covered in 13th-century paintings, decipherable with the aid of Professor Tristram's drawings which hang on the north wall.

Wissington is the *hors d'oeuvre* to the feast which Nayland offers to the senses, a neat, pretty village of narrow winding streets and houses of great charm; Alston Court, in the centre, is especially fine and the big hooded doorcase, added around 1700, was the most recent addition to a house that dates to around 1480.

In Suffolk, where we are so used to churches standing well away from the villages, Nayland is a delightful exception. St James's is right in the centre, reached down a narrow path and ringed by cottages whose colourful gardens spill into the churchyard. Constable's painting of *Christ blessing bread and wine* remains in its intended place over the altar, though sensibly protected by an alarm system. Painted in 1809, it was his second and last attempt at a religious theme (his first, once in the church at nearby Brantham, has now been removed to IPSWICH, where it is displayed in Christchurch Mansion).

The B1087 north-east to **Stoke by Nayland** offers one of the most dramatic views of the Stour valley: all you see of the village is the 120-foot high church tower, standing proudly on top of the hill, above wooded slopes falling away to the valley below. Not until you round the bend that leads up the steep hill to the church do you discover the rows of exceptional timber-framed houses that form the core of the old village, consisting of the 16th-century Guildhall and Maltings.

St Mary's north porch is 16th-century, of brick, with trefoil-headed arcading like that at OXBURGH HALL (Norfolk). The south porch shelters a sumptuous door covered in the little figures, standing in niches, of a Jesse Tree. Inside, the noble nave arcade and the tall narrow tower arch, reaching right up to the roof, are a memorable sight. Among the outstanding brasses are those of Sir William Tendring (d. 1408), who fought at Agincourt, and of Dorothea Sanders (d. 1632), dressed in gorgeous lace and jewellery.

Needham Market (5/3D)

This growing town, 3 miles south-east of Stowmarket, has two highlights: one of them is the most deceptive church of St John the Baptist on the High Street. The little church was once a chapel to neighbouring Barking and looks undistinguished, its dusty flint walls rising from the pavement and an odd skylight poking up from the roof. Inside, the purpose of the skylight is revealed: the finest roof, by common agreement, in the whole of East Anglia, if not England. H. Munro Cautley, who wrote the first detailed studies of Suffolk churches, called it 'the culminating achievement of the English carpenter'. Needham's other hidden delight is

The roof in the church of St John the Baptist at Needham Market is one of the finest in England

the River Gipping which runs east of the High Street. On both roads out of the town, the B1078 and the by-road to Creeting, there are beautiful mill groups. The walk northwards along the river bank is a great delight.

Barking, 1½ miles south-west of Needham, was once the more populous parish until a plague struck in 1685. St Mary's church sits in the well-wooded grounds of the Hall. That building has gone, but the Rectory of 1819 stands above the church; yellow brick, the colour chosen to imitate stone, is used for the façade, while red brick is relegated to the less visible sides. The church has a fine terracotta window with Renaissance foliage ornamentation, one of a batch made for nearby Shrubland Hall in the 16th century that perhaps proved surplus to requirements. Inside, there are many examples of excellent carpentry – especially the roofs, the

delicate screens and the 14th-century vestry door.

The remote and unspoiled church of St Mary at **Badley** is reached by taking the B1113 towards Stowmarket and turning left about a mile out of Needham Market. A mile-long metalled track passes through cultivated fields; at the end you find the little church in a wild, overgrown hollow, where the only sound in summer is that of the larks. The key is held at the Hall, in the trees a little further on, which provides an excuse to see the 15th-century house with its dovecote and barns. Scarcely any change has taken place here in three centuries and the church, with its scrubbed oak pews, crown-post roof and quarry-tiled floor, is full of rustic atmosphere.

St Mary's church at neighbouring **Combs** was equally remote until Stowmarket began to throw out its post-war suburbs. Housing stops just short of the flower-filled meadows below the church.

Newmarket

SIR IAN TRETHOWAN

North from Six Mile Bottom, the road runs straight until a roundabout and a warning sign: 'Racehorses for 5 miles'. This is Newmarket. Ahead are two of Britain's most famous racecourses, over 60 training stables housing nearly 3,000 racehorses, one for every five of the town's human inhabitants. Stretching out on either side of the town are 4 square miles of training grounds, providing 40 miles of gallops or canters open on any one day. Within a few miles radius are over 50 stud farms, holding hundreds more thoroughbreds – famous horses which have become stallions, like Dancing Brave and Reference Point, well-bred mares to pleasure them and in due time produce the wide-eyed foals and the bucking yearlings which can be seen through the neat railed fencing which lines so many of the roads in the areas.

Newmarket is the undisputed headquarters of British racing and bloodstock breeding. It represents as great a concentration of thoroughbred racehorses as anywhere in the world, exceeding even that of the blue grass country of Kentucky.

According to legend, racing began here some 2,000 years ago, when Boudicca was encamped 2 miles down the road at Exning. It seems likely, however, that if she established any sport it would have been chariot racing rather than the Iceni Derby. What is more certain is that by 1200 the town was established as a staging post between Cambridge and Mildenhall. It was named after the purpose it served – a 'new market'. The records show that the little town remained in utter obscurity for 400 years, emerging only through chance; one day James I stopped on his way north to course some local hares, enjoyed himself and decided to come again to the Newmarket heathland which seemed to offer such good opportunities for sport. At first he came mainly to indulge his passion for harecoursing, but in time horse races became established and the roots were planted of today's large and highly sophisticated equine industry.

James I was an unlikely founder of a great racing centre. He was an ungainly, if enthusiastic, horseman himself and the roistering, gaming Newmarket of late Stuart times was a far cry from his strict, gloomy childhood under the forbidding glare of the Scottish Presbyters. His son, Charles I, also enjoyed Newmarket, but became increasingly and disastrously distracted by politics. The Cromwellian interregnum was scarcely conducive to sport, and it was left to Charles II to establish racing at Newmarket on a formal, regulated basis. Charles was an excellent horseman and twice won the Newmarket Town Plate, the oldest race in England – and the longest, at nearly 4 miles – still to be run. He laid down the first known rules of racing.

Charles II also, by all accounts, turned Newmarket into a place of unbridled pleasure. During his two annual visits, corresponding roughly to the present spring and autumn meetings, the whole court followed in his wake. Nell Gwynn used to stay in Palace Street, appropriately convenient to the Palace which had been built to house the King and his retinue. The Palace has long disappeared but Nell Gwyn's house still stands. The diarist John Evelyn spent a night in Newmarket in Charles's time and found it, 'more resembling a luxurious and abandoned rout than a Christian Court'. Charles never found too much difficulty in relaxing, particularly nocturnally, and when he sought anonymity he took the name of his favourite stallion – 'Old Rowley'. In memory of its founder, the larger and older of Newmarket's two racecourses calls itself 'The Rowley Mile'.

Throughout his reign Charles was never far from treasonable plots, and in 1683 a group of dissidents planned to use his regular trips to Newmarket to seize him at a convenient point on the road back to London, at Rye House. But there was a fire at Newmarket, Charles left early, and it was the plotters who died.

Charles's Stuart successors maintained an interest in Newmarket, but it abruptly fell from favour with the arrival of the Hanoverian Kings, who had scant interest in England as a whole, let alone a small town in one of its bleaker corners. Deprived of Royal patronage, racing on the Heath declined for a time, but by the mid-1700s the young London bucks were back and the seal was set on Newmarket's racing presence by the foundation of the Jockey Club. (The word 'Jockey' is today a complete misnomer, but in the 18th century owners as well as riders were called 'Jockeys'.) The Jockey Club assumed the regulation of racing, which it holds to this day, and has headquarters in both London and Newmarket.

Stud farm paddocks, Newmarket

The Jockey Club Rooms at Newmarket stand on the right in the High Street, about a third of the way down. The original 18th-century building was badly damaged by fire, but part of it still remains and the rest was rebuilt in the 1930s with a care for preserving the original style.

Before reaching the High Street, however, there is much to see. On the left at the roundabout is the National Stud, originally an Irish stud farm, given to the nation in 1916. It was transported to England when Southern Ireland became independent and, after a sojourn in Dorset, found a final home at Newmarket, where at one stage it housed three Derby winners – Blakeney, Mill Reef and Grundy.

Next to the Stud is the entrance to the July Course, where Newmarket races in the summer and across the Heath – beyond the Devil's Ditch, which stretches for 6 miles and is believed to be an ancient fortification – is the Rowley Mile course, which races in spring and autumn. They are very different. The July Course on a sunny afternoon has a garden party air – straw hats,

pretty summer dresses, the crowds free to mingle with the horses quietly ambling under the trees before moving into the paddock to meet their jockeys. The evening meetings have more of a fairground atmosphere, with larger, more boisterous crowds.

Racing on the Rowley Mile is altogether a more serious affair. Here, for the big races – in the spring the first two Classics, the 1,000 and 2,000 Guineas, in the autumn the Champion Stakes and the big two-year-old tests – gather racing's professionals, owners, breeders, trainers and bloodstock agents. They come not only for the races, but for the major bloodstock sales at Tattersalls on the other side of the High Street.

Most of the best known horses in racing history have won big races at Newmarket, particularly the two Classics. In the 19th century the 2,000 Guineas winners included Bay Middleton, Stockwell and West Australian, while in the 20th century there have been such famous names as

Newmarket gallops

Blue Peter, Sir Ivor and Nijinsky (all of whom went on to win the Derby), together with Tudor Minstrel and Brigadier Gerard – the list is endless. Recent 1,000 Guineas winners have included the remarkable Pebbles and the legendary French filly Miesque.

In one respect racing at Newmarket is unique. American visitors used to their tight, oval tracks, with every yard of the running clearly visible, are stunned to discover that races on the Rowley Mile take place on a dead straight track, stretching away for 1¼ miles. Even the long distance races, like the 2¼ mile Cesarewitch, have only one bend and actually start in the next county. As Newmarket people say: 'You hang around in Suffolk for a race which starts in Cambridgeshire.' Clearly the Newmarket courses are not ideal for viewing, but they represent a tough, fair test of a horse's stamina and courage and there are plenty of television sets around on which to watch the opening furlongs. Visitors with little experience of racing can gain from a day at Newmarket some sense of the institution created by 'Old Rowley'.

Newmarket appropriately houses the National Horseracing Museum, just a few yards down from the Jockey Club. Its centre piece is the skeleton of the great Eclipse and there are interesting photographs and memorabilia from many sources of British racing. The Museum organises tours not only of the Museum itself, but of the National Stud, the racecourses and the gallops, as well as visits to a training stable and sometimes a nearby private stud farm.

The tour can also sometimes take in the Jockey Club Rooms, elegant in themselves and housing some of the finest of British sporting paintings, including in the Morning Room Stubbs's pictures of Eclipse and Gimcrack. Visitors can see other famous paintings and such memorabilia as the Jockey Club Whip allegedly made with hairs from Eclipse's tail. The Stewards' Room is racing's court of justice, where serious disciplinary cases are heard. The Stewards sit round a horseshoe table and the defendant jockey or trainer faces them, standing on a strip of carpet just inside the door – from which comes the term 'on the mat'.

But if the Jockey Club Rooms exemplify the administration of racing, it is in the stables and on the training grounds that you find working Newmarket. The stables vary, from the elegance of the phenomenally successful Henry Cecil's, with nearly 200 horses, all beautifully bred, to smaller yards, where eager newcomers try to scratch a living from 20 or 30 much humbler horses.

The routine is much the same. Starting in the early morning, the horses are exercised in shifts (which racing people call 'lots'). A stable lad (or increasingly, girl) will look after at least two horses, sometimes even four. It is a hard life and they are not well paid, but the younger stable staff dream of moving on to become professional jockeys and – who knows – a Piggott or a Carson.

Newmarket has two main areas of gallops – to the south-west of the town, by the racecourse, and to the north-west, along the road to Bury St Edmunds. The turf on Newmarket Heath, centuries old, provides a wonderful, springy, sympathetic surface for horses at exercise, but even the finest, carefully maintained grass will eventually become uncomfortably hard in fine weather and unpleasantly soggy after much rain. In recent years, therefore, Newmarket has developed a number of artificial gallops, impervious to changes in the weather. One of the first and most successful was laid down through the generosity of one of the Arab owners who are playing an increasingly prominent, even dominant, part in modern British racing.

One does not have to be a racing fanatic, or even knowledgeable, to relish the sights of Newmarket – the neat, trim stables, the well tended gallops and, perhaps above all, the strings of horses threading their way through the streets of the town, stretching into a trot or a careful canter as they reach the training grounds and then, under the watchful eye of their trainer, moving into a full gallop. There appears to be no particular pattern to the movement of the horses, but each one is being worked to a careful schedule set by his trainer: often just walking exercise, sometimes cantering and only occasionally a flat out gallop. The pattern of training racehorses in Newmarket was set over 200 years ago and the skills have been passed down racing families which have lived and worked in Newmarket for generations – Armstrong, Jarvis, Piggott, the names recur in the town's history.

Newmarket is also the centre of the bloodstock sales industry. Tattersalls, the firm which has been prominent in the English market for over 200 years, has its headquarters in The Avenue, just off the High Street. Richard Tattersall held his first sales near Hyde Park Corner in London, but the firm gradually became established in Newmarket and all that is left in the modern sales

complex of its London persona is a little statue of a fox set under a rotunda. In Newmarket there are also other ancillary racing activities: an apprentice training school and the Horseracing Forensic Laboratory, which tests whether or not horses have been doped.

But the town is not all horses. Apart from the famous Newmarket sausages, large and highly spiced, there has in recent years been a growth of light industry – a caravan firm, for instance, and another manufacturing computers. During the Second World War, there was a bomber airfield sited near the racecourse. A hole in the Devil's Ditch shows the line on which the planes took off and the control tower remains as part of the racecourse buildings.

Leaving Newmarket on the Bury road, 2 miles out on the left hand side, at the Chippenham crossroads, there is a little enclosure which always holds a cluster of fresh flowers. This is the Boy's Grave. According to legend, a shepherd boy fell asleep on the Heath and when he woke up he found a dog, or a wolf, had killed a number of his sheep. Mortified, he killed himself and was buried here. Who leaves the flowers on the grave no one seems to know – possibly gypsies.

According to another legend, the colour of the flowers on Derby Day will be those of the winner. Sadly, history shows that legend hardly ever accords with fact. But in a town which lives on horseracing, which in turn lives on hope, one should not spurn the fanciful.

The heaths around Newmarket make poor farming land and there are few settlements of any antiquity in the vicinity. The lovely pack-horse bridge over the River Kennet at **Moulton**, 4 miles east of Newmarket, marks the ancient route between Cambridge and Bury St Edmunds. At **Gazeley**, another 2 miles to the east, the Earl of Clare built a short-lived motte-and-bailey castle whose earthworks, east of the village, have reverted to nature. The village itself has early 19th-century flint-and-brick houses grouped around the green, and All Staints' church is remarkable for the unusual form of the Early English chancel windows.

At neighbouring Dalham, 2 miles to the south, the scenery changes from flat, windswept fields to gently wooded hills, cut by the River Kennet, which is here little more than a stream. This flows through the gardens of the pretty village cottages. The village hall was built in memory of Cecil Rhodes, who purchased Dalham Hall but died before taking up residence. The Hall, a fine Queen Anne building, stands high above the village to the north, next to St Mary's church, a large Perpendicular building with a low tower, rebuilt after the steeple collapsed in about 1625.

North Cove (6/3A) *see* Beccles

Norton (5/2C) *see* Stowlangtoft

Orford (6/3E)
Those who like to get well away from the crowds should seek out Orford, 10 miles east of Woodbridge, on a weekday out of season, and enjoy the peacefulness of this fascinating village perched on the edge of the River Alde. It consists simply of a broad market place, with a castle to the west, church to the east, quay to the south and miles of lonely marsh stretching up to ALDEBURGH and down to BAWDSEY.

St Bartholomew's church is famous as the setting for the first performance of Britten's *Noye's Fludde* (1958). The great broad nave and aisles are built of the local septaria, a soft, young stone that looks like sun-dried mud. At the east end of the nave pointed arches rest on massive Norman piers and blocked arches represent the beginning of the tower crossing of a once-magnificent 12th-century church. The original chancel lies in ruins to the east, with enough of its piers remaining to hint at the lost Romanesque splendour.

The history of the church is tied up with that of the castle, whose Norman keep towers above the coast to a height of 90 feet west of the market place. It is now maintained by English Heritage. Both were built for Henry II in 1165–67 and the castle, sited here for coastal defence, was of a revolutionary new type, polygonal in shape and less likely to collapse if undermined. Magnificent views of the village and coast are to be enjoyed from the summit.

Down by the little quay, where fishing boats and leisure yachts are moored, you can take a boat (book in advance with the warden) to the R.S.P.B. reserve on Havergate Island, where avocets have returned to breed after a long absence (*see* 'Coastal Birds of East Anglia,' p. 32).

Orford Ness, a 6-mile long shingle bank and site of a pre-war radar research station, is accessible only by boat. At the north end a huge colony of lesser black-backed and herring gulls comes here to breed in the spring.

Five miles north of Orford at **Iken**, the church of St Botolph stands above the muddy tidal reaches of the River Alde, remote from the busy world. There was a monastic cell here as early as AD 647 and the chancel contains a Saxon cross shaft carved with interlace knots and intertwined dragons. The nave was all but destroyed by fire in 1968, and the parish of only 60 people is grateful for any contribution towards its restoration.

At **Blaxhall**, 3 miles to the west, St Peter's church is enlivened by delightful Arts and Crafts stained glass and monuments designed by Margaret and Dorothy Rope. West of the church, Stone Farm is named after a great slab of rock which, according to local legend, has grown from the size of a small loaf over the last 100 years.

Otley (6/1D) *see* Helmingham

Oulton Broad (3/4F) *see* Lowestoft

Packenham (5/2C) *see* Ixworth

Peasenhall (6/2C)
The main street of Peasenhall, 6 miles north-west of Saxmundham, perpetuates the line of a Roman road and is accompanied for the whole of its length by a rivulet that drains water from the surrounding fields. On either side, painted cottages stand side by side like slabs of colour in a Victorian candy jar.

Some 15th-century linenfold panelling from the Swan Inn was recently rescued by the vicar and reused in the church of St Michael, at the west end of the village. The church porch has a boldly carved dragon and club-wielding wode-hose carved in its spandrels.

The southern edge of the churchyard is bordered by the 1805 Drill Mill, in which the village wheelwright, James Smyth, manufactured his 'Nonpareil' seed drills, progenitor of those that are still used widely in the country to this day.

East of Peasenhall, the pretty River Yor flows through several formally landscaped parks to the former coaching town of **Yoxford**, now a local centre of arts and crafts galleries and antique shops. Outside St Peter's church stands an ornate cast-iron signpost of 1830, with hands pointing to London, Yarmouth and Framlingham.

Playford (6/1E) *see* Grundisburgh

Polstead (5/2F)
Three miles north-east of Nayland, this village nestles in wooded, hilly countryside, threaded with high-banked narrow lanes, the genuine Suffolk as many still remember it before the great robbery of our hedges.

Orford Castle

In this idyllic setting, a murder took place 150 years ago which shocked the nation. Time has now lent the Red Barn Murder an almost fictional glamour and tourists come in search of the scenes of the crime, armed with the excellent village guide, available at the church. The truth was horrible enough; Maria Marten was brutally murdered by the father of her illegitimate child, William Corder, and the crime remained undiscovered until Maria's stepmother dreamed that the corpse was buried under the floor of the Red Barn. So it was, and Corder was hanged for the murder at Bury St Edmunds in 1828.

Polstead means 'place of pools' and a large and picturesque duck pond fills the centre of the village. Opposite and to the west, a leafy track leads uphill to St Mary's, a most intriguing church. Built around 1160, almost the entire fabric is of Roman tile, brick and ragstone, which suggests that a substantial Roman building survived here well into the 12th century. To confuse matters further, some of the brick is of different proportions and of rougher texture than the Roman material, which seems to suggest that the Norman builders had mastered the technique of brick-making before, or simultaneously with, the first revival of the craft in the Low Countries.

Two miles to the north-west, **Boxford** is another delightful, quiet and unspoiled vilage, offering beautiful vistas over the meadows watered by the River Box. All the houses are painted, even the council houses, in idiosyncratic colour combinations which may seem garish to some visitors, lovable to others. The north porch of St Mary's church is the oldest surviving in Suffolk and very unusual. It is built of timber, with 13th-century Decorated tracery and curving timbers that meet in the centre of the roof to form a large suspended boss. Perhaps many more porches like this once existed, but most, like the south porch here, were replaced by stone and flint flushwork extravaganzas in the 15th century.

Immediately west of the church is the delightful garden of Chequers, which is open under the National Gardens Scheme. The River Box flows through the grounds, which are planted naturalistically with bulbs chosen to provide year-round colour, from the earliest snowdrops to the last colchicums of the autumn.

Two miles north-west, at **Edwardstone**, the church of St Mary lies within the grounds of the Hall, most of which was pulled down in 1952, leaving only a simple, timber-framed farm-house. The Jacobean pulpit in the church is one of the most ornate in Suffolk; Victorian restorers enhanced the atmospheric building, with its earthy brick floors, by providing pews with stepped gable ends and wrought-iron chandeliers.

Redgrave (5/3B)

The village of Redgrave, 4 miles south-west of Diss, has shifted over the years, leaving the church of St Mary all alone a mile to the west. Perhaps the church was already isolated by the 15th century, for it escaped being rebuilt in the Perpendicular style. It stands, instead, as a rare example in East Anglia of near complete 14th-century Decorated architecture, with a lovely east window of flowing reticulated tracery.

Nearby Redgrave Park once had a Tudor house, built for Lord Keeper Bacon, that was pulled down in the 1940s after having served as a prisoner-of-war camp. The family name survives in the outstanding group of memorials in St Mary's church. The source of the Waveney is a mile north of Redgrave (see also LOPHAMS, THE, Norfolk) and the river forms the county boundary, flowing through marshy commons that are a haven for wildlife.

St Mary's church at **Wortham**, 1½ miles east, is similarly isolated. The round tower is the broadest in England, with a diameter of 29 feet. The upper stages collapsed in 1780, so that the two remaining stages are scarcely taller than the nave, which is lit by a fine series of Perpendicular windows linked by a frieze of flushwork panels. The tower may well have served a defensive function, for the River Waveney to the north was a route used by Scandinavian invaders as late as the 11th century.

At Burgate a mile south of Wortham, the church of St Mary contains one of Suffolk's foremost brasses, that of Sir William Burgate (d. 1409) and his wife.

Rendlesham (6/2E) see Woodbridge

Rickinghall Inferior and Superior (5/3B) see Botesdale

Rougham (5/2C) see Hessett

Rumburgh (6/2A)

Six miles north-west of Halesworth, the church of St Michael and St Felix at Rumburgh stands alongside the late 17th-century Abbey Farmhouse, and both are contained within a moat. A priory founded here in 1064 was given to St Mary's Abbey in York in the late 12th century; the broad west tower was built shortly afterwards, with its three lancet windows. The tower looks incomplete, as if further height was intended, and the church itself is very simple, with a lovely ornate traceried screen.

Bloomsbury *aficionados* may recognise the name of **Wissett**, 2 miles to the south-east; it was here, at Wissett Lodge, that Duncan Grant and David Garnett worked as farm labourers during the First World War, after appearing before a conscientious objectors' tribunal. They chose a pretty village, with a stream crossed by white footbridges all along the length of the principal street. St Andrew's church stands by the same stream and has a good Norman doorway, carved with primitive beakheads.

Rushbrooke (5/1C) *see* Hessett.

Saxhams, The (4/3C)
The churches of Great and Little Saxham, 3 miles west of Bury St Edmunds, both contain monuments to colourful characters. St Andrew's, **Great Saxham**, lies along a delightful leafy lane and contains the bust of John Eldred (d. 1632), whose travels in Turkey are described in Hakluyt's *Voyages*. Eldred made a fortune from importing spices and built himself a mansion called Nutmeg Hall, which, alas, does not survive.

St Nicholas's, **Little Saxham**, has a lovely ornate Saxo-Norman round tower and inside, in the north chapel, is an outstanding monument to William Lucas (d. 1677) and his wife, carved by Abraham Storey, one of Christopher Wren's top masons. Lucas was Gentleman of the Bedchamber to Charles II during the king's exile.

Nearly 3 miles to the south, All Saints' church at **Chevington** is full of fine woodwork and has an unusually tall and narrow chancel arch – only 7 feet wide – and a fine 14th-century chest carved with traceried panels.

Saxmundham (6/2C)
The character of Saxmundham, 6 miles north-west of Aldeburgh on the A12, was much altered in the 19th century when the railway arrived and the ancient market town became an important centre of iron working and engineering. It is now a town of brick: the Market Place, formerly 7 acres in extent, has been filled in with Victorian structures, including the Bell Hotel of

Lychgate, Kelsale

Somerleyton Hall

1842 and Town Hall of 1846. Next to the Post Office, Wells the Ironmonger retains much of its florid Art Nouveau shop front.

Neighbouring **Kelsale**, just over a mile to the north, has a splendid guildhall, built around 1495 and enhanced by excellent 1891 additions in early Arts and Crafts style. It is now used as the Suffolk Teachers' Centre. The Arts and Crafts influence continues in the fine lychgate leading to a lime avenue and the church of St Mary and St Peter. The highly ornate Jacobean pulpit was so admired by the parishioners of nearby ALDEBURGH that in 1631 they sent their carpenter to see it and ordered one of similar design.

Saxstead Green (6/1C) *see* Sohams, The

Shotley (6/1F)
Nine miles south-east of Ipswich, Shotley Gate stands on the very tip of the peninsula formed by the estuaries of the Rivers Stour and Orwell.

north are best, up the Orwell, past HMS *Ganges*, not a ship but a land-based former naval training station, over to the Frimley Marshes. The view may soon be lost, however, as plans have been announced for a major yacht marina off Shotley Point.

The little church of St Mary is in Shotley Street, a mile inland and pebble-dashed like a seaside bungalow. The chancel within is nevertheless delightful. Rebuilt in 1745, it has a coved ceiling decorated with stucco cherubs, floating above a chequerboard floor, and an elegant communion table.

At **Erwarton**, a mile to the west, the church of St Mary is built of the local sandy septaria stone. There is a persistent legend that Anne Boleyn's heart was buried here, in the family vault of her uncle, Philip Calthorpe (d. 1549). This is just one of the many fine monuments in the church. The Calthorpes' home, Erwarton Hall, can be seen from the road north of the church. It is fronted by an extraordinary red-brick Jacobean gatehouse, sprouting numerous chimney-shaped finials.

Two miles west again at **Harkstead**, the flat countryside is enlivened by numerous trees and small fields enclosed by thick hedges, full of white blossom in summer. The simple church of St Mary was enlarged by Victorian restorers in 1875, who added an altar surround of blue, white and gold tiles ornamented with vines, wheatsheaves, lily flowers and Evangelists' symbols.

Snape (6/2D) *see* Aldeburgh

Sohams, The (6/1C)
Earl Soham was named after the Earls of Norfolk, whose seat was 3 miles east at FRAMLINGHAM, and a lake which has since disappeared (Old English *sae* originally meant 'lake' rather than 'sea'). Handsome houses now back on to the hollow where the lake once was. St Mary's church, at the east end of the village, has a very varied set of bench ends, some of which are restored, some probably Victorian, but none the less enjoyable for that.

Neighbouring **Monk Soham** had an abbey which, like the lake, has gone; but we are reminded of it in the four monks seated around the stem of the fine Seven Sacraments font in St Peter's church. There is a fine hammerbeam roof to the nave, minus its angels, flowing Decorated tracery in the chancel and a huge 14th-century iron-bound chest.

The village seems almost a part of Harwich, whose spired church, across the bay in Essex, rises above the marshes. The bay is full of ships of all kinds, from lightships and tiny fishing boats to the giant ferries that cross the North Sea to the Hook of Holland. Except at weekends, the village is remarkably tranquil; the only sounds are the lapping of water against the wooden landing stages which project from the short quay and the distant clank of gantries in the container port at Harwich. Footpaths thread through the marshes of the estuary: the views

Saxstead Green, 2 miles east, does indeed sit around a green, a large marshy one that is covered with moisture-loving wild flowers and drifts of buttercups in early summer. This sets off to perfection the beautiful four-sailed corn mill that stands on the green, preserved in immaculate working order by English Heritage. It is open daily except Sundays in summer.

Somerleyton (3/3F)

Sir Morton Peto, who developed Lowestoft, 4 miles to the south-east, as a seaside resort, built this village and its extravagant Hall. He began Somerleyton Hall in 1844, was elected M.P. for Norwich in 1847, was one of the guarantors of the 1851 Great Exhibition and was created baronet in 1855. This glittering career collapsed in 1866 when his firm went bankrupt and Peto disappeared into obscurity. Trollope had men such as Peto in mind when he wrote his great novel *The Way We Live Now*. (Carbury, the setting for much of that novel, is based on SOUTH ELMHAM, less than 15 miles from here.)

The house that Peto built is now open to the public in summer, a wonderful example of *nouveau riche* taste on which no expense was spared. The gardens are equally fascinating as an example of mid-Victorian formal planting. Paxton's glass houses have been fully restored and there is a notable yew maze, planted in 1846, as well as magnificent stands of azaleas and rhododendrons, with much garden statuary mixed in.

The village to the west of the house is a little more restrained, but even here the neo-Tudor cottages are highly fanciful, with patterned thatched roofs and large shaped chimneys. By contrast the church of St Mary, rebuilt in 1854 by the same architect as the Hall, John Thomas, is not at all eccentric; a copy-book Suffolk flint church in Perpendicular style.

At **Herringfleet**, scarcely a mile to the west, the church of St Margaret stands on a bank above the River Waveney. It is an endearing church with a Saxon round tower, pierced by pairs of triangular-headed windows and an assemblage of glass – some 15th-century English, the rest brought from the Franciscan friary at Cologne in the 19th century.

Two miles to the east at **Lound**, the church of St John the Baptist also has a Saxon tower, but the real interest is the furnishings of 1912–14. There is a jolly organ at the west end, painted as gaily as a fairground organ and with two flute-playing angels to either side of the bank of pipes;

a great tall spire of a gilded font cover, a sumptuous gilded, ribbed, painted and coved chancel screen and lovely rich altar curtains of Spanish silk, dyed to an old rose pink. Only one person in England could have been responsible for this – Sir Ninian Comper, employed at his own expense by the incumbent, the Revd Lynes. Comper rewarded him with a church of great grace, medieval in spirit and yet of its own time; spiritual but also great fun. There is even a joke in the big St Christopher wall painting on the north wall, for Comper wittily added himself driving his Rolls-Royce; in 1964, restorers also added a Bristol Britannia aircraft, in the sky above St Christopher's head.

South Elmhams, The (6/2A)

Seven hamlets, beginning 2 miles south of Bungay, share the suffix South Elmham, each of them little more than a church and a scatter of farms and collectively known to local people as 'The Saints'. The churches are unfortunately all rather dull, but the landscape is very unusual, especially the unenclosed commons to the east, linking All Saints, St Michael and St Peter.

The historian Norman Scarfe has argued convincingly (in *The Suffolk Landscape*, Alastair Press, 1987) that all seven parishes, together with Flixton and Homersfield to the north, were originally units within a late Saxon episcopal estate. What is more, he suggests that the Minster was founded in the 7th century as a result of the missionary work of St Felix. The Minster lies across a barley field, midway between St Cross and St James, a building of national importance but difficult of access. The surviving ruins have long fascinated historians but archaeological excavations have failed to resolve the date or explain the purpose of the church. Victorian antiquarians chose to believe that it was the Saxon cathedral of the South Folk (Suffolk) diocese: the counterpart to the North Folk cathedral at NORTH ELMHAM (Norfolk).

Southwold (6/4B)

This small town is the jewel of the Suffolk coast, 'a residential resort for discriminating persons', as Norman Scarfe put it in the original Shell Guide. How the town has managed to stay unspoilt is quite remarkable. There are no gimcrack souvenir shops, no fast-food outlets or amusement arcades – just a beach, famous for its coloured pebbles, and rows of pastel-painted beach huts, which give the resort an Edwardian air – local caterers even serve pots of tea on the beach. When it is too cold to swim there are long walks through the marshes to the north and, when the weather is too bad even for that, there is the compensation of the excellent Adnams beer, brewed in the heart of the town and delivered by horse-drawn dray to the several pubs.

The brewery, the church and the gleaming white pepperpot lighthouse are all near neighbours around the town green, mixed in with Georgian brick houses and colourful pantiled former fishermen's cottages. St Edmund's is one of Suffolk's most celebrated churches, admirable in its sheer height and airiness; the Second World War was partly responsible for this, as the Victorian glass was blown out and replaced by clear windows – all except for Sir Ninian Comper's east window of 1954 which shows the martyrdom of St Edmund. The division between the nave and chancel is marked only by a set of 15th-century screens; the roof, which is carved with angels in the nave, is painted with stars against a blue sky in the chancel. By the tower at the rear of the church is the figure known as 'Southwold Jack', who strikes a bell with the battle-axe in his right hand to mark the beginning of services. He dates from about 1480 and is dressed in the basinet helmet and armour of the men-at-arms who fought in the Wars of the Roses.

South of the church on Bartholomew Green is an excellent small museum of local history, which shows how several unsuccessful attempts were made to establish a major harbour and fishery here in the 18th century, each effort defeated by the unrelenting seas.

Stoke by Clare (4/3E) *see* Clare

Stoke by Nayland (5/2F) *see* Nayland

Stonham Aspal (5/4D) *see* Stonhams, The

Stonhams, The (5/4D)
The churches of the three Stonham villages, 4 miles east of Stowmarket, all display magnificent woodwork. St Mary's **Earl Stonham** has one of the richest roofs in the county, a *tour de force* of the carpenter's skill. Below, excellent Victorian pews with poppyheads fill the nave.

A mile north, St Mary's church at **Little Stonham** is tucked in between the old barns of Hall Farm. Here an equally splendid roof has sadly lost its angels, and woodwork panelling lines the church. Just to the north, on the A140,

the Magpie Inn is a well-loved local landmark, with its 16th-century wrought-iron magpie perched on a frame that spans the width of the road.

Visitors to the church of St Mary and St Lambert at **Stonham Aspal** are greeted by the effigy of the Revd Anthony Wingfield, a bewigged figure in stone reclining in the churchyard. The splendid set of bench ends is Jacobean and therefore an unusually late example.

Two miles south, All Saints' church at **Crowfield** has a delightful timber-framed chancel, unique in Suffolk and rare enough anywhere. It looks as if a domestic house or wool merchants' guildhall has been added to a small Perpendicular church. The interior is as heavily timbered as the exterior and the arched braces of the fine 15th-century porch are carved with angels, flowers and a broody hen.

Stowlangtoft (5/2C)
In this village 2 miles south-east of Ixworth, the raised position of St George's church shows off the magnificent building to great advantage. The whole church was rebuilt by Robert Davey de Ashfield, 'servant to the Black Prince', in 1401 and the exceptionally tall windows contain some of the original glass as well as Flemish 16th-century work added during 19th-century restoration. From the pre-1401 church the fine though mutilated font survives, carved with saints and their emblems rather than with the standard Suffolk Evangelists. Outstanding Flemish carvings were stolen in 1986 and have been traced to Amsterdam; efforts for their recovery continue. Fortunately the outstanding and varied bench ends and misericords remain intact. They comprise a complete bestiary and include grotesques that are unusual or unique in England.

Equally fine misericords are found in St Andrew's church at **Norton**, 2 miles to the south, but these almost certainly came from elsewhere: perhaps BURY ST EDMUNDS'S abbey. The excellent 15th-century glass includes depictions of St Christopher and St Appollonia, patron saint of toothache sufferers, who holds a pair of massive pincers.

Stowmarket (5/3D)
This lively town in the heart of Suffolk has few buildings of any architectural pretension but serves as the shopping centre for a prosperous agricultural region, and the streets are full of colour and bustle on market days. The town grew rapidly in the 19th century when the River

Museum of East Anglian Life, Stowmarket

Gipping was canalised, creating a navigable link to Ipswich; there is a delightful walk along the old towpath through the town and into open countryside to the south-east.

West of the market place is the award-winning Museum of East Anglian Life, situated in 70 acres of the former Abbots Hall estate. The open-air section contains carefully reconstructed buildings from the region: a working water mill, engineering workshop, and a 14th-century aisled farmhouse. The museum covers rural crafts, with working demonstrations by wheelwrights, coopers, basket-, harness- and rake-makers, but also the important industrial heritage of East Anglia: fertiliser production, brickmaking and agricultural engineering. Throughout the year there is a lively programme of lectures and temporary exhibitions.

At **Haughley**, 3 miles north-west of Stowmarket, St Mary's church has a collection of 18th-century fire buckets and an unusual arch-braced roof, ornamented with large florid bosses. The church stands in the shadow of Suffolk's largest Norman motte and bailey: the mound 80 foot high and the bailey enclosing 7 acres. Haughley Park, which is open on Tuesdays in summer, is well to the west of the village. Built in 1620, but in a conservative style that is as much Elizabethan as Jacobean, the charming red-brick house has been very well restored after a fire in 1961 and is surrounded by acres of lovely gardens and woodland.

At **Wetherden** village, just north of this estate, St Mary's church stands beside a tributary of the River Gipping, surrounded by huge lime trees planted in 1750 by the Revd Richard Ray.

Elmswell, the next village to the north-west, grew when the railway arrived in the 1840s and continues to spread. The church of St John stands at the western extremity of the town, its noble tower recently restored to pristine condition so that the flushwork can be seen as it must have looked when new in 1476.

Stratford St Mary (5/3F) *see* East Bergholt

Stutton (5/4F) *see* Tattingstone

Sudbury (5/1E)
This ancient borough just over the south-

western border with Essex, centre of wool-weaving and later of silk production, is well on the way towards a massive growth in its population, from 7,000 at the beginning of the 1960s to a projected 16,000. New roads into the town lie at the bottom of cuttings, so you do not see much of the mass housing and utilitarian factory sheds that now ring the town.

Sudbury never was a town immune from change. St Peter's church, which stands proudly at the top of Market Hill, is now redundant and used principally as a concert hall. A bronze statue of Gainsborough, Sudbury's most famous son, stands outside the church, looking down over the commercial heart of the town and its splendid Victorian buildings.

On the right, the Black Boy Hotel is the only example of timber-framing, its neo-Tudor front hiding an older structure. Opposite is a fine run of decorative brick houses, now all banks except for the flamboyant Italianate baroque Corn Exchange, designed by H. E. Kendall in 1841. It has recently been converted with great sympathy by the county architect Jack Digby, into a library and information centre, worth visiting for the airy, skylit interior.

At the bottom of Market Hill, the road divides: Gainsborough Street to the right leads to the birthplace of the great painter. The grand red-brick façade was added by Gainsborough's father, perhaps in 1727, the year in which Thomas was born. The house is now a museum used to display paintings by Gainsborough and his contemporaries and to host the occasional exhibition of contemporary art. Further west, Gainsborough Street becomes Stour Street. Here several ornate timber-framed houses survive, notably Salters Hall, a merchant's house, and the Old Moot Hall. Both are 15th-century, with oriel windows and much carving.

The left fork out of Market Hill leads to the long and winding Friars Street, with its pleasing westward prospect of Regency houses. A little way down on the left, Bullocks Lane leads past the fragmentary remains of the Dominican priory, founded in 1248 and now incorporated into a Georgian house. The lane leads on to Friars Meadows and the Valley Walk, which follows the course of the old Stour Valley railway, parallel with the river. After this path crosses the A131, south-west of the town, there are some fine views of the willow-fringed banks of the river, of Sudbury Basin, used by Stour barges until 1913, and of the 19th-century waterside mill, now converted to an hotel.

St Gregory's church, standing on the northern fringes of the town, was rebuilt in about 1365 by Simon Sudbury, who was made Archbishop of

Gainsborough's House, Sudbury

Canterbury in 1375 and was beheaded in 1381 in the Peasants' Revolt. His skull is preserved in the vestry and there is an exhibition covering his life and times in the south chapel. The splendid 15th-century font cover compares in magnificence to the famous one at UFFORD. Southwest of the church, the stone and brick gateway once led to a college founded by Archbishop Sudbury. The view through the gate is to the former workhouse, now a hospital.

Sutton (6/2E)

On the east bank of the River Deben opposite Woodbridge, Sutton is the gateway to the sparsely populated peninsula formed by the Deben to the west and the complex river system of the Butley and the Alde to the east. It is an area of sandy heath which is intensively farmed; to the north, great stretches of pine forest were wiped from the map in the storms of October 1987, but replanting has taken place on an extensive scale. To the south, fields are kept productive only by continual irrigation.

Sutton Hoo, perhaps England's most famous archaeological site after Stonehenge, represents one of the highest points (at 30 metres) in this windswept landscape. The site, which includes a dozen burial mounds, is open at weekends in summer and is accessible from the B1083 or by ferry from Woodbridge. The original ship burial, excavated in 1939, was found to contain an extraordinary wealth of material, now displayed in the British Museum. It may have been the grave of Raedwald, king of East Anglia, who died in AD 625. Early in the 1980s there began a new campaign of excavation, survey and research which will reveal more information about the Anglo-Saxon people, who began their immigration from northern Europe in the 5th century and made such an impact on our language as well as leaving a rich legacy of art.

In Sutton village, 3 miles south of the necropolis, All Saints' church contains a fine example of a typical 15th-century Suffolk font, carved with the symbols of the Evangelists and the Annunciation.

Four miles to the east, All Saints' church at **Hollesley** is enjoyable for its excellent Victorian bench ends which copy genuine medieval examples (such as the sciapod from DENNINGTON and the Seven Deadly Sins from BLYTHBURGH). South-east of the village, Shingle Street is exactly what its name suggests: a great bank of shingle thrown up by storms and now a Site of Special Scientific Interest for its rare seashore flora.

Three miles south from Hollesley is **Bawdsey**, where the late Victorian manor, converted to a radar research station, played a vital role throughout the Second World War, warning of German bombing raids. The long, lovely shingle beaches are dotted with Martello towers, built by the Royal Engineers in 1810–12 when England was once again expecting invasion, this time from Napoleon.

Tattingstone (5/4F)

Five miles south of Ipswich, Tattingstone is a leafy village on the edge of an estate. St Mary's church contains a good monument by Flaxman to Rear Admiral Thomas Western (d. 1814) and stands opposite the former House of Correction, built in 1765 and now a home for the elderly.

Convoluted lanes lead south out of the village, skirting the gorse-covered grounds of Tattingstone Place and its expanse of ornamental lake, maintained as a conservation area. The large red-brick house, built in 1764, looks over to what seems to be a church; in fact the church, known as the Tattingstone Wonder, is a pair of cottages, built in 1790 to enhance the view from the Place.

Three miles south at **Stutton**, St Peter's church enjoys an idyllic situation, perched on the edge of Holbrook Bay. From the church, footpaths follow the rim of the bay and the banks of the Stour estuary for many miles.

The lane north from Stutton church to **Holbrook** is lined with huge over-arching trees: olive-green holm oaks interplanted with the fresher green of English oak. Through the gaps you catch occasional glimpses of the tall spire of the Royal Hospital School and the whole sweep of the massive neo-Georgian school complex becomes visible as you join the B1080. The school, founded in 1712 for the sons of seafarers and originally attached to Greenwich Hospital, moved here in 1933. The sheer scale of the project is impressive, with its Hawksmoor-like central tower rising above the long arms of the main teaching blocks and facing a crescent of staff housing.

A little further north, the entrance to Holbrook village proper is marked by a pleasing clapboard mill, standing by a tributary of the River Stour.

Thorington (6/3B) see Bramfield

Thornhams, The (5/4B)

The little church of St Mary, **Thornham Parva**,

2 miles west of Eye, is all thatched, including the low tower, and contains a medieval retable of national importance. Painted in about 1300, it depicts Christ on the Cross, flanked by saints, painted in pure brilliant colour and in perfect condition. Recent research suggests that it was made by artists working in the Royal Workshops linked to Westminster Abbey and that it originally graced the high altar of the Dominican priory at Thetford. Another panel from the same group is on display in the Musée de Cluny in Paris. This work of art would alone justify a visit to the church but there is an added interest now that the extensive 15th-century wall paintings have been restored. Buried to the south-east of this simplest of medieval churches is Sir Basil Spence (1907–76), architect of one of this century's greatest buildings, Coventry cathedral.

The House In The Clouds, Thorpeness

St Mary's church at **Thornham Magna** lies a mile to the south and contains an accomplished monument to Lord Henniker (d. 1821) and his wife Emily, former occupants of Thornham Hall, which burnt down in 1955; the beautifully wooded estate is, however, open daily to the public. Guides to the 12 miles of footpaths are available from the Thornham Field Centre at Redhouse Farm; guided walks, led by experts in the local flora and fauna, are conducted on most Sundays in summer.

Thorpeness (6/3D)

Two miles north of Aldeburgh, this seaside resort is almost entirely the creation of Stuart Ogilvie (d. 1932), who turned a scattered farming and fishing hamlet into a remarkable model village in memory of his mother. Work began in 1910 with the digging of The Meare, an oversize village pond. The Country Club was built alongside it in 1912. There followed a number of mildly neo-Tudor cottages, built of cement panels with timber studs to hide the joins. To supply the village with water, an 1803 windmill was moved to the ridge north of The Meare from nearby Aldringham. This was used to pump water into a wonderful folly of a tower, whose tank is disguised as a clapboard house with windows, tiled roof and chimney, perched 85 feet high in the air. Below the tank is a genuine five-storey house. The better and more solid housing to the north of the village was constructed in the late 1920s; it reflects both the contemporary taste for neo-Tudor half-timbering and the emerging Modernist style.

After Stuart Ogilvie's death his son, Lt. Col. Sholto S. Ogilvie, carried on the good work, including the construction of St Mary's, a simple non-denominational church, whose completion was interrupted by the war.

At **Aldringham**, 2 miles north-west and also part of the Ogilvie estate, the little church of St Andrew was rebuilt in 1842; it contains one of Suffolk's best 15th-century fonts, showing few signs of damage and carved with symbols of the Evangelists.

Thurlows, The (4/2D)

Great and **Little Thurlow**, 4 miles north of Haverhill, form one continuous village, delightfully situated on the west bank of the River Stour. At the south end, the river flows beneath a pretty but dilapidated little cast-iron bridge of 1830, with a cart wash alongside and beneath the rose-covered garden walls of the Hall.

The Hall itself is Georgian, and the grounds are open under the National Gardens Scheme in spring, when the grassy river banks are carpeted with multi-coloured flowers. All Saints' church is essentially Norman. It offers a lovely view southwards to the well-restored barns of Hall Farm and westwards to the smock mill on the hill outside the village.

The main north-south village street is lined with pleasing houses; Lavender Cottage, a 15th-century hall house with both cross wings, stands next to The Cock, 18th-century Gothick. Further north, the tall and handsome School, dated 1614, was founded by Sir Stephen Soame, a former Lord Mayor of London. He also endowed the attractive almshouses which stand

alone by the side of the B1061 at the north end of the village, and he is buried in the bulky mausoleum which projects from the chancel of St Peter's church, Little Thurlow.

Half a mile further on, a turning leads to the pretty Saxon church of All Saints at Little Bradley, where a delightful brass commemorates John Daye (d. 1584), the printer famous for publishing the first edition of Foxe's popular *Book of Martyrs* in 1563.

Troston (5/1B) *see* Ixworth

Ufford (6/1D)

Three miles north of Woodbridge, Ufford is a beautiful village by the River Deben, its old thatched cottages and substantial farmhouses immaculately maintained. The village stocks are carefully preserved by the gate to St Mary's church, famous for its prodigious telescopic font cover, a great ornate spire that reaches 18 feet to the ceiling. Much original colour remains on this and on the richly decorated timbers of the nave and chancel roofs. Equally gorgeous is the stained glass of Saints Salome and Anna, mothers of St James and St John. It is Victorian, but a very convincing copy of the 15th-century work at All Souls College, Oxford. (*See* 'East Anglian Parish Churches', p. 88.)

Walberswick (6/3B) *see* Blythburgh

Waldingfields, The (5/2E)

Little Waldingfield, 4 miles north-east of Sudbury, has a most endearing church, St Lawrence, with ornamented Tudor roofs rising above walls coloured white, pink and green. Here, traditional limewash has been used and the soft powdery colours blend harmoniously with the old quarry tile and brick floor.

At **Great Waldingfield** a mile to the south, the church is also dedicated to St Lawrence. Stately from the outside and surrounded by picturesque cottages, the interior was substantially restored in 1866, when the excellent mid-17th-century communion rails, carved with garlands, were brought here from the church of St Michael, Cornhill, in the City of London.

The road to **Acton**, one mile to the north-west, skirts the wartime airfield, R.A.F. Sudbury. The village is all new housing estates, part of the overspill from rapidly growing Sudbury, 2 miles south. Here, at All Saints' church, the snowcem menace has struck. Once this paint has been applied, will it be possible to remove it from the porous stone which it so badly disfigures? Even so, the church contains one of England's finest brasses: Sir Robert de Bures (d. 1302) in chain mail and long fur-trimmed surcoat, beautifully engraved with minute attention to the details of his armour.

Walsham le Willows (5/2B)

The village, 4 miles north-east of Ixworth, is as picturesque as its name with cottages of all periods fronting a stream and entered by a choice of leafy lanes. St Mary's church has not only a splendid roof but also the only example in Suffolk of a virgin's wreath, or 'crant'. This consists of a wooden disk suspended from the nave wall, carved with the name of Mary Boyce, who died in 1685 'of a broken heart'. Until the late 18th century, the young men of the village would hang garlands on the crant on the anniversary of Mary's death.

At **Badwell Ash**, 2 miles to the south, the tower and porch display fine examples of flushwork. The south-east buttress of the porch contains a display of blacksmith's tools. Exactly the same motif appears on a bench end in the neighbouring church of All Saints, **Great Ashfield**, which suggests that a local blacksmith or farrier might have been a patron of both churches. The bench end has been reused as part of a reader's desk below the magnificent square pulpit of 1619.

Westhall (6/3A) *see* Halesworth

Westhorpe (5/3C) *see* Finningham

West Stow (4/4B) *see* Icklingham

Wetherden (5/3C) *see* Stowmarket

Wetheringsett (5/4C) *see* Mendlesham

Wickhambrook (4/3D) *see* Cowlinge

Wilby (6/1B) *see* Wingfield

Wingfield (6/1B)

This scattered hamlet, 5 miles north-east of Eye, consists of only a handful of buildings but several of them are of great historical interest. A college of priests was founded here in 1362 under the will of Sir John Wingfield, Chief of Council to the Black Prince. His money was used to rebuild the sumptuous church and his manor was demolished to make way for the

Brass to Sir Robert de Bures, Acton

college, now deceptively disguised as an 18th-century farmhouse but hiding within it the remains of the original 14th-century aisled hall. The College is often used for concerts and other cultural events, and is open to the public at weekends in summer (*see* p. 143).

Sir John now lies buried on the north side of the chancel of St Andrew's church, facing the extraordinarily flamboyant south chapel built by his successors, the de la Poles. Parts of the castle built in 1382 by Michael de la Pole, first Earl of Suffolk, stand up on a hill, north of the village.

Two miles to the east, in the church of St Peter and St Paul at **Fressingfield**, another de la Pole left her mark. Alice, the grand-daughter of Chaucer and wife of William de la Pole, Duke of Suffolk, carved her initials in one of the benches, proving that even high-born ladies can sometimes be frivolous. These benches are of the same rich-hued oak as the lovely roof, and the seat backs as well as the bench ends are carved with ornate

Tide Mill, Woodbridge

tracery. Backing on to the churchyard, the timber-framed Fox and Goose Inn dates to the 15th century and was built as a guildhall.

Wilby is a hamlet of multi-coloured cottages, 3 miles south of Wingfield; even the modern bungalows are gaily painted. A bulky tomb chest almost blocks the entrance to St Mary's church. It was clearly built to be noticed and is lit from above by a skylight. Above, and far more

graceful, are portrait medallions to the 18th- and 19th-century members of the Green family. The rest of the church is filled with excellent woodwork: bench ends illustrating the Sacraments, the Seven Works of Mercy and the Seven Deadly Sins, a fine Jacobean pulpit and the south aisle roof carried on angel corbels.

At **Horham**, 2 miles west, the benches are an intriguing patchwork of wood of different ages and styles, from reused Elizabethan domestic linenfold panelling to 19th-century copies of

of a small cathedral town, with its Georgian façades, ambitious church and the Abbey School alongside.

Traffic is excluded for much of the day and as a result the town can be experienced with all the senses: Woodbridge is not only handsome to look at – you also smell old wood and beeswax polish and hear the sound of furniture restorers in their back alley workshops (for Woodbridge is an important centre of the antiques trade). It is pleasant, too, to hang about the market place listening to the gentle lilt of the Suffolk dialect, or to wander down cobbled alleys to the church where the sounds of the practising choir and organist drift through the open porch door.

The absence of traffic also allows for leisurely exploration, and there is much to see. High above the town, Market Hill is lined with handsome houses, many of them much older than their 18th-century red-brick façades suggest. Shire Hall, standing on an island in the middle of the Square, was built originally in 1575, but was given Dutch gables and a sweeping double staircase to the upper rooms in the early 18th century. In every direction the roads which lead off the Hill present vistas of leaning timber-framed buildings.

On the south side of the hill is an excellent museum about maritime Woodbridge and some of the local notables: Thomas Seckford who built Shire Hall and was the town's most generous patron, as well as being Master of the Rolls in Elizabeth I's day and the brains behind this country's first ever accurate road maps; Edward Fitzgerald, the eccentric translator of Omar Khayyam's poem *Rubaiyat* and leading light of the 'Woodbridge Wits'; and Jeffrye Pitman, Sheriff of Suffolk, to name only a few.

Seckford and Pitman are commemorated in the magnificent church of St Mary, which is reached down a cobbled alley alongside the museum and is completely encircled by back gardens that spill on to the churchyard. The fine dado of the original chancel screen is preserved behind glass, showing lively, well-drawn saints against a background of green and gold, like a William Morris wallhanging.

To the east of the church, in the shadow of its 108-foot high knapped flint tower, is the Abbey School, once the Manor House of Woodbridge and the site of an Augustinian priory. Beyond lies Church Street, with its numerous alleys and courtyards behind Georgian houses, which leads to the main street of Woodbridge, 'The Thoroughfare'.

earlier carving. Only the pulpit, dated 1631, was tailor-made.

Wissett (6/2B) *see* Rumburgh

Wissington (5/2F) *see* Nayland

Withersfield (4/2E) *see* Kedington

Woodbridge (6/1E)
This town on the River Deben is a sophisticated, cosmopolitan place. It has something of the air

This long street stretches for nearly a mile, running parallel to the River Deben – although the river is not yet visible. Instead, the view is of an uninterrupted sequence of red-brick and multi-coloured half-timbered houses, many with original Victorian shop fronts. The shops here consist not only of the usual national chain stores but also high-quality bakers shoemakers, cheese-mongers and delicatessens with, further north, second-hand booksellers and art galleries. A good number have hanging signs suspended from their façades, all excellent examples of the modern signwriter's craft.

The Woodbridge waterfront lies to the east of The Thoroughfare, beyond car parks, new supermarkets and a busy road, so that it no longer seems an integral part of the town. Indeed, as early as the 19th century this former port had already begun to change its character, with the insensitive siting of the town's gas works and railway station. In the mid 17th century, 350 ships were registered here and the town's shipyards built many a fine sea-going vessel as well as warships for the Admiralty. The boat-building tradition lives on, now largely centred on leisure yachts.

Standing on the busy quayside is the Wood-bridge Tide Mill, restored to working order and open throughout the summer. As the name suggests, the 18th-century clapboard mill, with its boat-shaped roof, uses the tide to drive its grinding machinery. By contrast Buttrum's Mill, to the west of the town, is the more familiar four-sailed windmill, built in 1835 and now also returned to working order. It is open at week-ends.

At Kyson Hill, a mile south of the town centre, the National Trust owns 4 acres of parkland from which there are excellent views of the winding River Deben and of the heaths on the eastern bank, site of the Sutton Hoo burials (see SUTTON).

Rendlesham, 4 miles north-east of Wood-bridge, was the site of a royal village founded by the Wuffingas, the dynasty that ruled East Anglia in the 6th and 7th centuries and whose kings were buried at nearby SUTTON HOO. It is now dominated by R.A.F. Bentwaters and St Gregory's churchyard backs on to typical military housing estates. The lovely east window in the church is most deceptive: it looks 14th-century, in the Decorated style, but was inserted in 1783 and is made of wood.

Eyke (meaning oak) is a mile to the south. The church of All Saints has two fine Norman

arches which once supported a crossing tower. Excellent bench ends, deceptively medieval in appearance, feature a python and a penguin amid the more usual menagerie of monsters, owls and leaping fish.

Woolpit (5/2C)

Pre-Norman documents call this town, 6 miles west of Stowmarket on the A45, 'Wulfpytt', suggesting that wolves were still being trapped here in the 10th century. The brickworks, now closed, flourished from the 17th century on-wards, producing a yellowish-white brick that was then much favoured because it resembled stone. Large quantities were exported to America and used to build the Senate Wing of the Capitol in Washington. In Woolpit itself, many builders seemed to favour red bricks, or even half-timber, rather than the local product as the Swan Inn and the houses lining the small green at the centre of the village demonstrate. Yellow brick first appears at the margins in early 19th-century terraces, enlivened by contrasting red brick for window surrounds and pilaster strips.

An angel flutters in the roof of Woolpit church

St Mary's church has a surprising and successful Victorian tower and spire with flying buttresses, the spaces between the clerestory windows being enlivened by much inventive flushwork. The church suffered badly at the hands of iconoclasts, but later restorers did an admirable job in replacing the glorious host of feathery angels that flutter among the great beams of the soaring roof.

At Shelland, 2 miles south-east, royalist sympathies were still strong in 1767, when the little Gothick church was built and dedicated to King Charles the Martyr. In 1896 the church was decorated by a local wainwright, using the same gay colours which he used to paint farm waggons; recent restoration has brightened up the vivid colour scheme.

Woolverstone (5/4F) *see* Chelmondiston

Worlingworth (6/1C)

Five miles north-west of Framlingham, Worlingworth is a long, sprawling village with much recent infill but a highly rewarding church at its eastern end.

Visitors to St Mary's are greeted by a crisp St George and menacing dragon fighting their eternal battle in the spandrels of the porch. Inside, there is a spire of a font cover to compete with the best in the county, painted in gay colours and reaching to the roof. The graceful box pews that fill the nave are Carolean, dating from 1630 and all of a piece with the pulpit, which is carved with lion masks and crowned by a tester suspended from the ceiling. At the back of the church is a lovely Bruegelesque oil painting of the Worlingworth Feast, which took place in 1810 to celebrate George III's jubilee.

Three miles east on the A1120 at **Dennington**, the church of St Mary is filled with splendid woodwork. The 15th-century benches alone have no less than 76 different and intricately carved poppy heads and armrests, one of which features a now-famous sciapod, a mythical

The sciapod in Dennington church

African whose giant foot serves as a sunshade.

The 1628 three-decker pulpit is a maze of interconnected boxes and passageways, with projecting hat pegs. Two delicate painted screens survive, complete with their lofts; even rarer, a pyx canopy of around 1500 hangs above the altar. Used to expose the Blessed Sacrament, most were destroyed by Protestant reformers and only a handful survive in England.

Two miles further north-east, the plain stalwart church of St John the Baptist at **Badingham** hides all its treasures inside. The nave, under a rich hammerbeam roof, slopes steeply up to the rebuilt Victorian chancel and the font is one of Suffolk's best. Minor defacement has not destroyed its charming realism.

Wortham (5/3B) *see* Redgrave

Yaxley (5/4B) *see* Eye

Yoxford (6/2C) *see* Peasenhall

Bibliography

Blythe, R. *Akenfield*, Allen Lane, London 1969.

Clifton Taylor, A. *The Pattern of English Building*, Faber & Faber, London 1972.

Crewe, S. *Stained Glass in England: 1180–1540*, RCHME/HMSO, Norwich 1987.

Dymond, D. *The Norfolk Landscape*, Hodder & Stoughton, London 1985.

Dymond, D. and Northeast, P. *A History of Suffolk*, Phillimore Press, Chichester 1985.

Harrod, W. *The Norfolk Guide*, Alastair Press, Bury St Edmunds 1988.

Pevsner, N. *The Buildings of England: North-East Norfolk and Norwich*, Penguin, Harmondsworth 1982.

Pevsner, N. *The Buildings of England: North-West and South Norfolk*, Penguin, Harmondsworth 1962.

Pevsner, N. and Radcliffe, E. *The Buildings of England: Suffolk* (revised edition), Penguin, Harmondsworth 1974.

Rackham, O. *A History of the Countryside*, Dent, London 1986.

Ravensdale, J. and Muir, R. *East Anglian Landscapes*, Michael Joseph, London 1984.

Scarfe, N. *The Suffolk Guide*, Alastair Press, Bury St Edmunds 1988.

Scarfe, N. *The Suffolk Landscape*, Hodder & Stoughton, London 1972.

Seymour, J. *East Anglia*, Collins, London 1970.

Wade Martins, P. (editor) *Norfolk From the Air*, Norfolk Museums Service, Norwich 1987.

Wade Martins, S. *A History of Norfolk*, Phillimore Press, Chichester 1984.

Key to Maps

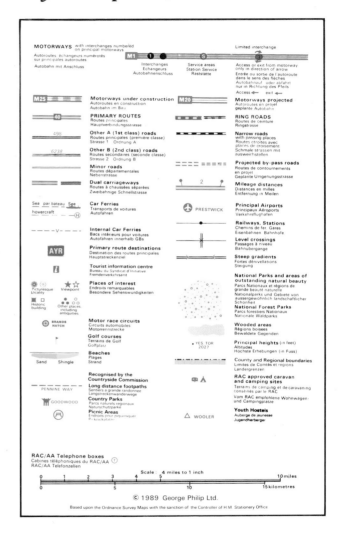

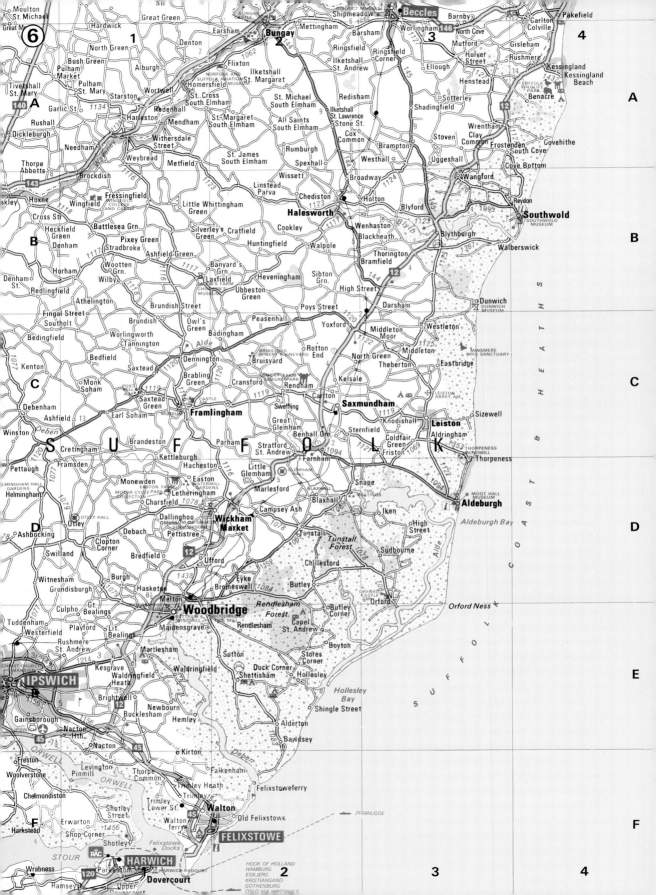

INDEX

Numbers in italics refer to illustrations